OUT IN THE CENTER

OUT IN THE CENTER

Public Controversies and Private Struggles

EDITED BY
HARRY DENNY
ROBERT MUNDY
LILIANA M. NAYDAN
RICHARD SÉVÈRE
ANNA SICARI

UTAH STATE UNIVERSITY PRESS
Logan

© 2018 by University Press of Colorado

Published by University Press of Colorado
245 Century Circle, Suite 202
Louisville, Colorado 80027

 The University Press of Colorado is a proud member of
the Association of University Presses.

The University Press of Colorado is a cooperative publishing enterprise supported, in part, by Adams State University, Colorado State University, Fort Lewis College, Metropolitan State University of Denver, Regis University, University of Colorado, University of Northern Colorado, Utah State University, and Western State Colorado University.

∞ This paper meets the requirements of the ANSI/NISO Z39.48–1992 (Permanence of Paper).

ISBN: 978-1-60732-782-0 (paperback)
ISBN: 978-1-60732-783-7 (ebook)
DOI: https://doi.org/10.7330/9781607327837

Library of Congress Cataloging-in-Publication Data

Names: Denny, Harry C., author. | Mundy, Robert, author. | Naydan, Liliana M., author. | Severe, Richard, author. | Sicari, Anna, author.
Title: Out in the center : public controversies and private struggles / Harry Denny, Robert Mundy, Liliana M. Naydan, Richard Severe, Anna Sicari.
Description: Logan : Utah State University Press, [2018] | Includes bibliographical references and index.
Identifiers: LCCN 2018000465| ISBN 9781607327820 (pbk.) | ISBN 9781607327837 (ebook)
Subjects: LCSH: Writing centers—Social aspects—United States. | English language—Rhetoric—Study and teaching (Higher)—Social aspects—United States. | Writing centers—Psychological aspects. | English language—Rhetoric—Study and teaching (Higher)—Psychological aspects. | Identity (Psychology) | Critical pedagogy—United States.
Classification: LCC PE1405.U6 D46 2018 | DDC 808/.0420711—dc23
LC record available at https://lccn.loc.gov/2018000465

To those who teach and learn in writing centers, to those whose bodies and actions challenge the status quo in our spaces, to those who embody and perform the rich tapestry of what writing centers strive to be, and to those who search for voice and validation.

CONTENTS

ACKNOWLEDGMENTS

This edited collection has its origins in numerous conversations among the editors and contributing authors—conversations that began in our offices and in our writing centers, that moved into digital spaces, and that developed into conference presentations at the Conference on College Composition and Communication and the International Writing Centers Association Conference. These events served as the few times in which we could meet in person, and given our inability to grasp the simple math associated with understanding time zones and thus successfully schedule online meetings, we are thankful for the community of writers we are a part of that brings us together with such frequency. Otherwise, we might still be attempting to determine the time in Stillwater, Oklahoma, or Valparaiso, Indiana. Without generous support from our institutions that made our conference travel possible, what began as an idea about the intersection of identity politics and public controversies never would have developed into this published book. We would like to thank Oklahoma State University, Pace University, Penn State Abington, Purdue University, St. John's University, and Valparaiso University for funding conference travel that helped us present at conferences and develop our ideas.

We would also like to extend special thanks to Pace, Penn State Abington, and Purdue for providing funds to help us finalize our book. In addition, we would like to thank Michael Spooner and everyone at Utah State University Press for seeing the importance of putting the authors included in our collection into conversation with one another and with the wider writing center and composition studies community. We appreciate the thoughtful criticism of our manuscript reviewers who challenged us to revise our approach to the collection; their insight made it stronger, more cohesive, and better rooted in wider scholarship. We feel honored to have received such thoughtful feedback on our work from Michael along the way and to have had him shepherd this collection into print during the final year of his distinguished career at USUP. Likewise, we would like to thank Sam Brawand for her thoughtful and thorough editing of our manuscript. She noticed inconsistencies that helped us polish our work, and her approach to editing allowed us to retain the unique voices in which our contributors write—voices that speak to existing and necessary diversity in the field of writing center studies. Finally, we would like to thank Michele Eodice for the work and guidance she continues to provide for those of us in the writing center community and for her support of this project.

OUT IN THE CENTER

INTRODUCTION
Public Controversies and Identity Politics in Writing Center Theory and Practice

Harry Denny, Robert Mundy, Liliana M. Naydan, Richard Sévère, and Anna Sicari

Scan a given week's worth of WCenter listserv messages or attend a writing center staff meeting at any given writing center and you'll see everyday struggles with identity that are faced by the diverse members of our writing center community. How should a writing center director handle a complaint that a tutor is wearing a top another tutor deems as overly provocative? How should a writing center staff respond to a racist cartoon printed in the school newspaper? In what ways might a writing center fashion itself as a safe(r) or brave space—if such a fashioning is even possible—in the face of hate crimes and everyday microaggressions being committed on campus? These questions point to the notion that writing centers involve complicated work that draws attention to the interfacing identities of practitioners and patrons alike—identities Harry Denny (2010) in large part explores in *Facing the Center*. He argues that diversity underpins writing center work and that writing center practitioners must take up conversations about identity politics in tutor education, fostering dialogue about how difference is negotiated in order to create more socially just spaces. He notes that "identity and the politics of negotiation and face are always present and require inventory and mapping" (28). And he offers his "text as a starting point, launching pad, or intervention in conversations yet to begin" (28).

Certainly, Denny succeeds in starting a line of inquiry in our field. His book is part of a wider conversation that includes books such as Laura Greenfield and Karen Rowan's *Writing Centers and the New Racism* and Frankie Condon's *I Hope I Join the Band*, works that focus on the subjects of race and racism (Condon 2012; Greenfield and Rowan 2011b). These texts call for social activism—specifically antiracist work—and they argue for a process of decentering in order for contemporary centers to work toward racial justice via their pedagogies. In our collection, we attempt to

DOI: 10.7330/9781607327837.c000

broaden the focus these and other texts present and continue to complicate how we understand the role identity politics play in writing centers.
We aim to explore the very public and yet also personal nature of writing
center sessions and of individuals working and collaborating in an environment that necessitates dialogue and negotiation within the self and
with others. We put a diverse collection of voices into dialogue with one
another about a range of identities including race, gender, class, sexuality, language, ethnicity, positionality, disability, and faith. And we draw
attention to the ways in which these identities come to interweave with
one another in our writing spaces in the academy. We also look to contemporary public controversies and sociocultural/socioeconomic crises
that shape public perceptions of identity. In doing so, we suggest that
writing center practitioners must engage in dialogue involving the ways
in which tutors, writing center administrators, and writers can most pro-
ductively and effectively navigate personal or public issues that involve
identity. And we suggest that conflict is a means of access that brings to
light conversations that have not yet been fully realized in our field. *Out
in the Center* recognizes the writing center exists as a social and cultural
creation that extends into the world and not just within the confines
of an academic institution. This collection recognizes that moments of
crisis, whether they involve public controversies or private meditations,
serve as points of entry into an extended dialogue regarding the bodies
that enter the writing center space and the subsequent politics that intersect as notions of self are shaped through collaborative work.

WRITING CENTERS BEYOND THE VACUUM

Writing centers, as Andrea Lunsford (1991) writes in "Collaboration,
Control, and the Idea of a Writing Center," fancy themselves as storehouses or resource spaces where writers go for efficient tip sheets for this
grammar issue or that genre question; as garrets where writers produce in
monastic solitude; or as Burkean parlors where people can talk with and
push one another to create knowledge (3–10). Yet each of these notions
of the space assumes writers, writing as a product, and the process of writing can be separated out from the social, cultural, economic, and political. They assume writing—its production and its circulation—operates
within a vacuum from all that shapes and consumes it. Storehouses,
however, are contextual and never provide blanket solutions to every
problem; garrets might be illusory; and parlors are never egalitarian or
void of the privilege, power, and stakes that pour through the institutions
and society that make their existence possible. Writing centers are never

safe harbors or neutral zones, as if any place like that could exist or has ever existed. They exist as spaces in dynamic interplay with the environments around them. Writing centers are sites where a truism is always in play: the personal is political and the political is personal.

Writing centers are pulsing with activity and conversation, and their walls are permeable, permitting the outside in and the inside out. In other words, in the writing center, the external and the internal have no distinct boundaries, and hence there is no such thing as being only in the center. We are always *out in the center*, as this collection's title suggests, because the lives of those entering writing centers are never compartmentalized or siloed. The work of becoming and supporting writers is never walled off from the influence of infinite social, cultural, political, and economic currents. Rather, every*body* entering a writing center makes public the messy hodgepodges that they are, that they have been, and that they are becoming beyond the moment of their entry. Individuals in a writing center are never distinct from the societal forces that make possible the meaning and legibility of who they are. In turn, writing centers and the campuses on which they are situated can never separate themselves from the communities that surround them.

Certainly, writing centers are agents of institutions that seek to interpolate their subjects to assume their proper positions through education (even when education involves remediation). Institutions that house writing centers seek to reify the boundary between public and private in order to police bodies, identities, and rhetorics. Writing centers depend on a fictive distinction that purports to isolate the everyday intellectual labor of education in disciplinarity, reason, and expression from a world beyond where public and private engage in a never-ending tango. Yet writing centers can and do also function as sites of slippage and subversion where agents can challenge institutionality and where institutions fail to deliver on their objectives. In this sense, all of us who teach and learn in writing centers engage in a certain everyday improvisation, as Beth Boquet (2002) terms it in *Noise from the Writing Center*, or act as tricksters, as Anne Ellen Geller, Michele Eodice, Frankie Condon, Meg Carroll, and Beth Boquet, the authors of *The Everyday Writing Center*, describe (Geller et al. 2007). They can and should be spaces in which the tensions of communities can and do manifest. And these tensions become most legible when the tidy operation of tutoring genre, argument, development, sentence clarity, and grammar gets upended by perceptions, preconceived notions, and power dynamics—by compelled disclosure of identity formations such as those that accents or belief systems represent.

Sometimes tutoring can't happen when personal struggles slip into interactions—or at least it can't happen in textbook ways. Students and staff alike rush to and from class, diving into sessions that can involve first-year writers hashing out their first college essays; upper-level undergraduates orienting themselves to their initial professional group work; graduate students learning to signify as experts; and faculty struggling to overcome time constraints. Yet cutting across these common features and populations in writing centers might also be murkier dynamics: those involving the first-generation college student, the multilingual writer, the learner struggling with intercultural conflict, the biracial tutor, the faculty director who is Other, the graduate student coming out of the closet, or the consultant navigating classes and providing for her child in a single-parent household. The private experiences and internal struggles of these writing center inhabitants are not always visible to passersby, whether passersby are outside administrators or incoming students. Moreover, the intersections that always already define identity are rarely visible to passersby, reinforcing in everyday writing center reality what Jonathan Alexander and David Wallace write with regard to the theoretical work that defines the field of rhetoric and composition: that "little work in our field explores multiple intersections of identity and difference" (Alexander and Wallace 2009, 315–16).

Often, the writing center serves as a space for individuals to come out, to reveal or uncover their identities to relative strangers—consultants or writers who might be working with them to develop ideas for compositions but who in so doing travel down conversational rabbit holes to explore key facets of identity and tensions that accompany them. To appropriate Alexander and Wallace's (2009) words, people in writing centers experience how "a woman may be homophobic, a working-class man may resent the efforts extended to those who are seen as disabled, and a gay man may be prejudiced against those in interracial relationships" (316). Tutors and directors witness (or experience themselves) the struggles of Generation 1.5 writers who feel what Homi K. Bhabha (2004 [1994]) might term as their relative hybridities—the ways in which they are US citizens by nationality but linguistically neither here nor there. Tutors and directors see and may also share the anxieties black men might bring with them when entering spaces following news reports of violence against individuals who look much like them. Instead, writing centers emerge as spaces where features of identity, and intersectionality as it connects those features, make emotionally charged appearances to relative strangers. Writing centers exist as spaces that bolster and challenge identity formation and reify identity by way of conversations that always already involve identity—conversations that involve the writer behind the writing and the identity-oriented ideologies that shape any given individual, as well as the language that they produce.

To complement the dynamic social situations that define writing centers, time and again, national crises or media firestorms create flash politics that infiltrate the everyday routine of sessions and staff development within writing centers. While writing, we find ourselves in the midst of many great national tumults—talk of banning Muslims from entering the United States, the injustice of a college student sentenced to only six months imprisonment for the rape of an unconscious woman, or the use of the phrase *black-on-black crime* to dismiss the Black Lives Matter movement. We read stories of fraternity brothers chanting a racist song that is captured on video and goes viral on the Internet. We see that survey-research documents validate women's more-common-than-not experiences with sexual violence. We see images of men and women of color who are dying at the hands of law enforcement. And we see the failure to change law enforcement in the killings of people of color. As a result, we see protests that manifest in response in most major cities make their way into our centers, whether overtly or covertly. Major media report on first-generation students struggling to find connections at elite universities; a coach is fired after being caught using antigay slurs to motivate his athletes; anti-Muslim rhetoric dominates reports of a shooting at a gay nightclub in Orlando: all these infiltrate writing center consultations because they speak to the identities of writing center inhabitants.

Indeed, as we were drafting this project, conversation drifted to a school shooting that had recently taken place at a community college in Oregon. It happened in a writing classroom, and one of us observed that "this kind of thing always happens in a writing space, doesn't it?" The shooter's writing was said to have involved anger and violence, so all of us wondered how a writing instructor or a writing tutor would negotiate the work of a student dealing with anger and rage. We also imagined the challenge of students healing from the trauma of a shooting, whether it be a mass murder or a less publicized everyday act of gun violence. With open-carry laws a reality on more and more campuses, public and private anxiety is legitimately high in the wake of what seems to be a never-ending series of collective traumas, such as those witnessed at the Pulse nightclub in Orlando or senseless random shootings taking place daily in Chicago neighborhoods. These events and the generalized sociocultural anxiety that amplifies them underscore their ubiquity (or at least what we imagine it to be) and the zeitgeist in which writing centers exist. It is not as though writing center staff need permission or occasion to discuss and process events such as these. These events are almost hegemonic in their presence in our collective conscience; they feed what people are thinking about and experiencing, and they often drive what professors are assigning for writing and research projects. Writing centers can never be rarified spaces where teaching and learning around writing happens outside a wider (and even micro) social and cultural context. Writing centers must engage the social (and the cultural, political, and economic) because they are part of it.

IDENTITY POLITICS AND THE EDUCATIONAL MISSIONS OF WRITING CENTERS

Issues of inequitable power that are synonymous with the institution and the larger culture are easily replicated in the center unless we are cognizant of existing power dynamics. Without dialogue, an opportunity to draw parallels between the local and the global, writing centers risk reinforcing division and marginalization and therefore paradoxically working against the educational missions that should be driving them. To prepare for the crises that may emerge in writing sessions, we look to leverage national and global events as teaching moments, occasions Linda Adler-Kassner (2008), Vershawn Ashanti Young (2007, 2011), and Nancy M. Grimm (1999, 2006) have identified as organic activism with material consequences. We challenge readers to ask critical questions of these crises in order to learn from them. For instance, what role do we serve in dynamics in which composition classrooms seek to polish students into proper middle-class vernacular and thinking? And how might our experiences and work challenge this agenda and ensure students make informed decisions about how they mark and produce their languages and membership in communities of practice? How might we further imagine ways to position writing centers as subversive spaces that advocate for those who have a marginal status in the academy and who might benefit from the support because of our relative privilege as agents of institutionality? We have no doubt that writing centers speak to the diverse identities of their inhabitants and to identity politics that play out in politically charged spaces.

Like writing centers and those who inhabit them, crises are not self-contained, nor do they operate independently of a complex social context; they are not confined to the public domain of water-cooler debate. They sustain a pressing relevance, especially for educators who see learning and advocacy as intertwined and who also desire to develop writing center staff education and training that scaffolds from abstract theory to enigmatic *real-world* application. Certainly, many campuses lack the lived experience with diversity and the complexity of identity. Everyday oppression is both material and felt. To echo bell hooks's 1994 *Teaching to Transgress*, in her chapter "Theory as Liberatory Practice," "When our lived experience of theorizing is fundamentally linked to processes of self-recovery, of collective liberation, no gap exists between theory and practice. Indeed, what such experience makes more evident is the bond between the two" (61). Hence, the personal struggles and negotiations our essays address model the kind of critical dialogue that must happen in tutor education and how we, as writing center inhabitants, must respond to and take on these conversations to promote self-actualization and agency for individuals in order to create spaces of advocacy and social justice in the academy.

What we ask is for our readers to reexamine the work we do and to rethink writing center pedagogy to address the questions we ask in this edited collection: How are we using identity politics as a theoretical framework to address moments of public and personal crisis? How are we teaching people who enter into our spaces about the concept of intersectionality and how to best serve those who seek us out? In a recent *Writing Center Journal* (*WCJ*) article, Lori Salem (2016) writes, "I would argue we have nothing to lose and everything to gain from reinventing writing center pedagogy. To be clear, I am not saying that we should look for ways to tinker with or expand our traditional practices. Rather, I am arguing for completely rethinking what we do and why we do it" (164). Salem, in responding to Grimm (2011) and Jackie Grutsch McKinney (2013), calls for writing center practitioners and scholars to respond more directly to the students who enter our spaces and their needs and argues for practices to be more grounded in research. This edited collection takes on Salem's call—we ask readers to not just incorporate this text, or a chapter from this text, into their next *tutor training* but also to completely rethink the way we understand writing center work in order to best serve the individuals who enter our spaces. How are we understanding collaboration in the writing center and truly using collaborative work to empower individual agency? To echo Grutsch McKinney, this edited collection sees the work in our writing centers extend far beyond one-on-one writing center sessions, and we argue that this book serves as a model for the types of educational work that can occur in the writing center. How are we teaching our tutors to enter into critical dialogue with the individuals with whom they work, as well as with one another? And, more important, how are writing center administrators listening to and learning from their tutors and their private experiences in the writing center?

While we are addressing the space of the writing center in an institutional context, this edited collection also seeks to challenge more broadly the field of writing center work. At a recent International Writing Centers Association (IWCA) conference, very few panels addressed identity politics in the writing center. Of the few that did, two were fraught with conflict: one panel that addressed identity politics of race, sexuality, and language was packed with a large audience and yet placed in the smallest room the conference offered. People who wanted to attend this session and engage in the educational experience of the discussion were not able to because of the overpacked room. While it is a good sign that people wanted to attend this session, is puzzling, if not telling; what does the organization stand for if it puts such a panel in a small room? Another panel, consisting of a diverse group of undergraduate tutors discussing their bodies in the space of the writing center, went well—a responsive audience filled a room that accommodated all the participants. However, the lack of institutional support this group of tutors received was astonishing. The group of tutors had to rent a car to drive from New York to Pittsburgh, with no funding for accommodations. The five-plus-hour drive made a rather dangerous day trip, allowing the tutors no time to enjoy the conference the way they should. And as Karen Keaton Jackson (2016) points out in her March 7, 2016, post to the *WCJ Blog*, there is very little institutional or organizational support for historically black colleges and universities (HBCUs) and Hispanic-serving institutions (HSIs) to attend regional and national conferences. It must be pointed out that these experiences and conversations all took place in the 2015–2016 academic year, a year in which national conversations about racism, bigotry, xenophobia, and misogyny trickled down into the private and daily experiences of individuals. To what extent do these national conversations inform our everyday thought and practice?

The editors of this collection are very aware of the marginalized voices in the field and the importance of collaboration and support, with all of us working on current research projects that address issues of contingent labor, of systemic issues of sexism and racism, of working-class identities and their place in the institution and specifically in the writing center. We hope, with this collection of narratives and our focus on critical dialogue in our centers, the field takes up identity politics and addresses everyday real and felt issues of sexism, racism, classism, and homophobia. Through these personal narratives and the essays that follow them, we hope writing center practitioners pay closer attention to how public controversies and concerns inform the everyday private moments that occur in our spaces. We hope the conversation this collection constitutes serves as a model for how we, as writing center staff, can have informed, essential conversations that can inform the larger field of composition studies in grassroots ways. If we, as educators and instructors of writing, are not having these conversations with our students, we must ask ourselves, *who is?* In a climate in which education is being trivialized, with national figures proclaiming a love for the uneducated in an attempt to appear anti-elitist, and with laws passed in states in which anyone can teach in public education, it is vital to make relevant the importance of writing and education to students who enter our spaces. Writing centers must make urgent conversations on the complexity of identity and of oppression in order to create meaningful educational experiences and to promote agency for social justice—not solely in an institutional context but also in a social one.

Who Is Out in the Center? Overviews of Parts and Chapter Summaries

Given the multitude of narratives and theoretical discussions involving identity that have emerged in the field of rhetoric and composition (Alexander 2008; Gilyard 1991; LeCourt 2004, 2006; Matsuda 1999; Miller 1991; Royster and Kirsch 2012; Schell 1997; Villanueva 2003; Young 2007, 2011), only a small percentage gets translated into scholarship for and about writing centers as spaces that involve both public controversies and private struggles and that house students and professionals who understand intersectionality as a lived experience. We are often unprepared to understand, speak, and educate in these moments, moments in which students and staff alike experience private struggles with race, class, gender, sexuality, language, culture, disability, and faith, along with the competing intersections that problematize essential notions of self. Yet each contributor to this collection explores how identities and everyday work around identity politics produce risks and rewards; influence the journeys of teachers/scholars; and make writing centers and the writing programs that at times house them or exist in dynamic interplay with them into transformative arenas for ongoing dialogue. Such a conversation, one with many invested parties, begs for contributions from across the spectrum of practitioners. The voices of students, tutors, writing center and program directors, and composition instructors, both on and off the tenure track, that make up our collection speak with attention to intersectionality about their varied experiences.

In part 1, we explore questions involving race through essays authored by a current graduate student tutor, two former tutors, and a former writing center director. Talisha Haltiwanger Morrison writes about the embodiment of race in the writing center, her search for community at predominantly white institutions, and the everyday microaggressions and flat-out racism she confronts as a black woman tutoring and teaching writing. Alexandria Lockett reflects on her work with a variety of students at her graduate institution, noting that black bodies are under constant scrutiny and suspicion in writing centers, just as they are in any other social space. To contest that dynamic, Lockett worked to challenge that surveillance by actively participating in how her sessions were documented and reported and by changing protocols to ensure all tutors' experiences were captured in narratives. Richard Sévère further extends this discussion of bodies and race, drawing on writing center scholarship and critical theory to address how his physicality as a black man affects perceptions and dynamics in writing centers. Allia Abdullah-Matta bridges experiences with race in the classroom to those in the writing center and theorizes that there are connections between bodies and the politics of race. Rochell Isaac makes connections among the students with whom she has worked, their struggles to think critically about writing tasks, and their deeper ambivalence and reluctance, even resistance, to share their experiences in an academic arena predicated on judgement and evaluation of experiences. Isaac argues that education, as a liberatory practice, and the constellation of pedagogies that translate it into action place working-class African American students in paradoxical learning spaces, trying to assimilate standards while maintaining access to a lived reality of their own.

In part 2 of this collection, we further extend the critical race conversation begun in part 1. Nancy Alvarez's essay takes up the lessons of tutoring in Spanish at a community college in the Bronx and her transition to tutoring in an English de facto environment, ironically in one of the most linguistically diverse urban areas in the world. The whiteness of the seemingly English-only writing center at her graduate institution caused her deep conflict, and she pushed that writing center to begin to think about the demographics of its staffing and clients, as well as how it put multilingual policies into practice. Tammy S. Conard-Salvo further deepens this intersectionality of race and linguistics by addressing how she has navigated being a multilingual administrator by learning to embrace but also to be wary of the ability to code switch in sessions.

Part 3 begins a subtle movement from identity as more or less embodied to discussions of gender and sexuality that force tutors and administrators alike to disclose identities with clients and staff. Anna Sicari writes about navigating her identity as a junior writing center professional, all the while confronting institutional and societal sexism, whether in the form of peer administrators challenging her place in and knowledge of the field or in the shape of gendered dynamics with male colleagues. Sicari turns to feminist theory both to light a path forward for writing center professionals and to underscore the material reality generations of women academics and their peers directing writing centers have experienced. Harry Denny reflects on instances of harassment, pointing to the conflicting pressures for LGBTQ+ writing center tutors and professionals to be out, to disclose their identities, or to be visible figures and leaders, all the while underscoring the risk and threat of being out. He recognizes the implicit privilege of having the ability to choose to be out when some have bodies and performativities that signify them in advance of speaking, particularly people of color. Robert Mundy takes up the tensions inherent to masculinity in the context of seeking help, help with anything, and the result of making oneself vulnerable and in need of support in a culture that stigmatizes men seeking and providing nurturance to one another. Mundy addresses how a certain sort of machismo makes possible giving support without undermining a certain "guy's code" of masculinity.

Just as our public genders and sexualities can mask private struggles to negotiate the everyday reality of tutoring sessions, a person's spirituality is not always carried on their sleeve or hung around their neck. And, of course, clients, tutors, and administrators more often than not come from religious traditions that inform how they think, how they express themselves, and, more broadly, who they are. Yet our literature in writing centers provides little guidance or opportunity for writing center training on the topic. In part 4, Sami Korgan writes in her piece about navigating writing center sessions and breakroom conversations about religion at a religious institution where her faith is in the minority. Much like the other people in this collection who reflect on *coming out* in sessions and to peers, Korgan also speaks to how she addresses the pressure to confess her identity and theology. Like Korgan, Ella Leviyeva reflects on being another religious minority, Jewish, at the same institution and on facing the pressure to be a spokesperson for her faith as well as contesting the assumptions of the majority religion among her peers and clients in the writing center. Hadi Banat shares the complexities of being Muslim and multilingual at a predominantly white institution and how it plays out in everyday interactions in a writing center context. He details occasions in which clients and peers ask him to speak on behalf of his faith in a wider social and political environment that is generally hostile and uneducated about the diversity of theologies in Islam.

Parts 5 and 6 advance discussions of tutor experiences with economic class and disability in sessions. Both these foci document additional aspects of identity that are ubiquitous (yet often invisible) and that tutors and clients bring to sessions and struggle to disclose. Tutor-education texts rarely push readers to imagine how classed identity impacts one-to-one learning. Elizabeth Weaver writes about being a professional contingent academic worker, moving around New York City for gigs as a tutor and an adjunct instructor. She connects these working conditions to her roots as a working-class, first-generation student from the Midwest who earned a graduate degree from an Ivy League institution. Like Weaver, Liliana M. Naydan speaks to the experiences of contingent writing center work in graduate school, of the dynamics of labor contingency within universities, and of the need for graduate tutors to unionize. Beth A. Towle addresses moments when class is foregrounded in sessions and therefore makes her contend with her own negotiation of class through education and the need to *come out* as working class, frequently to her clients' disappointment, as they seem to wish for expert insight from those who possess inherent privilege. Anna Rita Napoleone complicates notions of privilege by exploring times in which her standing was checked by her working-class affect and/or register, leaving her frustrated by the limited options available to her as a student and professional. Although she is compelled to challenge the labels assigned to her as an immigrant and member of the working class, she echoes the sentiment and frustration others have expressed: how long can one fight this fight and how possible is success given the rigidity of higher education? Following these tutors' and directors' discussions of class identity, Tim Zmudka offers insight on the experience of being learning disabled in a writing center. While many disabilities are embodied, Zmudka writes about himself and the difficult negotiation learning disabled tutors must undertake. He notes that having attention deficit hyperactivity disorder (ADHD), even though it is always present in education and writing centers, carries great stigma in society and culture, which makes disclosing this aspect of who he is precarious for his credibility in sessions but crucial for building awareness of its presence in education and writing centers.

We wrap up the collection with a concluding chapter that brings together the lessons from all our contributors. This collaborative essay calls for sustainable action and research in writing centers, encouraging tutors and directors to imagine local ways in which they can call attention to identity, document its impact through inquiry, and shape policy both within and beyond the center and their institutions. While we each know and have experienced the marginality of writing centers in a host of ways, we argue that writing center practitioners have an obligation to move leadership in ways that makes sense in their contexts, to continue to foster change and inclusiveness in institutions that intrinsically tend toward the status quo instead of challenging it.

A Reader's Guide to Our Collection

Any attempt at addressing the complexities of identity in writing centers is a tall order, and some might wonder why we structure the book the way we do, or why a part on race precedes those on other aspects of identity. Others might wonder whether our authors could have complicated their identities a bit more, recognizing nobody ever occupies a position of complete marginality or of absolute domination. We do not intend the structure to represent some sort of parable of oppression Olympics ordered from most to least. As editors, we recognize, along with our authors, the privilege and complexity from which we express our reflections. We know that as tutors, directors, faculty, and administrators we always already inhabit some degree of interiority to the tactics and relations of power and status in the academy writ large but also on the everyday level of how our local units operate and the missions that guide them. We also began this project thinking about the absence of theory in so many of the texts in our profession that have taken up identity politics, however well intended, and about the underexplored range of experiences and the authenticity of the multiple ways in which diversity and oppression play out, particularly for bodies that aren't white, male, middle class, straight, Christian, or able bodied. We are also aware, with few exceptions, that our current texts have rarely foregrounded the actual voices of real tutors who have experienced the very phenomena our classic texts channel obliquely but without, for want of a better term, *street cred.* We enter this dialogue fully recognizing that capturing every voice and every perspective would be a fool's errand, a folly of political correctness. Instead, we ask readers to riff on our authors' narratives and our responses through their own experiences. We also hope readers will find spaces and opportunities to extend the conversations we begin, as we don't intend this collection to shut down or offer a supposed last word on the dynamics and insights we offer across these pages.

Pragmatically, we had to make decisions about the order of the authors' essays and decided to structure the collection along an index of the intensity of the politics of identity, both historically and in relation to our present sociocultural moment. Quite simply, race, and especially the experiences of African Americans, occupies a powerful center in the United States and academia that just cannot be denied; it, of course, does not diminish the power and felt experience of the innumerable other aspects of who we are as humans, citizens, educators, students, and leaders. Our colleagues who authored the *Everyday Writing Center* capture the crux of our values and thinking so well:

> A common objection to studying and working against racism specifi-
> cally is that there are other forms of oppression, such as sexism, classism,
> and homophobia for which critical race theory and anti-racism do not
> account. While we acknowledge the importance of working for justice in
> these other crucial areas, we offer anti-racism work as a place to begin for
> what we believe to be compelling reasons: Racism cuts through multiple
> identities and magnifies the effects and impact of other manifestations of
> oppression. The experience of people of color who are also women, work-
> ing class, and/or gay is markedly different from the experiences of whites
> who share those other identities. (Geller et al. 2007, 91–92)

As a result of the wise insights of our reviewers and Michael Spooner, our intrepid editor, we go further, we think, than Geller et al. and other collections that take up race. We revised our manuscript with a specific mission to foreground the complexity and intersectionality of identity. No other current text has such a self-awareness and an antifoundation-alist mission; we pushed our contributors to revise with a sense of how their narratives might refuse to stop with just another contribution to the ever-expanding lore, or what Grutsch McKinney terms the "grand narratives" on which writing center scholarship tends to depend (too much, some might argue). Readers will notice that the complexity and nuance that comes with perspective and age, as a tutor *graduates* to other professional experiences or as a tutor (or director) recognizes that their unique privilege in a situation is different from those who occupy other positions. Following part 1, on race, we turn to a discussion of multilingualism. The politics of language commingles in our society with the politics of race; in practice, they cannot be separated because the bodies and the voices whose accented English or vernaculars are policed are easily racialized bodies, albeit often different from the bod-ies involved in the centuries-long struggle against racial oppression and white supremacy as exercised in the United States.

Just like race and the politics of language, gender and sexual identi-ties are ubiquitous in the landscapes of writing centers. The fluidity and fear of transgressing conventions makes the recognition and perfor-mance of gender and sex more charged today than ever before. That tension and its heat lead us to share the perspectives of our authors, who push at the boundaries and implications of gender and sexuality in the everyday work of writing centers. Everyone who enters our spaces embodies and performs gender and sexuality as part of the amalgam of who they are, and those practices are rife with both personal and institutional complexity. Like all spaces, writing centers function within patriarchy; however, confronting our gendered/sexual selves is amplified by the intimacy of writing and by the conferences in which it is discussed. That work happening in writing centers operates from pedagogical principles that value the feminist influences of collaborative learning and collective support and encouragement. The very movement that made possible the mantra "the personal is political" also fostered teaching moments that encourage individual, deep connection to the writing process. The insights the feminist movement made possible for challenging the wider dynamics and relations of sex and gender also contributed to a questioning of sexuality, another intrinsic component to who we are and how we identify. Queering our sexual politics isn't just the stuff of protest surrounding antidiscrimination and equal treatment under the law. The assumptions and hegemony of sexuality are ever present in sessions and tutor education, just as whiteness and patriarchy are.

We conclude by turning to parts on faith, class, and disability, all of which are less visible aspects of identity but no less critical to who we are and what influences how we perform our sense of self. Each of these elements of our identities requires a performance, if not an explicit disclosure, in interactions, particularly in sessions. We grant that any of these features of identity might be legible, as race, ethnicity, gender, and sexuality are, but they require a certain literacy for recognition that is different from the literacy required for recognition of those other components of identity. We also readily concede that in coming out, in disclosing their class, faith, or disability, individuals can be the objects of prejudice, stereotypes, bigotry, and even discrimination. All these effects of oppression, whoever the object, are always deplorable and immoral, by our view. We cluster these subjects in the latter part of the text not to minimize or marginalize them but out of pure recognition that their histories and frequency are far less intense or charged in US society and education.

We do, however, caution our readers to avoid using identity politics as a tactic to leverage over other groups, to jockey for status, or to privilege one performativity over another. Although the collection is organized by aspects of who we are as consultants, directors, and those in between, we are fully aware that seeing these components of who we are as totalizing and galvanizing, even stable, presents its own unique set of concerns, namely the inability to fully espouse a perspective that embodies intersectionality. At the same time, we realize how difficult perspective can be, particularly when contemplating and reacting to moments that may have elicited fear, pain, or frustration. With great ease, we can invoke a rhetoric that essentializes experience, and in doing so, we risk keeping others from engaging with us—holding them to a hard line of who can and should identify accordingly. Instead, we ask readers to find and build alliances on the nuance of experience. We encourage readers to discover our gaps or lapses and to imagine how they might individually, or in collaboration, further complicate and extend the conversation with others and through others. We invite readers to talk with one another and with all the writers in this collection, to praise, to challenge, to speculate, to deepen, and to build toward further inquiry.

PART I

Race

1

BEING SEEN AND NOT SEEN
A Black Female Body in the Writing Center

Talisha Haltiwanger Morrison

Growing up in a small town in Oklahoma, I was very often, and very noticeably, a Black body in White spaces. When I was very young, I was curious about what made Black people different from White people. My grandma used to say White people smelled funny, but I could never tell any difference. We all smelled the same to me: White, Black, and the other races too. There was one White kid who smelled funny, but I think he was an exception. In elementary school, I wondered whether the White kids were smarter than I was, if maybe that's why some of them got to go off to that special class. But I made straight pluses (+) in elementary school and then straight As, so that wasn't it. I think they just got to go because their parents were doctors and stuff, so it was a race and a class thing, but not an intelligence thing. I don't know why, but when I was around six years old, I also wondered if White girls' pee made a sound when it hit the toilet water like mine did. Personally conducted bathroom studies confirmed that it did, so this, also, was not the difference between White people and Black people.

Eventually I realized that physically, the difference was mostly just skin and hair. But there was also something else, which I would later identify as cultural differences. One of these differences was that Black people talked about race, at least with other Black people. Black people talked about being Black. White people did not talk about being White, did not talk about White and Black, did not talk about Latino or Native or Asian Americans. Over time I heard them say they did not "see" race. Did that mean they did not *see* me?

Of course, they did see me, how could they not? I was a Black body in White spaces. They just didn't want to talk about it. And being a Black kid in White spaces, I learned I was not supposed to talk about it either (at least not until one of my White teachers called upon me to explain how all Black people feel about the use of word *nigger* in

DOI: 10.7330/9781607327837.c001

Huckleberry Finn). Other Black kids in White spaces also learn not to talk about it.

TO THE CENTER

I am working as an undergraduate tutor at the University of Oklahoma when a Black female student walks in with a paper. She is assigned to me and we sit down and begin working. The student is a friend, a coworker from one of my other jobs on campus. I can't remember now what her paper was about exactly, just that in it, she describes a racist incident, but she's circling around the word *racist*, leading up to it but never getting there. I don't at the time, and still do not now, assume all Black people and other people of color are comfortable talking about race, especially in White spaces, and especially since at this point in my life, I'm still finding ways to do so myself. But this student knows me. Our outside relationship lessens the hierarchy and blurs the line between "peer" and "consultant" (Zhang et al. 2013), and I can speak as a friend and as one Black woman to another. I ask her to explain what happened, just in her own words, and when she does, I can push her further. "Racism," I say, "you're talking about racism."

"I know," she says, giving an embarrassed giggle. "I was just trying to . . . I just didn't know if I could say . . . ," leaving her sentence unfinished.

Earlier I noted as an aside that teachers wanted me to speak on behalf of *all* Black people to determine whether or not the novel *Huckleberry Finn* is racist (Twain 1884). That was and wasn't an aside because that happens, all the time, and many people have talked about it—people of color expected to be representatives or spokespersons for their entire race. But it happens despite our acknowledgment of its wrongfulness and harmfulness to people of color.

Example: my first year in graduate school I took a required class in composition theory. One week into the class, we had a discussion about racial privilege, and a White student brought up how White people have the privilege of never having to speak for their entire race. The entire class, all White except me, agreed people of color shouldn't have to do this either. Two weeks later, the teacher shared a story about her first semester teaching when a White student wrote a racist paper arguing for the resegregation of schools. She told us how she responded, and the class had a discussion in which I did not participate at first, not for any particular reason other than that I was listening to others. Then, it happened. My teacher turned to me, the single Black student not only in the class or program but also in the entire English department: "Well,

I think we're ignoring the *obvious* perspective in the room." I had been called OUT. Again. I was uncomfortable with the way I had been called to enter the conversation, but as a first-semester graduate student, I was a bit unsure of myself in the new setting. I offered my opinion that yes, the paper was horrible, the student's viewpoint offensive, but given his background and lack of exposure to Black people, I could see why he might hold such a bigoted viewpoint, and I thought the teacher had responded as appropriately and effectively as she could have. Several of the White students in the class roared back with an odd kind of righteousness. I was wrong! How could I not be outraged by such ignorance from this eighteen-year-old kid (who had never actually met a Black person before attending college)? Later we would read Jacqueline Jones Royster's "When the First Voice You Hear Is Not Your Own." I came to understand that from my classmates' perspective, I had not spoken "authentically" as a Black person nor shared an appropriate Black response (Royster 1996). At the time, I sat shocked, falling silent while my teacher engaged my classmates in further discussion without me.

BACK TO THE CENTER

Spending so much time as the only or one of few people of color in White spaces, I should be very familiar with how isolating it is. But it's a strange thing, you almost forget you're alone. A Black student at Purdue, however, reminds me when he walks into the writing lab to work on a paper for his English composition course. The assignment asks him to write about an organization he participates in and why it is important. He's chosen an organization providing academic and social support for minorities in business. The student writes about how helpful the organization is, about how without the organization, Black men like himself might not make it in a place like Purdue. I ask him what he means by that. He hesitates before going on to state the obvious: there are few Black people at Purdue. He says the organization helps him feel connected because he did not when he first arrived on campus. He felt invisible and alone. "So why didn't you write that?" I ask.

"Well, I just, I didn't know if I could just say that," he tells me. Like the student at Oklahoma, he is wary of speaking openly, of calling attention to the Whiteness of this space. The student sees me, the lone Black face in the writing lab, but I still bring myself further out. I tell him about my first experience walking onto my undergraduate campus. College was a whole new world from high school, and I had been fortunate enough to find friends and resources to help me, but when I came to Purdue, I realized it had not been intended for me, or people like me; despite decades of access, some things about the place still resisted me. I tell him I know about the isolation, about reaching out and trying to grasp something familiar, which I had experienced even more while earning my master's degree. Unlike this student, I am not new here or to this experience. I am in my third year at my third large predominantly White research institution. I also don't know this student the way I knew the young Black woman at Oklahoma, but elements of his experience still speak to me. I tell him I do understand some of what he is trying to convey and that it's okay to put those feelings into words if they are his truth. As far as I know, he has not come back to the writing lab. I did see him a few more times that semester in the building for his class and elsewhere on campus. Each time, we both smiled and said hello to one another, a small bond that might not still exist were we to see each other now, but it accomplished what we each needed to keep going at that time.

During the same semester I worked with the Black student discussed above, I had a Nigerian international student in my English composition course. I ended up developing a more lasting bond with this student, who sometimes shared her struggles and confusion about being Black in the United States. She visited the writing lab several times that semester and had trouble filling out the demographic information: she identified as Black, but not African American, and these things were lumped together, *Black/African American.* In class, we frequently discussed racism. The student shared an experience in which someone had told her she was "smart, for a Black girl." I remember smiling, knowingly, wearily, and telling her I had had several similar experiences: White people who were shocked that I could be Black AND intelligent, Black AND articulate, and who commonly extended this line of thought to my appearance, Black AND pretty. My student and I chatted when she came in for tutorials at the lab, and she often visited my office hours. She shared more of her experiences about being a Nigerian international student, which seemed to be much different from the experiences of Chinese and Indian students, perhaps due to the much smaller community as well as the different way Black and Asian bodies are racialized the in United States. We talked about our hair, and she shared her frustration with trying to find products while confined to campus. I gave her the name of the website where I order my hair supplies because I know the struggle for sufficient Black haircare products gets better but does not end with access to the Greater Lafayette community.

TO THE CENTER AGAIN

Later that semester I end up working with an Asian international graduate student. He is working on a business proposal for a mobile app for Black women with natural hair. The app would allow women to take photos of their hair, which could then be sent in and analyzed for texture, consistency, curl pattern, and so forth, and the app would recommend products for specific hair types. Women could even cut off a piece and mail in a sample of their hair for more specific analysis. I sit there, a Black woman with a head full of dark, curly, natural hair, slowly coming to the realization that this man's text is about, but not for, me.

Reading this man's work I find myself having a response I've never truly experienced in the writing center: anger. I am growing more and more upset at how Black women's hair, which is a very touchy topic for Black women, is being described. I am upset that this man is looking to make money from exploiting Black women's struggles to care for our hair—to make *money*. I am upset he can sit here beside me and discuss it so objectively, analytically. I am having a physical reaction to this student's project. My back goes rigid; my chest feels tight; I am hyperaware of my dark-brown curls, held back by an elastic band at the crown of my head. This tutorial is the most vivid experience of *feeling* my body, including my curly hair, in a session. And, the most bizarre part is that the student remains completely oblivious to my discomfort. I am, at times, literally squirming in my seat as he discusses Black women, and he takes no note of me or of my hair.

During the session I look around the lab, almost for an escape route. There are no other free tutors, and no one seems to be aware of my distress. I consider excusing myself from the session anyway because I am so upset. But I do not. The student has come for help, and despite my discomfort, is it not my obligation to help him? This is a legitimate question. Am I obligated to help him when I feel so physically uncomfortable? At the time, I decide yes, so I keep going, helping to increase his sentence clarity, which is his primary concern as a multilingual writer speaking to an audience he is hoping will give him money. I sit through the session, concerned about my emotional safety but also about my obligation. I am feeling angry for the first time in a session, but as Audre Lorde acknowledges in one of my favorite essays, "The Uses of Anger," even she, Black, woman, and a lesbian, has privilege based on her class and education that allows her to feed her children without worry (Lorde 1997, 284). I am called to think about my positionality. I am a Black woman whose identity is being commodified, but I am also a tutor at the Purdue Writing Lab. Before me is a male researcher seeking funds for a project, but he is also an international student who may be penalized because he possesses less command over standardized, academic American English than I do. Also, being an international student and growing up outside the United States, the student is less likely to be accustomed to paying attention to race and racial difference in the particular ways Americans do. Knowing this, still I feel I must speak. I cannot be what J Quaynor calls a "bystander" for the sake of professionalism (Zhang et al. 2013)

I begin by asking the student for more information. The proposal had grown out of the student's dissertation project. I ask if the faculty sponsor is a Black woman. She is, which gives me some hope that some of my concerns may be addressed by her when she looks at his proposal (I have looked at the first draft). I ask if he has considered whether or not Black women will be resistant to the technology, where it came from, and how it deals with Black hair. During our conversation I even, cautiously, express my concern that this product is a way to capitalize on Black women's constant struggle to find the right products. The student's app may meet a need, but I am worried about how he is suggesting it be met and worried that the affective component of finding Black hair blogs/vlogs/tutorials, which is where many Black women turn to for advice, will be lost. The writer is very open to my questions, and by the end of our conversation many of my concerns have faded away—though not completely.

He says the conversation has been useful for identifying some changes he needs to make because he wants to be careful about how he talks about Black women and their hair and about how to include Black women as part of the process of helping other Black women find the right products. The conversation is beneficial to him, as I've ultimately drawn not just on my knowledge of the English language but also on my knowledge and experience as a Black woman to help the student make rhetorical decisions, an effective use and balance of power and authority (Carino 2003). An important difference between the successful session Peter Carino describes in "Power and Authority in Peer Tutoring" and my tutorial, however, is that in my tutorial, my very personal self is part of the session, and not really on my terms. And despite the good that resulted from our conversation, I question, even now, whether or not I should have remained in the session in the first place. Carino (2003) says that "students who enter writing centers should be made to feel as comfortable as possible, if for no other reason than basic human decency" (98). But what of tutors? Where was the line between my obligation to the student and my own personal safety?

Fast forward to the following summer. I am doing an online tutorial chat session, also with an international student writing about Black women's hair. The student has watched Chris Rock's documentary *Good Hair* as part of a sociology class and must write a response paper (Stilson 2009). Most of the paper is a summary, or putting the film in conversation with what the student has read about domination and how Black people, in this case Black women, have had to change their appearance to try to assimilate with dominant culture. Toward the end of the paper, the student writes that Black people should resist this domination, and that if Black women took more pride in their hair, then maybe natural hair would become the dominant mainstream style. I find myself in a new situation, one that has never happened before: as I respond to this student, I must *choose* to come out, to disclose my Blackness. Or, I could choose not to. I know this student likely does not mean what her sentence suggests: that Black women's lack of pride is the reason for their subordination. I know this is an issue of phrasing, most likely arising from her being a second language writer. At the end of our session, I raise this thought. She quickly confirms my belief that the sentence conveys something she did not intend. But unlike the former student, she *cannot* see me. I wonder, if I tell her—that I am a Black woman, that I have natural hair—will I do her harm? Will she be concerned she has offended me? Should this be my primary concern? I tell her I know she did not intend a negative inference and that was why I brought it to her attention. And then I continue: I tell her that as a Black woman with natural hair, I can say we are very proud of our hair, but she is correct that there is still discrimination and that sometimes, even now, this discrimination comes from other Black women. I also tell her things have gotten a little better since Rock's film was released seven years prior. She thanks me for my honesty and perspective. The appointment time has ended. I give a couple of last-minute suggestions, wish her luck, and sign off to begin the next appointment.

2

A TOUCHING PLACE
Womanist Approaches to the Center

Alexandria Lockett

Every day I worked in the undergraduate or graduate writing center, someone hugged me. This should not be a remarkable observation, but I consciously avoided any physical contact with students as a writing teacher in the same institutional space. Student interactions in my classes were detached, even steely. Bodies sat across from one another with firm distance as we maintained a procedural boundary. Occasionally, a student embraced me after the term was over, usually when seeing me to request a recommendation and follow-up after the course. Such rare instances of touch caused me to remember the first time I realized how often I was touched in writing center spaces.

In my personal tutoring experience with both undergraduate and graduate student writers, touch operated in ways that opened up the possibility of confronting how dynamics of race, nationality, religion, gender, sexuality, age, social class, and body size affect student learning. This chapter critically examines some of the ways in which touch, as a literal and figurative act, contributed to intersectional writing tutoring practice. When interpreted through a black feminist ideology, touch can be used as a way of doing, seeing, reading, or coming to know power. Moreover, I discuss how touch can be strategically incorporated into the reporting practices of tutors through the structured use of personal narrative and autoethnography.

In particular, this chapter presents ten reflections on my tutoring practices in both an undergraduate writing center (UWC) and a graduate writing center (GWC) for the purposes of articulating an antiracist, decolonial black feminist tutoring methodology. By interpreting my personal experiences through a critical analysis of touch, I demonstrate how narrative reporting is capable of showcasing what happens during a tutoring session. These radical acts of disclosure seek to touch the reader in ways that may seem outside the scope of traditional research

DOI: 10.7330/9781607327837.c002

writing. However, writing center work warrants creative interpretation of tutoring practices. This unique learning environment hosts all kinds of social relationships emerging from the shared goal of improving language learning for the purposes of expanding the capacity and range of participants' writing and communication performances.

Throughout this theoretical exploration, I argue that touch is not a singular occurrence that can be easily observed through simple categories like good touch and bad touch. When considering the herstorical significance of touch, and how touch has been legally and socially regulated among different genders, sexualities, ethnicities, and so forth, we must recognize that touch is both a biological necessity for human beings and a symbolic act of power exchange. Thus, if we consider touch as a sequence of embodied acts of relating across spatiotemporal environments and media, we can simultaneously comprehend the nature of some of the cultural conflicts occurring in the center, as well as facilitate more positive social relationships among the writing center's numerous stakeholders.

Ultimately, this chapter seeks to negotiate the dissonance between "natural" and constructed responses to touch by candidly discussing how a black woman's body affected the movement of other bodies in both an undergraduate writing center shared by graduate and undergraduate tutors and a graduate writing center frequented by graduate students and the occasional faculty member.

TOUCH HAPPENS: EMBODIED LEARNING IS A TOUCHY SUBJECT

By touch, I mean *physical interaction* rather than an emotional response to some witty remark in a first-year undergraduate student paper or a brilliant observation in someone's research. According to a rare study by Angela M. Legg and Janie H. Wilson (2003) about touch in college settings, an instructor's simply touching students' wrists when taking their pulse during a single lecture positively affected their motivation, ability to attain learning outcomes, and attitudes toward faculty compared to students who were not touched (325). They concluded that if "necessary touch," which requires physical interaction between two people (e.g., touching a wrist to take a pulse or a fitness instructor firmly planting their hand on a client's back to support a greater range of motion), could improve a student's learning experience, "non-necessary touch," such as a tutor briefly touching a client's arm, may do so as well. Thus, Legg and Wilson propose that "as teachers, perhaps we should further explore appropriate touch as part of our professional relationships with students" (326). Indeed, Legg and Wilson's recommendation is essential to observing the unique learning affordances possible in the writing center space.

Although touch among strangers, especially across genders and races, may conjure uncomfortable and even potentially traumatic emotions, it must be acknowledged as a way of knowing. Writing centers are uniquely positioned to subvert the notion that touch is inappropriate in educational spaces, which introduces exciting possibilities for reconceptualizing a more humane definition of professionalism and a potential for cultivating friendship.

For example, a first-year graduate student, an international student from China who became a dear friend, set up appointments to see me every week. After a few visits, she came in, sat down next to me, and linked her arm in mine after she set up her laptop on the table. She snuggled against me, and we worked on improving her syntax because English was her third language. My initial reaction was to move away because I wondered how people would interpret our closeness (even though the door was open). However, I did not want to give her the impression that I did not appreciate her comfort and cause her to shut down during the rest of the session. If she didn't care, why should I?

After our sessions concluded, I wondered whether our visible touch was pushing the boundaries of the consultant/the consulted too far. Since I was not technically her teacher, I knew no institutional policies could penalize me for cuddling in the writing center. Yet, I felt guilty because I never seemed to see other people hugging, holding hands, or crying in the writing center. Is a professional space signified by a lack of touch between those bodies moving in it?

I always wonder what some mean when they describe writing centers as potentially *subversive* spaces. Too often the meaning of this evaluation goes unstated. The word *subversive* certainly implies a certain kind of political value, but not in a fully actualized sense. It is one of those concepts that feels deviant without being anomalous, provocative—and even bold—but not edgy or overt. Writing centers sometimes function as a *queer* space because they offer the possibility for a kind of physical and intellectual intimacy largely unavailable in the majority of institutional ("professional") space. As a textual place, writing centers are a sexual place, but not in the sense of genital contact. Depending on the configuration of bodies willing and able to move in ways that disrupt white bourgeois heterosexual norms of interaction, the subversion possible in writing centers is the redefinition of public displays of emotion and touch.

As an embodied concept, touch signifies *interaction*. The consent of the touched may never be known to the person touching, as silence offers no indication of permission or desire. A verbal cue of yes may not be useful either, as some people may find themselves uncomfortable with touch after the fact. A simple phrase, "No, don't do that," is unequivocally a request to stop touching another person immediately. Yet, this remark could be a proprietary reaction. Ideologies of politeness mediate touch variously in human-centered spaces. We may avoid it altogether when it seems too risky and ambiguous.

In simple terms, touch communicates a desire for intimacy, which is similar to touch in its lack of neutrality. A gentle stroke of a thigh could be creepy or thoughtful—depending on our gender, the place, or the nature of our relationship. A smack of the hand to prevent that same touch is touch too. We also touch without hands. The breeze of breath from a pair of lips uttering "Stop," or a rapid heart flutter from a quicker pulse reacting to fingertips grazing against the arm, initiates a sequence of touch. We should pause to consider how we know when touch will be permitted or rejected, or considered lewd and inappropriate. In our meditation, we may realize avoiding touch doesn't make touch go away. We always touch, we just aren't always aware we do.

The complexity of consent creates superficial touch discourses. Of course you should not invade another person's space. In fact, keeping your hands to yourself is a primary method of embodying nondirective technique in writing center space. One might observe an undergraduate tutor frequently notifying new clients that the tutor won't touch the paper with a pen, or even with their hands. The hands-off-the-paper approach honors Western ideologies of property ownership. If I don't touch the paper, despite my intellectual assistance, it remains *yours* somehow. After all, writing centers must oblige academic-honesty policies that may readily interpret the transformations unfolding in the writing center as outside the scope of authorized collaboration.

Closely examining the meaning of touch in writing centers moves us into a very generative theoretical space. Of course, the semantics of touch and the role of consent must be considered through the fraught history of colonialism and capitalism—both of which rely on each other to terrorize, exploit, commodify, and exhaust human bodies. However, it is also true that several studies support the fact that appropriate touch may improve student learning as a consequence of multiple physiological benefits such as stress reduction, mood enhancement, positive behavior, enhanced mental functioning, and increased positive affect toward the toucher (Legg and Wilson 2013, 318, 326). As writing center professionals discuss *best practices* and assert their *professional-ness* to their colleagues and their social media audiences, have they considered the extent to which their narratives of writing centers involve the issue of touch in tutoring?

OUT OF TOUCH: WRITING CENTERS AS A FUGITIVE SPACE

I worked as an English 005 tutor at the Pennsylvania State University's UWC from 2011 to 2014 and as a GWC tutor from 2013 to 2014. My writing center experiences spanned being an ABD PhD student to securing a tenure-track assistant professor of English position at Spelman College. These details matter for two major reasons. First, I was the oldest tutor working in both the UWC and the GWC. When I assumed the position, I did not realize it was a somewhat stigmatized job. Younger tutors often discussed that some of their peers thought tutoring in the writing center was probably the *lowest* job one could do as a grad student. However, a friend's positive experience made them curious, or the likeability of the director drew them there. Some stayed longer than a semester or two; most did not. Thus, it did not take long for me to recognize I was working in a "queer space."

By *queer*, I mean it was considered neither a *normal* place for most graduate teaching assistants nor a *normal* place for the typical student to obtain assistance. Although the undergraduate students with whom I worked ranged from honors to developmental, they came to the writing center because they considered the circumstance to be exceptional, or out of the norm.

Furthermore, I deliberately chose to work at the writing center because I did not feel safe teaching (predominantly white) male students at my historically white university (HWCU). I had experienced too many public confrontations with red-faced young men loudly questioning my grading practices and course content—most of which were part of the writing program's approved curriculum. On several occasions, my colleagues and I observed spectacular displays of disrespect—hands slamming down on my cubicle desk, eyes darting frantically around the room, and muscular arms flexing and folding across chests—all of which appeared to me as signs of danger. Their bodies moved quickly with backpacks filled with unknown contents. Our interactions occurred alongside a steady stream of national news headlines about mass shootings that made me especially cautious, and terrified, of white male rage.

By producing more narratives about tutoring in the writing center, I recognize I am disrupting the emerging discourse of "data-driven" or "evidence-based" research (Babcock and Thonus 2012; Driscoll and Perdue 2012; Nordstrom 2015; Ryan and Kane 2015). However, the lack of narratives from the perspective of Black women tutors warrants my qualitative approach. We should be cautious about privileging replicable and aggregable data (RAD) research over more explicitly subjective methods. The language of RAD tends to strip the human experience of its nuance and may risk diminishing the various ways we might interpret experience as data.

When researchers use adjectives such as *data-driven* or *evidence-based* to make rhetorical appeals for the validity of their research, they unnecessarily create a rigid separation between RAD and other kinds of information. What kind of research, for instance, isn't data or evidence?

Through such language, some RAD discourse asserts a claim to objectivism that effectively narrows the scope of observation to quantification. When we research the way people experience teaching and tutoring, we are investigating an inherently subjective phenomenon. What the observed do under observation, and how observers recognize certain performances, constitutes a rich cultural and socially situated exchange. Indeed, qualitative, artistic investigation about the human experience is a legitimate form of data collection. Any information that can be recognized as data emerges from a context in which the researcher recognizes how some story is being told or some representation is happening.

Moreover, the notion of RAD is applicable in any and all kinds of circumstances in which researchers are capable of acquiring a data set large enough to make claims about the existence of some phenomenon. As Neil Simpkins and Virginia Schwarz argue in their November 9, 2015, post to the blog *Another World*, "Queering RAD Research in Writing Center Studies," "Queer and trans ways of being in the world frequently resist creating patterns of data that are replicable and aggregable. For example, trans people may change their names and gender markers officially and/or unofficially, and this might affect individual data writing centers collect." This observation reinforces one of their other critiques, which is that marginal identities skew the data. Unfortunately, representations of historically underserved writing center tutors is so statistically insignificant that even anecdotal evidence from these populations remains absent in scholarship about writing centers. Thus, as researchers increasingly look to data science to appeal to the current educational bias toward the academics of science, technology, engineering, and math, today referred to as STEM, they inadvertently, and perhaps unknowingly, seek to depoliticize (and thus deracialize) writing center workers and their work. Our experiences matter and could generate more comprehensive strategies for further developing the value and significance of writing centers.

WOMANIST NARRATIVE REPORTING AS A TUTORING METHOD

As a first-generation, black woman college student at a college with a less than 2 percent black population, I found it impossible to ignore the misrepresentation and/or absence of my lived experience in so-called learning spaces. Black feminism, or womanism, has always been informing my intellectual engagement with the world. It offers a language and a methodology to describe black women's lived experiences. Scholars such as Irma McClaurin, an anthropologist like the great Zora Neale Hurston before her, draws on ethnography as a methodology for illustrating the significance of experience (2001). Similar to Jacqueline Jones Royster (1996), bell hooks (2000), Patricia Hill (2002, 1996), Beverly Guy-Sheftall (1995), Angela Davis (1999), Toni Cade Bambara (1970), and countless other black writers, McClaurin (2001) argues that black feminism is an epistemological, logical response to multiple oppressions women of all colors face—some occurring more simultaneously than others (5). There is no *one* definition of black feminism, and black women do not live a monolithic existence. This is why Collins refers to it as "a consciousness" and hooks and McClaurin call it "activism" (McClaurin 2001, 5).

Some writers, such as Alice Walker (1983), who dubs black feminism as "womanist" in *In Search of Our Mother's Gardens*, acknowledge that black women cannot ignore the effects of the intersectional relationship among race, class, gender, and sexuality (xi). For Walker (1983), "Womanist is to feminism as purple to lavender" (i). Walker (1983) vividly describes this relationship in her claim that "acting Womanish . . . usually refers to outrageous, audacious, courageous or *willful* behavior. . . . A woman who loves other women, sexually and nonsexually. Appreciates and prefers women's culture, women's emotional flexibility . . . , and women's strength" (xi; emphasis in original). Black feminism, then, is a multivocal struggle to articulate, contest, and eradicate oppression.

In writing centers, as elsewhere, I recognize that language, culture, and technology—as interlocking structures of power and privilege—affect any category conceived, transmitted, and circulated as part of standard white English. Communication is a *leaky* process in which we can directly observe some of the ways in which the bodies of humans, the words and phrases that come out of their mouths, the facial expressions they wear, and the physical gestures they make contribute meanings of the concepts race, class, gender, sexuality, geographic location, nationality, religion, and able-bodiedness. Since each term illustrates and impacts humans' perceptions of ability, access, and, ultimately, intelligence, they are functionally similar and thus interdependent.

I recognize that my body in a writing center, and any formal site of instruction, has a tendency to render it an *uncontrolled* space. Writers responded to my body variously, but its presence unsettled the "normal" practices of white undergraduate and graduate tutors. My body, when situated in a writing center, corresponded to the writer's discussion of personal experience. My body and its knowledge production were appropriated by other graduate tutors. My body was also praised and critiqued by some of the undergraduate tutors. Some tutors complained to the director about how "direct" my tutoring was, whereas others started listening in and doing differently because they "didn't know they could do that." Their training wasn't at odds with my methods, but most people found it "best" to listen to someone read a paper and suggest a comma here or a clarification there. No stories were exchanged between them, just two people across the table from one another connected but parallel through a paper and the occasional polite interruption: "Does this make sense" or "You may want to put the thesis at the end of the first paragraph." Don't get me wrong, some of my white middle- to upper-class students took to this method very well. They expected the extent of academic help to be answers to "Is this right or wrong?" as opposed to "Is this an excellent expression of that?"

However, my sense was a tremendous lack of freedom. Tutors and writers didn't seem to know they could get up, walk around, use the whiteboard, use the computer, find a text, write a sample sentence, talk about the meaning of the assignment, walk across the hall to the Women's Resource Center when the space got too rowdy full of paper reading, or do anything active at all. They restrained themselves from becoming too close to the space and too close to each other in the center.

I inhabit a body whose default expectation of any learning space is scrutiny and surveillance. The excerpts below give you a glimpse of how I experienced tutoring both inside and outside the so-called task at hand. I knew what was happening would be affected by my embodiment, and I wanted to actively participate in that process—writing notes during my graduate writing center sessions, and thus institutionalizing narrative writing as part of the graduate tutor's protocols, was how I accomplished that.

TEN TOUCHING REFLECTIONS
The GWC Sessions

STUDENT 1: This student has scheduled a GWC appointment to revise a paper about economic conditions in Brazil. She is composing the paper for an education course, and she struggles with her grammar. The student exemplifies multilingualism, as she fluently speaks English, Spanish, Portuguese, and French. Our shared languages—English and French—facilitate a productive grammar session. She punctuates our conversation about poverty by asking me about my geographic literacy. She pulls up maps on her screen and excitedly shows me where she is from and where she is writing about. We practice describing these places and incorporating those adjectives in her evaluation of how education functions there. As with many students, reading aloud is not an appropriate protocol for her. Since English is actually her fourth language, she is unable to hear her errors.

***

STUDENT 2: This student refers to himself as a "nontraditional" student because he is pursuing graduate study in his midforties. He is a psychology major who identifies as "former good writer" and who feels as if he is "losing his voice." He identifies as a Caucasian male from a working-class background. Reading aloud does not make sense for this student because he is not interested in having his paper "corrected." Rather, he is seeking information about academic writing conventions. We briefly examine his work, and I notice certain kinds of repetition that exemplify a student struggling to follow rules rather than create meaning. I interpret those repetitions as anxiety-induced impotence. He relates to this sexual metaphor, and we begin to explicitly discuss writing as an inherently sexual performance. The session should only last fifty minutes, but I give him an hour and fifteen minutes. After our session, he gives me a long, tight hug. He says, "Writing is more intimate than sex," a quote that continues to shape my theory of writing pedagogy. He immediately recoils, and blushes. I smile at him and let him know I understand his spontaneous reaction as a natural response to human connection, not an invitation to have sexual contact. He smiles, and we chat at the door for several minutes about his realization. He admits that the idea of coming to the writing center made him feel "impotent," but after our discussion, he understands he is adapting to a different set of expectations and that this adaptation requires "real" intellectual work.

***

STUDENT 3: This international student has been referred to me by one of her friends. She is from India. She is enthusiastic about our session because she wasn't aware that the GWC could help her with multimodal composition needs. Her understanding of the GWC was that it was a place to "double-check grammar." This belief shows me that associations of writing centers with remedial writing persist, even in graduate writing center spaces. However, I wonder whether another tutor would have been able to assists her with her specific interest—choosing the best portfolio platform for showcasing her work as an instructional technology professional—without a familiarity with design and a language for talking about new media. I show her my portfolio, and we create a physical layout sketch of what a portfolio could look like for her objectives. Storyboarding elbow against elbow, peeking over arms, and revealing the images connect us from page to screen.

***

STUDENT 4: This student identifies as a "nontraditional" graduate student because she is returning to graduate studies in her fifties. She is an African American woman from New York City, and she has been working in secondary-education administration for decades. She appears to be meticulously organized. Every page is highlighted, every page with a Post-it affixed. But she knows this method is failing. She can't crack the code of grad-school communication. She is barely making passing grades in her seminar, and she feels uncomfortable with her instructor. When she realizes she can "keep it real" in the space, she opens up about her feelings toward her instructor, whom she feels is dismissive of her professional experience and possibly racist. She also lets me know I make her uncomfortable because it is as if she is getting advice from her daughter. I listen to her like she's my mama, and admire her resolve. We use Black English alone and the language of wider communication when my colleagues enter the space. I love that she code switches quickly, and it builds a trust between us. I give her tissues and hug her tightly when our sessions are over. She sees me several times. Her writing grades go from Ds to As, and she wants to introduce me to her daughter because we are the same age. It never happens because I'm on the job market and I'm scheduled to visit eight campuses in one month. I still regret that we never had dinner together.

The UWC Sessions

STUDENT 1: This student is enrolled in a first-year composition class. He identifies as a white male with an upper-middle-class background. His purpose for enrolling in English 05 is based on a life-long experience working with tutors. He tells me about golf courses and his strict parents.

He sometimes complains about the fact that he can't be as athletic as black men. I never interrogate this racial obsession, but I wonder whether I should have. After three weeks of meeting, he hugs me after every session. He also hugs me if he sees me anywhere else on campus. His friends stare at us strangely when he introduces me as "his tutor."

***

STUDENT 2: This student is enrolled in a first-year composition class. She identifies as a white female from a solid middle-class background. She also identifies herself as a confident, "open-minded" Catholic and a good writer. She complains a lot about stupid girls and says the majority of her friends are male. She is tall, athletic, and curvaceous. She has long dark-brown hair, large eyes, and full lips. She avoids fraternity parties because she worries about being raped or drugged. She chose to take English 05 because she was pursuing personal growth and writing excellence. We make a lot of eye contact. At the end of the semester, her hair becomes blond. She hugs me occasionally, usually after particularly intense sessions.

***

STUDENT 3: This student is enrolled in a writing-across-the-disciplines course titled Business Writing. She is from China and expresses a strong interest in returning to her country. She is a fashionista, often wearing four- to five-inch heels and dramatic dark eye makeup to her sessions. We share makeup tips, and she tells me to "dress up" and "go to the gym" more. Our laughter often receives icy stares from the undergraduate tutors. We never hug, but she touches my leg and shoulder often.

***

STUDENT 4: This student is enrolled in first-year composition. He identifies as Asian American and working class. He is very self-conscious and enrolled in English 05 to increase his confidence. He is from a poor, predominantly black part of Philadelphia. He doesn't identify with the large international Asian student population and complains about the homogeneity of Penn State University. He loves basketball. He used to be in an interracial relationship with a black girl, who broke up with him during the same term as our tutoring experience. He is often tired; he started a rigorous gym regimen because his girlfriend "broke up with him for some jacked black guy." I make him blush when I compliment his writing ability, and sometimes I give him hugs. He never initiates them, but he always returns them. I tell him he's awesome and good-looking and will make someone really happy one day. I probably made him feel very uncomfortable sometimes.

***

STUDENT 5: This student took English 005 for two semesters in a row. I had her as a student when she was enrolled in ESL 004 and ESL 015, basic and first-year writing courses for multilingual students. She is enrolled in a special program called College Assistance Migrant Program (CAMP), which is designed to assist students whose parents are migrant workers. English 005 is a requirement of the program. This student is native to Cambodia, and she speaks very little English. Initially she was very shy, but after working with her for a few months, she confides a lot to me. She tells me stories about extreme poverty in her country and how she struggles with adjusting to dating expectations in America. She tells me she has a secret boyfriend, another Cambodian student in the CAMP program. She worries about her family finding out because she is supposed to be in an arranged marriage when she returns to her country. He is too. She gives me a long hug before and after every session.

***

STUDENT 6: The student is enrolled in first-year composition. She is a native French speaker and African American. She speaks impeccable standard white English during every single communication with me regardless of how I opt to communicate. She is petite and shy but often surprises me with moments of intense passion triggered by any discussions about social stratification. I introduce her to one of my other English 005 writers—an outspoken, first-year student from Gabon. The two women become close friends during our English 005 experience. Sometimes one comes for the other and we talk to each other for a half an hour or so. I never have physical contact with this student.

CRITICAL REPORTING IN THE WRITING CENTER

I was the only black tutor in the UWC for most of the time I was there. One other black woman was hired the last semester I worked there, and she never ever spoke to me despite the fact that I greeted her and attempted to initiate contact with her several times. Furthermore, she was an undergraduate student. I was the only black tutor for the GWC as well, which correlated with the fact that I was the only black female graduate student in the entire program after Dr. Ersula Ore graduated in 2011. One student was admitted the year after, but she withdrew from the program due to mental illness. The only other black woman to be admitted to English graduate studies from 2009 to 2014 was my mentee Mudiwa Pettis, but I had already graduated by this time.

I stress these details to illustrate that insomuch as writing centers obtain labor from English graduate students, the center is almost guaranteed *not* to have tutors representing historically underserved groups, including tutors who openly disclose a multilingual background. This is due to the fact that we do not make up a significant percentage of students studying the humanities at any higher educational level. In my personal experience, the tutoring space was inhabited primarily by white women.

Why, then, would I choose to place myself where even most English graduate students refused to tread? As I previously mentioned, I was asked on countless occasions by both my colleagues and the writers why I worked at the UWC if I had obtained a PhD. The fact that my credentials were often in question illustrates the primary reason I could not utilize most of the theoretical perspectives I was learning from editors Christina Murphy and Steve Sherwood's *St. Martin's Sourcebook for Writing Tutors*, which was used in my tutoring seminar (Murphy and Sherwood 2003). How was I supposed to worry about my tutoring approach when I had to first grapple with the problem of convincing writers I was capable of helping them at all? I often wonder how I would have asserted that credibility if I hadn't first been ABD, then earned a PhD, then secured employment in one of the worst academic job markets in history.

Therefore, I strongly believe in note taking as a part of teaching and tutoring practice. The ten reflections above were part of over fifty sessions in which I took detailed notes during my experience tutoring for Penn State University. It was a critical process that enabled me to perpetually reflect on what tutoring means, and especially what writing centers mean. On the one hand, it was a very technical process. It functioned to provide the writer with a reminder of the experience and strategies discussed in the session. On the other hand, I am just now becoming aware of the degree to which note taking impacted the session activity. Did writing down the event cause the student to reinforce their purpose (e.g., to learn how to become an excellent writer)? Could it possibly have intimidated and silenced them? The latter is worth noticing in the event that a tutor wants to ask the client how they feel about their session being recorded and narrated.

I often wondered why I didn't see writing tutors writing with their students in the center more. So many sessions are just oral proofreading. Many tutors are (justifiably) terrified of being accused of plagiarism or writing on student's papers. However, this concern is not at all helpful to students who read better than they can listen to English. Note taking, then, is about coherency, accountability, and transparency. It is about data and ultimately about evidence. I need the writers being consulted to see that I can write, that I can help them create, and that

I will follow up. I left my "traces" at Penn State University in all kinds of ways—whiteboard screen shots on a student's phone, countless Google Docs shared, and e-mails exchanged.

In this space, the narrative-driven, note-taking method illustrates a black feminist response to a tendency for writing centers to oppress students. Through the notes, I sought to illustrate the depth of our engagement. I composed my perception of our interaction in hopes that it would challenge them to think more critically about how they know *and* how they learn, especially as it related to our very different bodies negotiating meaning. Note taking, then, was an attempt to put forth the effort to teach them, learn from them, and document our process.

Every single student I worked with received a copy of these notes and reports. However, the brief background descriptions in this chapter were created after our sessions were complete and in preparation for this research effort. I have compiled and published them with names redacted for your reading and research pleasure and practice. This practice of disclosure and documentation was crucial for me to confront students' assumptions about my (lack of) intelligence and recognize the purpose of us both being in the space. I saw note taking as an effort toward concretizing the fact of writing centers as a place where cultural and intellectual work is done and circulated. Note taking also sparked feedback from instructors whose varying reactions demonstrated that tutors have the potential to redefine the power structures that often relegate writing centers to a position of *service only* and faculty as simply persons who passively transfer the duty of writing to institutional sites other than the classroom.

I disclosed these profiles of ten distinct learners—four graduate student writers, six undergraduate writers—because I wanted to show you, not tell you about, what it meant for me to put to work a theoretical perspective toward learning that privileges my students' attitudes and experiences. What I came to know about the student depended on their opportunity to disclose information about their lives and the ways in which that disclosure may have affected their topic choices, their learning obstacles, and of course, their relationship to me—the tutor. I am inviting you to pay attention to what I noticed about the students and to match that information with the notes I took during certain sessions, as was the case with the graduate student writers, or over a span of an entire semester, which was the case with the undergraduate student writers.

You will notice I include information about whether I physically touched the writers. Because I was someone who wasn't their teacher, boundaries of touch were quite blurry. I often asked other tutors, "Do your writers touch you sometimes?" This query led to very interesting responses, which varied from "absolutely not" to "I have been hit on countless times by my clients, and I have a strict no-touch policy." It occurred to me that the petite white girls were having radically different experiences than I was. Was I mammy-fied by the writing center—a desexualized, nurturing figure whom Asian girls could hold hands with and white men could hug without apprehension? On the other hand, I wondered whether the writing center ignited taboo sexual feelings between me and some of the writers. Why, for instance, did some white male writers tell me about their genetic envy of black males, or how they preferred blondes to all other women when discussing evaluation arguments? What kind of response did they expect from such disclosure? Did it just leak out under the pressure of control collapsing in the midst of difference?

In sum, these profiles are telling in their discussion of what is happening to our bodies, their contact, our closeness, and our separation. I want you to compare our experiences and consider how your students disclose and how they hide. To what extent do they raise questions about how much you give your writing to the center, or whether you are required to?

At best, the writing center enables tutors to experiment with various methods of practicing cultural and intellectual work. When a tutors' care is interpreted by their clients/writers as permission to reveal empathy, sadness, frustration, anger, joy, and even love in tears, hugs, kisses on the cheek, the holding of hands, or fingers grazing a thigh in the public place of the writing center, we must examine the theoretical significance of these acts. We may find that touch, in its most radical sense, is a creative, deeply psychological engagement that spontaneously emerges from the unnecessary constraints of the policy and the program.

3

BLACK MALE BODIES IN THE CENTER

Richard Sévère

> *Sell cigarettes and your body will be destroyed. Resent the people trying*
> *to entrap your body and it can be destroyed. Turn into a dark stairwell*
> *and your body can be destroyed. . . . Why—for us and only us—is the*
> *other side of free will and free spirits assault upon our bodies.*
> —Ta-Nehisi Coates, *Between the World and Me*

As a man of color standing six feet two inches and weighing two hundred pounds, I have never been so aware of the anxiety my body causes others as I am now with the recent barrage of media images displaying similar black male bodies whose lives have been cut short at the hands of a system intended to serve and protect—bodies taken from this world because of perceived threats to the more privileged (white) male body. As an academic, I am even more attuned to my body and its nuances, a body that to some is a symbol of intimidation, aggression, and perceived anger—a body that speaks without an utterance. More important, my work in writing centers has cast an even greater light onto my body in ways that are equally alarming. Specifically, the perceived threat of the black male body (in media) has implored me to search for other bodies of color (directors and otherwise) in writing center work—a search for guidance, mentorship, comfort, empathy, and support from similar bodies that are at times silent, inherently political, and most often misinterpreted. Time and time again I am let down in finding such bodies. However, I did find some moments of solace in my former writing center, where five of the male writing consultants were of color, because I found that we shared similar stories in which our bodies are scrutinized, fetishized, and demoralized. Pivotal book-length studies on race in the writing center, particularly Harry Denny's 2010 *Facing the Center*, Laura Greenfield and Karen Rowan's 2011 *Writing Centers and the New Racism*, and Frankie Condon's 2012 *I Hope I Join the Band*, have called for writing

DOI: 10.7330/9781607327837.c003

center practitioners and scholars to pay critical attention to the ways in which racial identities shape/influence the work done in the writing center. Jason Esters's 2011 piece, "On the Edges: Black Maleness, Degrees of Racism, and Community on the Boundaries of the Writing Center," speaks specifically about the experiences and the challenges of overcoming stereotypes mapped onto Black male identities. As Denny (2005) points out in his essay "Queering the Writing Center," "For many people of color and women, their bodies encode their identity and speak for them" (9). While Denny's words ring true, absent from these critical works are the ways Black males and their coded bodies navigate and negotiate how they are perceived and received in writing centers—how these bodies are culturally coded and how those codes are interpreted in light of public controversies that incessantly convey Black men as inherently violent. What I have found is that conversations about Black males in the writing center are noticeably absent and that Black males themselves seem to be largely underrepresented in the field, thus nodding to Greenfield and Rowan's 2011 "new racism." This essay engages the intersectionality between race and gender, specifically representations of the Black male body in the media and how those images impact the writing center. My experiences and those of other Black male bodies in the writing center are intended to broaden the discussion about identity politics and how public discourses echo in these spaces.

AT THE CENTER—THESE BLACK BODIES

In his 2015 book *Between the World and Me*, Ta-Nehisi Coates speaks to his son about being Black in America and offers these words:

> But you are a black boy, and you must be responsible for your body in a way that other boys cannot know. Indeed, you must be responsible for the worst actions of other black bodies, which, somehow, will always be assigned to you. And you must be responsible for the bodies of the powerful—the policeman who cracks you with a nightstick will quickly find his excuse in your furtive movements. (Coates 2015, 71)

Coates's warning to his young son is disappointedly timeless and yet critical in pointing out how public controversies reinscribe personal bias that can infiltrate the writing center. To reiterate one of the many aims of this collection, we must be mindful that writing centers are not walled off from the influence of social, cultural, political, and economic currents. Coates's warning is not only to his son but to all men of color—which means men of color who work in the writing center and those who use it. And thus when former colleagues (in and out of the writing center) tell me, better yet confess to me, that I come off as very intimidating—even at times unapproachable—in writing center spaces that are supposed to be comfortable, at least according to the master narrative Jackie Grutsch McKinney's *Peripheral Visions for Writing Centers* says we create about ourselves, I am left to think about the many ways in which I am responsible for the codes ascribed to my body. I recognize that, undoubtedly, my physicality sends a message. Though I hope that message is positive and dynamic in nature, and I realize that in many instances it is depending on the context and who is receiving the message, there are moments in which my six-foot-two-inch-two-hundred-pound frame is engaging others in a negative dialogue unbeknownst to my consciousness. People have casually referenced the size of my upper body as justification for their intimidation or admiration. My chest, biceps, and shoulders aren't what some would describe as small, but how those features translate to violence, harm, or rejection is largely due in part to public perceptions oftentimes guided by either isolated experience or exposure to the reoccurring images projected by some form of media. As Lamar Johnson and Nathaniel Bryan point out, "Black males who are *spiritually* murdered are/were an already constructed text which vilifies Black boys and men because the Black body, even when unarmed, is armed in the eyes of white people"(Johnson and Bryan 2017, 163; emphasis in original). Only decades ago, the world watched the brutal beating of Rodney King at the hands of four white LAPD officers. The four men accused of beating King were acquitted, leading one of the jurors to point out that "he [King] was obviously a dangerous person, [with a] massive size and threatening action" (quoted in Hutchinson 1994, 9). Ellis Cose's 2003 *The Envy of the World* points out that the LAPD justified its tactics by portraying King as a "quasi-mythical beast, imbued with herculean strength and sub-human self-awareness" (8). Most recently, Michael Brown's mother, in commenting on her son's death at the hands of a white police officer in St. Louis, said he was killed because he was tall, big, and black. Such observations can certainly be read as affirmation of Earl Ofari Hutchinson's claim in *The Assassination of the Black Male Image* that the United States has made the Black man its universal boogeyman—a claim made nearly two decades ago (Hutchinson 1994, 00). In his reflection on how Black masculinity is perceived globally, Antonio D. Tillis, who serves as the dean of the College of Liberal Arts and Social Sciences at the University of Houston, points out that "the Black male is deconstructed globally . . . thus bearing the burden of stigmatization because 20th and 21st century popular media present, package and sell him in such a light for global consumption" (Tillis 2011, 215). As Cassandra Jackson's 2011 *Violence, Visual Culture, and the Black Male Body* also points out, the consumption of the Black male body has a long-standing tradition in US culture, from the auction block to the television set. Jackson argues, "Beauty and the threat of violence combine to produce a prurient experience that exploits the simultaneous cultural anxiety about and attraction to the black male body" (50). It is because of this consumption that despite intellect, education, location, intent, identity, or cultural heritage, Black male bodies remain in constant flux, concurrently traversing positions in the center and at the margins of society. Perhaps more important is Yolanda Sealy-Ruiz and Perry Greene's claim that "society often takes its cue on how to treat Black males based upon the past and current stereotypes about Black males and the (mis)representation of them" (Sealey-Ruiz and Perry Greene 2015, 55). Accordingly, writing centers are not immune to enacting such bias or exempt from engaging the ubiquitous gaze—in fact, it is one of the first steps in writing center practice. When we think of the face-to-face tutorial, physicality—one's immutable traits—is the first point of reference that unconsciously, or perhaps consciously, sets the tone for our interactions. And thus how we go about the work of the center is inherently rooted in a discourse that intersects with perceptions associated with race and gender.

To return to Grutsch McKinney's examinations of grand narratives in writing centers, specifically the archetype of the writing center as a space intended to replicate the home—or a spaced deemed as feminine and nurturing—two ideas come to mind: being male and, more important, being a male of color. When read against the paradigm of the home, the media has constructed the Black male body as an intruder, one who subverts the impression of safety and destabilizes the home. As Grutsch McKinney (2013) puts forth, "Home life may be abusive or dangerous" (26). More important, what does it mean for those who have never had a man of color in their home (socially or otherwise)? Or for some, what about the myth of the absent Black father who abandons the home? How do those codes manifest in writing center discourse? I and others who look like me occupy a space already coded with assumptions about our bodies, reminding us as Coates (2015) points out that Black men are "responsible for the worst actions of other black bodies" (71). The writing center space is not impervious to such public projections. As Denny points out, "Racial identity politics involves dynamics where marked bodies, those of people of color, come to signify with an excess of codes, a comprehensive set of meanings" (Denny 2010, 45). The Black male body is multicoded, signifying race, gender, class, and, in my case, physicality. In the midst of public cases involving Trayvon Martin, Eric Garner, Michael Brown, Laquan McDonald, Alton Sterling, Philando Castile, Keith Lamont Scott, Terence Crutcher, and countless other black victims represented by the Hands Up Movement and Black Lives Matter is a call for men of color to be on notice that that their bodies can be their enemies—bodies that need to be tamed, shrunk, and made less visible. Academic spaces, where cultural competence has not proven innate among academics, are no less problematic. I have found that men of color must metaphorically have our "hands up," not only to provide a sense of comfort for others who perceive us as naturally threatening but also as a means of acculturation. All emotional signs must be controlled so as to not incite fear or we risk relegation to being the "angry black man." Undoubtedly, it would be naïve to think my physicality does not impact the writing center as students, whether knowingly or unknowingly, associate my frame (the "big black guy") with my role in the writing center. Physically I represent the antithesis of nurturing and feminine and recognize such contradictions are bound to cause anxiety for some.

My experiences motivated me to seek the out often-silent bodies in writing center discourse. At two recent writing center conferences, we shared our stories, reflecting on what it means to exist in these bodies and how that existence impacts the work we do in the center. One male tutor, Ameer, whose physique I liken to Michael Brown's, reflected on the ways his body is coded and interpreted by others: "In correlation to a bear, with my stature, I'm considered a black bear. I stand six feet five inches and weigh 273 pounds, I'm husky, and I'm an African American male: all the signs of a threat to society as portrayed by the media." Ameer's awareness of his own body and his description of its semblance to what most would consider an unapproachable, outright dangerous animal is fodder for critical discussions about race and gender in the writing center. His presence is politically and socially tagged, exacerbated by images of Black males deemed dangerous by a system constructed to entice fear from others who come in contact with similar bodies. When played out in the writing center, Ameer's public and private worlds not only intersect but potentially collapse.

> I find myself continuously acting during my consultations. Because the writing center is supposed to be an inviting place, with no hierarchy, I shrink myself to make people feel comfortable. How can people feel comfortable with a tall black man hovering over them? It's like a black bear standing on his hinds at full height; it can be very intimidating. What I mean by continuously find myself acting—I'm talking about my

mannerisms. I find myself slouching to not feel as big as I am. I try to sit forward and crunch down or sometimes sit further back, away from the tutee, and I also speak with a softer voice than I normally would. (pers. comm.)

The need to *perform*, to physically shrink oneself, confirms the ways social biases are marked and coded onto the body—Ameer is not only aware of his own body but also aware of how that body compels other bodies to perform. The power dynamics between tutor and tutee become part of a discourse driven by each individual's personal, social, and political experience—how they see themselves in a larger, public context. Ameer reminds us of the ways he falls victim to the writing center grand narratives Grutsch McKinney (2013) challenges. Furthermore, Ameer's experience highlights why such paradigms are problematic in so many ways—the need to shrink himself to disestablish hierarchies and be seen as welcoming suggests his body is physically incapable of being viewed or coded as warm and inviting without conscious effort on his part. Individuals working in the center would likely characterize Ameer as a teddy bear whose theatrical antics are more prone to make others laugh than incite fear. However, how can such characteristics be made known when fear drives the narrative? Interestingly, it is the tutor—a six-foot-five-inch Black male—who remains in constant fear for his own body, both in and out of the center, because other bodies, more privileged bodies, are deemed far more worthy of protection. Historically, the Black male body has not been viewed as the victim, vulnerable to unwarranted violence and rage, although these are the exact images we are provided daily in the media—it is the Black male body that receives sixteen gunshots or is continuously beaten beyond recognition by the police. These are the ravaged and neglected bodies that are further silenced when individuals proclaim "All lives matter."

Reflections from other Black males in the writing center reveal that the fear of misperception is not specific to one certain body type. Marcus, an Afro-Caribbean writing tutor who stands at five feet seven inches and weighs135 pounds is significantly different in body shape and points out, "Students consider me more approachable and less intimidating in consultations because I am relatively shorter, and slender in build, in comparison to my fellow consultants and director" (pers. comm.). Marcus is aware of a particular type of privilege in that he embodies a smaller, less intimidating frame that allows him to build relationships and trust much faster and easier than Ameer or myself can. Marcus sees his role in the writing center as warranting a persona that counters the manufactured images portrayed in the media that are beyond his control. Being able to navigate the inherently political space of the writing center through his body is Marcus's method of code switching, another way in which we can interpret Vershawn Ashanti Young's framework for communication (Young 2011, 61–72). Young's work is especially relevant here in that we are reminded that it is up to the victims of oppression to ensure they are no longer victimized by the oppressor. It is upon Black males to make sure their bodies are sending the *right* message. In this context, Marcus is able to more easily present what is deemed as a tame and subdued Black body—one that does not incite fear upon initial contact. Marcus speaks further about his experience in the center as one of performance:

> Tutees and students have told me that I smile a lot, unlike my director, which makes it easier for them to overlook that I am a black male. Because of what the media has portrayed about men of color, I often find myself not genuinely performing my blackness in consultations and in the writing center in an attempt to overcome the stigma that the media has of people who look like me. The clothes that I wear, how I articulate myself, and my overall persona are a part of that performance. (pers. comm.)

Marcus's reflection is especially insightful in seeing how public controversies become private struggles that are enacted in the writing center. Although it is rare that I do not see Marcus smiling, the idea that he feels compelled to do so in order for others to see past his blackness is troubling. More important, like Ameer, Marcus is conscious of the political codes inscribed onto his body and thus compensates in a way that allows him to be successful, whether it is getting the tutee to engage in the consultation or simply to take him seriously.

Upon hearing these reflections, I am troubled that I have no substantial solution to offer these young men with whom I share similar struggles. In my short time in academia and even shorter time directing the writing center, I have not come upon a resolution for how to effectively deal with public perceptions of my body and other Black male bodies. I do find myself reflecting on the issue, thinking of ways I, too, perhaps, can alter the script of my performance in order to navigate the various academic and social communities of which I am a part. I rely on my roles as a director and mentor as means of setting an example that will allow these young men to find strength and comfort in their own bodies. Providing a platform for shared experiences while interrogating the work and common practices of the writing center seems a natural first step. However, that our narratives exist and persist signals there is much work to be done regarding race and identity, not just in the writing center. I turn to Denny's claim that "a day doesn't go by that somebody doesn't contend with the dilemma of assimilating, going with the flow, or challenging the well-worn path" (Denny 2010, 16–17), and I hope writing center scholars and practitioners will continue to seek out the narratives that further complicate the existing discourse on identity politics in writing centers.

4

BODIES IN SPACE
His, Hers, and My Race

Allia Abdullah-Matta

I remember standing with you in 2008 in front of 20 or so aspiring teachers in our course "Teaching to Change the World." We were so hopeful. Do you remember when we shared our stories and the students believed your story was mine and my story was yours? I can still see the look of surprise on their faces when they learned that I grew up poor and you middle class. I didn't go to college until my late thirties and you went right from high school. They made their assessment based solely on the color of our skin[s]. Nothing more but so powerful.
— Mary Grassetti, "Subject Line of Post if one"

I begin this discussion of "Bodies in Space" with the partial retelling of a teaching experience posted on my social media feed from a colleague in struggle, Mary Grassetti. Mary is of Irish descent and I am African American. We met in a new faculty seminar when we were both hired as full-time community college faculty in western Massachusetts. Our respective disciplinary backgrounds, education and English, enabled us to partner to develop and coteach a learning community that encompassed an introductory education course, Becoming a Teacher and English Composition. Our course, Teaching to Change the World, was designed and constructed to inspire *future teachers* and students who were thinking about careers in education to see their potential institutional roles as part of a larger, social justice initiative. Mary and I functioned as witnesses to the power of education to transform; we were/are slightly older women, and when we cotaught this course, we were in the process of completing our doctorate degrees at the University of Massachusetts Amherst after navigating marriage and motherhood. Our personal, professional, and scholarly experiences had provided specific instructions about how race, class, gender, age, and ethnicity functioned in our communities and affected our educational access and options in the marketplace.

DOI: 10.7330/9781607327837.c004

Mary and I represented an *intersectional coupling*; we had intentionally partnered, at Mary's suggestion, to entangle our respective disciplinary theories and methods and attach them to a larger cultural, social, and political agenda. We wanted students to understand and appreciate that as educators, they should consider intersectionality and the implications of race, class, gender, sexuality, ethnicity, nationality, and other social identity categories and that their classrooms, curriculums, and perceptions of others must reflect a critically conscious pedagogy. Our course curriculum and our presence (intersectional coupling) served as an important twenty-first-century educator–activist model. Our bodies were unmistakably *White* and *Black*, and we had reflected on and designed an important course; the title of the course indicated our mutual investment in social change. Further, in the midst of our course, the students witnessed and possibly participated in the historical nomination and election of the country's first African American president, Barack Obama.

The students' initial responses to our stories—that her story should be mine and my story must have been her experience—points to the *space of race* in which the embodiment of the Black body as text and lived experience is stereotypically negative. The students' reverse identification of our stories correlates to Faye V. Harrison's (1995) "The Persistent Power of 'Race' in the Cultural and Political Economy of Racism." Harrison historicizes the anthropology of race, which is an important backdrop to the constructions that "affirmed the superiority of certain Europeans over others" and the prevalence of ethnic, religious, and class stereotypes as racialized and part of the "long-standing disparities in power, privilege, and wealth [that] were legitimated by discourses emphasizing descent and heritability" (Harrison 1995, 52). Our students were largely of European descent, though we had a few who were African American and Latinx. They lacked significant exposure to people of color in institutional positions of authority. The class dynamics of this community also marked their expectations; however, as the local community consisted of White working-class and working-poor populations, their inability to even consider the possibility of Mary's lower-class past corroborates my assertion about the space of race. Fortunately, our students were able to overcome their initial racial biases, and we ended the course thinking that perhaps they learned to see the world through the prism of intersectionality. As Grassetti (2016) says, "We were so hopeful."

My notion of the space of race posits that race occupies a historical presence in contemporary society. This placement of race at the center even when folks say they "do not see race" is in fact a failure to acknowledge or discuss the ways in which race appears, and therefore results in, a spatial positioning of race. This spatial positioning of race reinforces and also colludes with the historical construction(s) of Black bodies in the mainstream society as stereotypically negative. Grassetti wrote to me in 2016 about her memories of our intersectional coupling and our hope as a visceral response to the escalation of police violence against Black bodies. She specifically mentioned my discussion of "the talk" and contrasted her own experience as a "White mother" to my experience as a "Black mother" raising sons in the twenty-first century. She recalled the difference; Black mothers have a specific talk that informs their children about the police and how their bodies are spatially positioned. It never occurred to her to have such a talk with her son because he is not racially at risk. Grassetti wanted to hear about what I remembered, and she was also checking in with me because she knew these are turbulent times for at-risk Black bodies in the United States. Her contact indicated an awareness of my body as spatially positioned and representative of the state of Black bodies in the public discourse and space. Further, her contact acknowledged she is affected by the tone of the racial narrative and the police violence as a human being and as an advocate for social justice. Grassetti was upset and understood that I was upset. She stood as an ally.

"Bodies in Space: His, Hers, and My Race" argues that race is present in the classroom, the text, and the writing center whether the actors (teachers, students, readers, and writing tutors/consultants) choose to overtly acknowledge and/or engage in a racially conscious teaching or tutoring praxis. I contend that while composition pedagogy employs an intersectional analysis, as indicated in the variety of texts in freshman and basic writing anthologies, the space of race elicits silence and conflict as contested terrains in the classroom and the writing center. The spatial positioning of bodies and texts complicates and can even prohibit an intellectual pathway for effectively engaging in an honest and politically productive discussion of race and interlocking oppressions. More specifically, how such a discussion manifests in writing products or as the subject of peer-editing and tutoring conferences warrants analysis as critically conscious pedagogy conforms to and addresses these turbulent times for at-risk Black bodies/bodies of color.

In *Space and Place*, Yi-Fu Tuan (2008) posits that space and place are basic components of the lived world, are taken for granted, and that when considered, "they may assume unexpected meanings and raise questions we have not thought to ask" (3). Tuan situates the cultural and spatial nuances in which complex human beings experience space and place, and he ponders "how we [as humans] attach meaning to and organize place and space?" (5). At the root of Tuan's discussion is a contemplation of culture and whether it emphasizes or distorts human dispositions, capacities, and needs. Tuan frames this phase of his discussion about culture and space by using contextual markers: biological facts; the relations of space and place as situated in experiences; and the range of experience or knowledge as "direct and intimate" or "indirect and conceptual mediated by symbols" (5–6). For the purposes of this discussion, I focus on Tuan's assertion that "people tend to suppress what they cannot express" and that if one works "to understand how people feel with respect to space and place, the modes of experience partially defined as tactile, visual, and conceptual are significant tools with which to interpret space and place as images of complex [and] often ambivalent feelings" (6–7). I am interested in the ways in which the space of race stems from historical constructs of race that mediate the police as symbolic and direct instruments of interlocking systems of power. How does this manifest as experiential and repetitive violence onto Black bodies/bodies of color?

Tuan's "Experiential Perspective" argues that experience is "a cover-all term for the various modes through which a person knows and constructs a reality," "is directed to the external world," "implies that one has the ability to learn from what one has undergone," and "is the overcoming of perils" (8–9). I contend that the space of race centers the overt and covert presence of race in the classroom and the writing center in terms of the body, the text, and the space. As twenty-first-century teaching and writing center practitioners, we must strive to acknowledge and implement mutually effective ways to address race as it appears in contemporary, critically conscious pedagogy and praxis.

COMPLEXES SPACES: RACE AS THE BODY AND THE TEXT

I bonded with the student population in western Massachusetts, well at least a few of them. They no longer looked at me as if I had walked into the wrong classroom when I arrived on the first day with my dark skin and dreadlocks.

It had become a ritual—my directed walk to the front of the room with books, bags, and handouts. Plop the materials down on the desk. Look out into the sea of whiteness with only one or two specks of brown, smile, and introduce myself. Occasionally, there were the one or two cheery-faced students who actually looked happy to see me. I am not sure whether, at least initially, they were in shock or just amused. The cheery ones were usually the high-achieving White students who excelled in the class. They were respectful, stayed after class or came to my office hours to talk, and indicated a genuine interest in the material. Their responses indicated that some students hunger and thirst to engage with race and that my body was welcomed in the space. There were always three or four salty students who thought I had no business teaching them anything. They were confrontational for no good reason except my race and gender. Combine that with the fact that they were assigned to read Gary Colombo, Robert Cullen, and Bonnie Lisle's *ReReading America* (Colombo, Cullen, and Lisle 1989), and folks like Frederick Douglass, Harriet Jacobs, Malcolm X, Toni Cade Bambara, Danzy Senna, and a host of other Black writers/writers of color, perhaps they did have a reason to be difficult.

I was used to this racial tension and potential conflict, just not necessarily from this side of the desk. I had experienced being the token Black person in many spaces. I was the only Black girl in my high-school honors English debate class in a working-middle-class residential neighborhood in Far Rockaway, Queens. Problem—you need a partner, and I was new to the school and neighborhood, so the white students did not know me from middle school and were less likely to want to partner with me. There were plenty of Black students in the school, just not in the honors debate class. Luckily for me, the only Latina in the class did not mind being my debate partner. She was one of them; she had lived in the community since elementary school, so actually, *she did me a solid.* Then there was the study-abroad program. I went to Paris as the only Black person in the group. In terms of culture and nation, I was in fact a US citizen, so it took me a while to adjust to the folks I later met who were of African descent. Until then, I mostly hung with the US (White) students. In the second semester, I eventually met a sister-friend (Black woman) from Canada, so at least I had one friend who was culturally and somewhat Black like me. Last, there were my experiences as a Black woman graduate-student writing center tutor in Brooklyn, tasked with tutoring mostly undergraduates but also graduate students. These students were Black, Jewish Orthodox, Latinx, and nonnative English speakers from Taiwan, Uzbekistan, and a few eastern European countries. Though these students were diverse in terms of race, class, ethnicity, and nation, they shared a common experience—they did not anticipate that their tutor would be a Black woman. These experiences serve as a small introduction to my academic life as an African American woman who had become accustomed to functioning in the midst of a sea of whiteness, or a mixed sea plagued by the implications of whiteness as the voice of authority.

What made teaching in western Massachusetts a different racial challenge is that I was in an institutional position of authority over the students—at least that was how they read the power dynamics. In terms of my discussion of the space of race, I was most struck by a poor white student who opened up to me about how much she enjoyed reading about slavery and was very sorry about what was happening to Black people in the text. She also shared that her father said that perhaps *I* was a racist because I mostly taught texts written by and about Black people, which was not entirely true. She also felt close enough to me to discuss her dilemma; she wanted to register for summer classes while receiving social service benefits and asked *me* what she should do to address that issue. I suggested she discuss the matter with the financial aid office counselor, and I chose not to address the fact that she had asked me for advice because she thought she could—I was nice to her and genuinely cared about her progress; moreover, she assumed I would understand the system of benefits. Shall I mention I have never collected social service benefits, though I worked in the field in another life, but she did not know about that previous work experience?

Another semester, I was teaching *The Autobiography of Malcolm X* (1940), and a White male student was very antagonistic. He argued with me all the time and also used to talk about me to two White women who sat at the back of the room. They were lovely; they were enthusiastic about the text and their learning progress. He submitted an essay that was a racial tirade against Malcolm X, and Black people in general, without using any textual evidence. I commented on his paper and reported the matter to the English department adjunct coordinator. I then told the student he should stay after class to discuss his paper. Those lovely ladies I mentioned were afraid for me, as they knew his attitude was hostile and potentially volatile. He was difficult, but because my comments on his paper mostly consisted of inquiries about his lack of supporting textual evidence, he calmed down. We had a productive talk about his race, my race, and how he was completely influenced by the space of race. He left after apologizing about his anger, and he agreed to do the paper over, based on the prompt. I advised that he support his discussion with textual evidence. Shall I mention that the tone of his next paper was completely different?

Both these scenarios highlight the ways in which my body clearly exemplified a particular spatial positioning. In the first scenario, the student has accepted my Black body as something she can relate to—she is interested in what I have to say because likes the texts, and she thinks we share a common experience of poverty because of my race and not hers. In the second scenario, the student attacks me because of what my Black body represents to him—he detests reading the text and resents our verbal and written discussions about race. Of course, both scenarios highlight the primary importance of my race, how it strikes these students, and how they receive its presence; however, they silently experience their *own* racial presence and the white-skin privilege that informs their conflictual interaction with me, the Black person in their midst. Both students *normalize* their racial and class positionalities. Shall I mention that the course theme encouraged students to reenvision and historicize US identity using an intersectional analysis?

My early experiences in the community college classroom space in western Massachusetts often played out in this way. My race was taken for granted, and in particular, some of my White students assumed unexpected meaning and did not even think to raise any questions. The obvious question should have been, how could I end up teaching *them* if I was actually from the stereotypically negative space of race in their minds?

OF WRITING CONCERNING BODIES, TEXTS, AND SPACES

According to Harry Denny in *Facing the Center*, "Beyond the everyday struggle for people of color—whether they're tutors or clients in writing centers or classrooms across the curriculum—to learn, assert, or contest ethos, from the words they produce to the essays and other writing they create, there's an ongoing struggle over face they must confront. Which faces are permitted and tolerated and which ones face scrutiny, challenge or oppression?" (Denny 2010, 37).

The space of race shows up in the writing center in terms of physical bodies, spoken and unspoken dialogues, and textual conversations. Racial dynamics occur between bodies and texts and also extend into the larger campus and world communities even after the tutoring sessions end. Denny's (2010) discussion of the "ongoing struggle over face" (37) gets at the core of these exchanges, which are historical in nature, and illustrates that "race's vitality and volatility have intensified. Rather than receding, it is progressing, although quite unevenly" (Harrison 1995, 49). Racial difference appears as racial pathology in the United States, though one would normally expect this would not be the case when entering an institution of higher learning in the twenty-first century. But it is the case, and it is apparent in the "recurrent notions of [the] 'culture of poverty' and [the] 'cultural capital deficits' [that successfully] encode, hierarchize, and pathologize difference" (Harrison 1995, 49).

To ponder the significance of Denny's (2010) questions, "Which faces are permitted and tolerated and which ones face scrutiny, challenge or oppression" (37), I would like to assess writing center experiences in two categories—when the tutor's Black body is raced and spatially positioned and when the racialized text is received as the combative body. Both these categories directly or indirectly engage outcomes of the culture of poverty as it pertains to assumptions and the ways in which cultural capital deficits encode, hierarchize, and pathologize difference.

As an African American woman who began graduate study in my late thirties, I came to the writing center after working in the public and private sectors in different capacities. I began as a graduate tutor, worked as a front-desk person, and was then hired to be the associate director. I began teaching composition while I was still a graduate-student tutor, so my composition pedagogy was/is greatly influenced by my simultaneous training in both spaces. My range of work and writing center experience(s) informs and contributes to my understanding of the complex ways in which my body was raced and spatially positioned in the workplace and in the center. I might also add that though my body can enter the institution and dwell in the academic space(s) of the classroom and the writing center because of my educational train-ing and professional experiences, my body also exists in these spaces as an outsider. My credentials let me (potentially) enter the space as an insider, yet my bodily presence and credentials can be, and have been, delegitimized by subtleties that question my abilities to legitimately occupy and work in the space.

I came to the writing center as a seasoned trainer and project analyst who was accustomed to having a professional writing life. I had con-ducted policy and systems studies via field interviews and audits that encompassed data compilation and qualitative and quantitative report writing. Over the years, I became acutely conscious of the ways in which my racialized and gendered body entered and occupied these profes-sional spaces. In addition, many of the workers who actually went into the field were folks of color, and the management teams we reported to were largely White; the various sites were social service agencies located in urban communities in New York City, and the workers were mostly folks of color. There was the occasional site where the workers were not mostly folks of color.

I recall the time I trained a group of hospital workers in Coney Island. Once the training ended, I was a part of the team tasked to provide systems onsite monitoring. At the site, the workers did not come to me with questions unless my White colleague *could not* help them and *she* had solicited my assistance. In the training classroom, the extent of my knowledge had been apparent as I was often the lead trainer, and I had been one of the curriculum developers. My cultural capital was accepted there as it was a classroom space and my body was positioned at the head of the class. There may have been unasked questions about how and why I was in the leadership position to oversee the trainees' learning. However, they were not overtly disrespectful. In the field, my body became spatially positioned as the *racialized Other* because I was now in an office with more White workers than workers of color. The space of race indicated I should not be *seen* as a body of competent knowledge—though inside, I was an outsider.

How my body was received in the social service center governed my access to the workers, the details they would reveal in the interviews, and the success of the field audit. If the workers did not open up to me, I could not competently assess their work and would not have adequate raw data to complete a field audit. Regardless of the racial composition of the center workforce, it was important that the workers could and would connect to my body to give me access to their work product. My cultural capital and authority were often in question. I learned how to assess how these folks received the presence of my race and began to understand the ways in which my race granted or prohibited access.

Navigating these experiences helped me understand how my body was read and received in the writing center. Working with ethnic, White, and immigrant students proved to be challenging at first. They were hesitant to accept my expertise, as they were also not used to having a Black person *teach* them something. Their cultural-capital deficits served to encode and pathologize my difference; their understanding of hierarchy translated as distrust, though I was the tutor and my presence in the space represented a level of *expertise* they were striving to achieve. They dismissed my authority and expertise based on their spatial positioning of my body. I also witnessed that students of color could experience conflict when working with a tutor in a Black body for the same reason, a dismissal of my authority and expertise. Both of these conflictual responses point to the space of race in the writing center and solidify the complexities raised in Denny's questions with respect to "which faces are permitted and tolerated and which ones face scrutiny, challenge or oppression" (Denny 2010, 37).

In this particular writing center, unless it was a walk-in appointment, students registered for the entire semester and were expected to keep weekly, hour-long appointments with one tutor. I experienced countless first-session visits in which the student looked shocked, hesitated to shake my extended hand, and questioned my advice to them about their writing product. I often navigated these conflicts with grace, as I had been dealing with the racialization of my body for years. If the student proved to be too difficult, I had options; more often than not, students realized I *could* not only help them but also that I was *willing* to help them.

Once I became the associate director of the writing center, I managed a diverse complement of undergraduate and graduate tutors, managed payroll activities and operations, developed tutor training, and hired tutors and staff to run the front desk. During the first year of my tenure as associate director, my racialized body was the cause for speculation. International graduate students from other departments flooded the writing center in search of a graduate assistantship. The center had a history of hiring these students to work the front desk, so we often received many resumes before the beginning of the semester. Many of these students were stunned that the associate director was a woman of color and specifically a Black woman. If I said, "I will be happy to take your resume and we will be in touch," some retorted, "When will the director be in?" Others left the resume and changed their tones once they realized I was in fact the decision maker and that they would report to me, if hired. Typically, their response to my body was raced and gendered, as many of the students who came to apply for these jobs were men of color who were unaccustomed to dealing with women; moreover, I was a Black woman, placed above them in terms of the institutional hierarchy. This truth was painfully apparent in their facial expressions, voice tones, and body language.

As associate director, I also served on the English Department Writing Program Committee, and I taught composition, developmental writing, research writing, and literature. Last, while in the position and for the first few years of my doctorate program, I taught a minicomposition course as part of a Summer Institute (a course designed to advance first-semester writing placement) and also for the Higher Education Opportunity Program (HEOP). The HEOP summer program enabled newly admitted HEOP students to take courses as preparation for their first semester. I was not only responsible for teaching the course, but I also served as a faculty mentor. In these capacities, I still had to reverse and overcome the ways in which my spatially positioned body was received in these spaces.

The racialized text as the combative body is indirectly and directly related to the racialized body, but not specifically just to the Black body. It would be interesting to analyze what happens when Mary teaches the very same texts I do. Is she seen as the politically conscious, social justice teacher-activist who has the courage to teach about police brutality and the Black Lives Matter movement? Do they read her body and use of these texts as progressive because she is Irish American? I assert that teaching about these topics in the contemporary moment shows the text is completely racialized and received by some students as the combative body. Moreover, is the writing center space a part of this racialized narrative, and if so, how do the student and tutor bodies connect and interact?

Given the climate of the at-risk Black body in the public sphere, many teaching and writing center practitioners are confronted with writing products that address discrimination in the criminal justice system, police brutality, and Black/people of color activism. In my current teaching life, I draw on my African diaspora and feminist studies training when teaching a variety of courses as an English faculty member at a very diverse community college in New York City. In my freshman composition and introductory literature courses, I intentionally assign texts that explore intersectionality and highlight the voices of the folks who are often left out of the mainstream narrative, or are included in only negative ways. I also teach African American literature and a number of other courses that emphasize the voices of women and people of color. My body aside, I am that practitioner who pushes my students to engage in contemporary racial discourse.

I accept that many students think I teach texts that discuss the complexities of race and gender (though I deal with much more) *because of* my race and gender. I hope my students read the curriculum as an indication of my political consciousness and social justice teacher-activism, but I am sure this is not always the case. I do know how my students read the curriculum is no longer my concern, as in my courses, the text serves as the space of race and is therefore situated as the racialized and combative body. As I continue to do this work, I think it is crucial to analyze how the text as combative body manifests in the student writing product on the page, is situated in the verbal discussion of texts, resonates during peer-editing or whole-class writing workshops, elicits a combative critique, and last, is at the center of a tutoring session in the writing center.

In a freshman composition course titled Shackles and Cages: Cultures of Lockdown and Liberation, I task students to critically engage with Michelle Alexander's *The New Jim Crow* and the Bill Haney film *American Violet*, directed by Tim Disney, to contextualize the complexities of the criminal justice system as it relates to racialized bodies and justice. These texts provide students with concrete examples of the injustices levied against Black bodies that make them at risk to receive unfair treatment in US society. I then ask them to concentrate their discussion of these texts using concepts such as power, intimidation, racial dynamics, racial biases, stereotypes, poverty, falsely charged, sentencing, and the material implications of a felony conviction. Students collaborate in small groups and then use this prewriting activity to write an essay that engages the two sources.

The writing produced is critically combative, as the Alexander (2012) text gives the students a solid ground for making sense of the criminal injustice that takes place in the film. After this type of exercise, the class discussion is quite intense and combative. The students are outraged, as they are able to connect these texts to a contemporary analysis of race in society and are therefore interested in doing battle. The battle takes place on the page and creates a particular space of race. In this case, the battle is revolutionary, and the students become more critically conscious. Here the text as combative body is positive. It is also important to discuss the corollary: what happens when the texts produce a writing product that makes other students very uncomfortable during peer-editing and whole-group writing workshops?

During one whole-group writing workshop, one student became verbally combative toward a student and her essay. The essay historicized lynching and connected it to police violence against Black bodies in contemporary society. The student discussed the significance of activism and pointed to the Black Lives Matter movement. The course was an African American literary survey, and the workshop addressed the final paper. The student writer was a woman of color with a complicated ethnic and national background. She is often mistaken for white and has decided to claim Blackness as her identity from a cultural and political standpoint. The student responder was a White male, and he was verbally violent and demeaning. He insisted that her discussion of the murders of Eric Garner (Staten Island, New York City, July 17, 2014) and of Sandra Bland (Waller County Jail, Hempstead, Texas, July 13, 2015) as lynching acts and indicative of improper police behavior was unwarranted and ill supported. Unfortunately, the student responder had not focused on the connection of the paper to the plight of African Americans; it was as though he had not read the assigned texts, which covered from slavery to the Black Arts movement. Ironically, he was a solid student and had written about some of these very texts. It was obvious he had personalized the discussion and had an affinity for the police. All of the historical knowledge gained from the texts was dismissed when it came to the contemporary discussion of these police acts. He kept saying the writer did not have proof and that she couldn't say these things or make these connections. He was responding to her body and the actual text; he was shocked that her defense of the Black Lives Matter movement was coming from her body and her text. The student writer was shocked by his hostility and did not respond to his critiques.

Of course, I intervened. I aligned with her essay by pointing to the historical support that was actually on the page and reminded him of our previous discussions of the inappropriate treatment of the Black body in society. We had read several slave narratives and a host of other texts, and we had watched the films of John Ridley, Solomon Northup's *12 Years a Slave*, and Gregory Poirier's *Rosewood*. His response to her paper was visceral and rooted in his race and his spatial positioning of Black people. His response in words and tone was as if she had physically assaulted him. He seemed unable to accept the parallel between what was in the literature and the realities Black people face in society. When I intervened and reminded him of these things, he became silent. Had this been a smaller peer-editing workshop, it would have been a disaster. He would have been unable to comment on the work as a legitimate piece of writing, as he was unable to see the merit of her content, and he was in effect too blinded by the content to identify or to mention any of the writing issues. Here the text was the combative body, and he responded with a combative critique.

The severity of this situation invites teaching and writing center practitioners to think about the space of race in significant ways. In part, I facilitate whole-group writing workshops to provide a safe space for writing critique. We can ponder and wrestle with the complexities of the text as racialized and combative. Many students need to learn *how* to engage with texts that address the complexities of race and intersectionality in productive ways. These issues undoubtedly seep into the tutoring session, as race is in the writing product whether one choses to see race or not. It is therefore important that tutors acknowledge these complexities and develop strategies that allow them to see race in all of its manifestations on the bodies of the student and the tutor, in and of the text, and as writing product. Race is ever present, as are other bodily positioning(s).

The escalation of police violence toward Black bodies/bodies of color and these turbulent times indicate that race and complex bodily positioning(s) will appear more concretely in the writing center. Teaching and tutoring praxis must ameliorate the silence and conflict around the space of race and unteach the consequences of seeing at-risk bodies as spatially positioned. As Tuan (2008) indicates, we must attach "meaning and raise questions" (3). Many of our students are engaged in activist efforts to combat societal inequities. Our students' writing products will address these intellectual and activist spaces if curriculums mirror the societal predicament around police violence and social justice initiatives. Race is out in the classroom and must be out in the writing center.

In my current position, I teach in the English department, and I have returned to the writing center in a community college setting that serves a very diverse population of students. I am not responsible for the administrative operations of the tutoring and front-desk staff of the center; I function as a faculty codirector in that I represent a pseudo-bridge from the department to the center (tutors) and from the center to the department (faculty). In this capacity, I engage with the tutors and the codirector, who is responsible for the administrative operations of the center. I have also elected to tutor students. In this writing center, most of the daily appointments are scheduled prior to the beginning of the tutoring-session hour.

Interestingly, in this environment, my bodily presence with the staff and tutors is not predicated on race or gender; it is derived from the power dynamics that exist with respect to my position as a faculty person. I entered and exist as English faculty in the writing center for two important reasons: (1) the tutors knew my name and my assignments before many of them had met me in person because of the students from my classes who came to the center for tutoring; (2) The codirector position is something that rotates over time, as the representative runs for a term and is elected by the English department faculty. Entering the writing center in this way centers my *authority* and status as a faculty member. Of course, this status can also call the very same *authority* and *status* into question—I am elected to enter, yet I enter as an outsider because of my bodily designation as a faculty member.

I do not think of myself as coded to speak as an insider in most of the spaces I occupy in the academic institution because of the ways in which my racialized and gendered body enters and is received in these spaces. I am a credentialed professor and educational practitioner, yet my racialized and gendered body must work to legitimize that I belong in and will be respected in these space(s). This has not been the case when tutoring students in the current writing center.

In my more recent tutoring encounters, I have not experienced the "you are the tutor?" look. I begin the session by introducing myself by my first name (something I do not do in the classroom space), and I do not reveal that I am a faculty person. I am careful not to reveal this at first, as I do not want the students to feel any unnecessary pressure, nor do I want them to feel as though they cannot fully express their anxiety or uncertainty about completing a colleague's assignment. Once the session is over, I might reveal that I am a codirector and a faculty member if they ask me about my hours at the center. My approach allows them to focus on the work and what they expect to gain from a session. I avoid the power-dynamic tensions that would exist if they knew my position before they entered the session. Of course, my raced and gendered body exists in the space, but it is not centered or positioned as potentially powerless or as proof of why it legitimately occupies the space.

Perhaps the levels of cultural, racial, and ethnic diversity that exist on this college campus define and predicate the bodily positioning and spatial energy? I am aware that my bodily presence models achievement and success to the students in particular ways. There are faculty of color on campus, though disproportionately in terms of the faculty-to-student ratio. The course and the classroom tensions previously discussed took place on the same culturally diverse campus, so perhaps the most striking difference is what happens in the classroom in the presence of the faculty, student, and textual bodies as opposed to the writing center.

I attempt to create a pseudo (peer) tutoring scenario and a collaborative-learning environment by not revealing my full identity and position. The essay "Diversity as Topography: The Benefits and Challenges of Cross Racial Interaction in the Writing Center" by Kathryn Valentine and Mónica F. Torres points to some of the literature that suggests "culturally diverse student populations, and more particularly meaningful interactions across those populations, offer students important opportunities for cognitive and social development. That is, interacting across cultural differences positions students to perceive and think and act in ways that contribute to their intellectual development" (Valentine and Torres 2011, 192–93). In these sessions, I witness my students' abilities to perceive themselves differently as a result of our positive interaction around their writing. If confident, they will then be able to think and act with a more focused approach to writing, which may advance their intellectual development, and in this moment my bodily positioning becomes an important instrument of success.

To return to Tuan's (2008) assertion about experience and its various modes that construct a reality (5–6), the space of race and intersectional manifestations exist on bodies and texts, in the classroom, and in the writing center. We, as twenty-first-century teaching and writing center practitioners, must strive to acknowledge and implement mutually effective ways to maintain and honor these many bodies in space(s) with respect to critically conscious pedagogy and praxis.

5

SACRED PAGES
Writing as a Discursive Political Act

Rochell Isaac

I know what I want to say but I can't explain it. These words were said to me so often during my time as a writing center tutor that I became rather immune to them. At some point during my tenure at the writing center, it simply meant the student wasn't really thinking critically or didn't know what he/she should be thinking about or saying. At another point, it became an indicator that there was going to be little analysis in whatever paper we were going to be working on. The truth was, and is, that many students come to their writing assignments laden with feelings of inadequacy and with much anxiety. The papers become something standing in the way of their successfully completing a course, checking off a requirement for their majors, or earning the elevated grades they desire. Already writing has become a joyless, meaningless chore, and therefore something they need to muddle through quickly to get done. Too often students come to the writing center at a critical junction: when required to by the instructor and/or when at risk of failing. Accordingly, students often associate the writing center with remediation rather than a supportive space where their specific needs can be addressed. I figured out pretty quickly that as a writing tutor I had to get past the negative emotions students brought to their writing assignments, as well as the lack of confidence on full display in their comments about their work. I realized too that those feelings of inadequacy must be legitimized so students can give themselves a fighting chance at succeeding in their academic endeavors. In fact, for colleges and institutions concerned with student success and retention, the writing center might very well prove to be a site rife with recipes for intervention and best practices.

It wasn't until I started to become more reflective about my teaching pedagogy—before that, I wasn't going into academia—that I began to realize perhaps I needed to pay more attention to the sentiment being

DOI: 10.7330/9781607327837.c005

expressed with the words *I know what I want to say but I can't explain it.* And what was the sentiment anyway? In either case, those words led me to wonder about two things: first, why were students so resistant to writing or completing their writing assignments? I thought they were since I was sure they were exhibiting signs of resistance. For instance, while it may be difficult to integrate a source into one's writing, it really isn't difficult at all to cite a last name and page number. Yet, students constantly fail to do this correctly. In addition, it was becoming commonplace to see students plagiarizing by copying chunks of information from the web with little, if any, attempt to camouflage the writing as their own. At least one reason for this is a simple refusal to do the work. Another more complicated reason is that students feel incapable of completing the assignment. "It's so hard!" they often say, or "It took me hours to do this much." Second, why were students so removed from what they had written on their pages? By that I simply mean, why didn't they feel connected to what they expressed on paper? I sometimes asked students to read a paragraph aloud, and they invariably stopped reading after a sentence or two and started speaking instead, often self-correcting (not a bad thing). I now think those reasons are going to be different for everyone. At the time, however, I concluded that students simply weren't engaging in deep thinking and that they were uncomfortable with taking positions that would reveal their not knowing (their non-knowing spaces). It became critical to me to help students find their voices, and I wanted to use their own thinking and words. I found myself having conversations and taking notes rather than getting to the paper and fixing things. My tutees were surprisingly willing to work with me, and the exercise quickly revealed students who needed to better understand the text they were responding to or the issues they were addressing. These conversations also quickly revealed the spaces, places, and gaps in the students' thinking. What they knew and what they needed to find out became clear.

In the hour-long sessions, I often tried moving their papers into the realm of tangible ideas and asking students to think critically and analytically about their topics. The conversations were sometimes enough to encourage student engagement with the material, but often I had to turn to my notes. I had gotten in the habit of writing down significant ideas so I could turn to them when needed. Students were constantly surprised by something they had said, by an argument they had inadvertently made, or by a critical question they had raised. From these notes, I was better able to get students to grasp the importance of their own thinking on an issue (although at some point I directed them to take notes as well). I began to judge the success of the hour-long sessions on whether or not students began to feel confident about the direction of their paper. I should admit here that in a number of cases we were not able to get to working on the actual paper. Instead, the session would be focused on reading comprehension. Students in that circumstance may not have been happy with me but, again, seemed willing to do the work.

So, why such resistance to writing? I wondered. An obvious answer was that students simply were not adequately prepared for college-level writing. But perhaps students were already ahead of me and knew their pages told on them, exposing their secrets. Maybe they were resistant to writing because they knew what showed up on the pages revealed them in ways they weren't ready to accept. In a *New York Times* article published in the Books section on July 29, 1979, James Baldwin notes this as well: "Language, incontestably, reveals the speaker. . . . To open your mouth in England is (if I may use black English) to 'put your business in the street': You have confessed your parents, your youth, your school, your salary, your self-esteem, and, alas, your future." Those students' pages were sacred, but they were going to be graded, and those grades often said they weren't good enough. Those grades often reinforced the notion that the students were pedestrian writers at best and/or that they really didn't belong in the academic environment. Baldwin explains this alienation: "It goes without saying, then, that language is also a political instrument, means, and proof of power. It is the most vivid and crucial key to identify: It reveals the private identity, and connects one with, or divorces one from, the larger, public, or communal identity." Language has long been known by linguists, psychologists, sociologists, and the like as a prime source of cultural identity. The Ebonics debate brought new insight into the politics of language and forced me to critically assess my role in the writing center, and I continued to do so as an instructor in my composition classes. The report *A Nation at Risk*, published in 1983 by the Commission on Excellence, sounded the alarm that our schools were failing, putting the country and democracy at risk, and within a short amount of time the at-risk label attributed to the nation would be used to describe children of color and or children who were otherwise different from the dominant culture (Ladson-Billings 1999, 219). Gloria Ladson-Billings (1999) argues that the shift is emblematic of the way the language of difference (disadvantage, diversity) recreates a position of inferiority (219). Moreover, Ladson-Billings (1995) explains that a major source of student failure and achievement is contained in the nexus of speech and language interactions. In this light, the goal of education becomes how to fit students viewed as Other by virtue of their race, class, ethnicity, gender, sexuality, language, or social class into a "hierarchical structure that is defined as a *meritocracy*" (467; emphasis in original). How was I going to balance teaching writing as process and praxis and as intellectual pursuit with teaching rhetorical skills and the more technical aspects of writing? I knew I needed to do this while still upholding the standards that allowed for real learning to occur. I still struggle to maintain this balance today.

William Zeiger (1985) argues that in college composition classes, writing is taught quite scientifically with the model of thesis and support (the expository essay) but with little room for inquiry or exploration that "aims to discover the fecundity of an idea" (456). He notes that proving an assertion in the modern sense is to earn undisputed acceptance of one's thinking, which serves to stop rather than further inquiry. For Zeiger, the art of inquiry allows for the examination of multiple sides of an issue, a willingness to entertain alternatives, and the allowance of contradictory elements to coexist. While the ability to construct a logical argument in exposition is a valuable skill, equally important is one's ability to explore. Zeiger contends that "by concentrating almost exclusively on thesis-support exposition in college composition classes, we are implicitly teaching that the ability to support an assertion is more important than the ability to examine an issue" (458). The result is the antithesis of a liberal education. Instead, students experience pressure to win an unequal "battle" with the teacher, and they begin to view the audience not as coinquirers or neutral players but as antagonists. In addition, the expectation of criticism lends to an excess of caution in which students only use information if it supports the thesis, suppressing contrary ideas. Alternatively, students produce an excess of "boldness" in which they dismiss counterargument with disdain (Zeiger 1985, 459). Finally, Zeiger calls for the open form of the essay "in the manner of Montaigne—an essay in an informal friendly tone, whose aim is to unfold the intellectual potential of an idea" (460). Zeiger presents a coherent case for the loosening of the rigid structures of form while emphasizing focus on ideas and cognition.

Similarly, I argue that we should recognize the cultural politics at play in higher education. Henry Giroux (1989) suggests that we come to view schools as "socially constructed sites of contestation actively involved in the production of knowledge, skills, and lived experience" (141). Furthermore, Giroux emphasizes that we must come to recognize pedagogical practice as "a cultural field" where knowledge, discourse, and power intersect, producing specific modes of authority and social regulation (141). In doing so, instructors determine the ways in which human experiences are produced, contested, and legitimized in the classroom (consider this with regard to language). In this way, instructors can create a language in which "a politics of culture, voice, and experience can be developed" (Giroux 1989, 141). In short, we can create a student-centered pedagogy. Also, we cannot ignore or be oblivious to the cultural wealth diverse students bring to the classroom and learning process. For instance, Tara J. Yosso's (2005) critical race theory (CRT) lens recognizes at least six forms of capital: (1) aspirational capital centers on the ability to maintain hope for the future even in the face of real and perceived barriers; (2) linguistic capital focuses on the intellectual and social skills gained through communication in multiple languages; (3) familial capital refers to the community history, memory, and cultural knowledge learned with family, including extended family; (4) social capital includes networks of people and community resources that provide instrumental and emotional support; (5) navigational capital emphasizes the skills gained maneuvering through social institutions not created with people of color in mind; and (6) resistant capital denotes oppositional behaviors that challenge inequality (Yasso 2005, 79–80).

Sadly, the students I encountered rarely expected to feel accomplished at the end of completing a writing assignment or to tune into a feeling of satisfaction of a job well done (although I've observed rising levels of confidence once students have gained a measure of success in their work). It became clear to me that students were not experiencing the learning environment as a safe place where they could reveal themselves. At the very least, they did not perceive the learning environment to be a safe haven. I wanted that feeling of accomplishment for the students I tutored mainly because it was that feeling that motivated me to complete those twenty-page papers in my own academic career. In the writing center, I rarely encountered students who viewed writing as a chance to delve deeply into a topic or to legitimize their thinking about a subject. It was that observation that made me begin to think we were failing our students in myriad ways and that there were systematic issues at play. It is not surprising then that critical pedagogy and its proponents, who invite students to examine social structures, began to appeal to me.

What were students supposed to be learning anyway? John Dewey thought the purpose of education was "to give the young the things they need in order to develop in an orderly, sequential way into members of society" (Reaburn 2016, 277). He continues, "Any education is, in its forms and methods, an outgrowth of the needs of the society in which it exists" (Dewey 1934). John Adams and Thomas Jefferson viewed knowledge and education as the path to freedom, as did Frederick Douglass. For transcendentalist Ralph Waldo Emerson, education was not simply about gaining knowledge but also about the ways in which knowledge transformed the self. Booker T. Washington's notion of the role of education was centered on economic freedom and independence for African Americans, while W. E. B. DuBois pushed back, arguing that "the function of the university is not simply to teach bread-winning, or to furnish teachers for the public schools, or to be a centre of polite society; it is above all, to be the organ of the fine adjustment between real life and the growing knowledge of life, an adjustment which forms the secret civilization" (DuBois 1986, 421). Paulo Freire's (1993) *Pedagogy of the Oppressed* rejects what he describes as the "banking concept" of education and instead presents us with the "problem-posing" method. Freire views education as "the practice of freedom" and liberating education as embodying "acts of cognition" (79). The goal of problem-posing education is to produce a space where "people develop their power to perceive critically the way they exist in the world with which and in which they find themselves" (Freire 1993, 83). In this way, "they come to see the world not as a static reality, but as a reality in process, in transformation" (Freire 1993, 83). Epistemologically, students begin to question the *hows* and the *whys* of certain conditions or phenomena, a radical activity for sure. In addition, Freire's concept of "critical consciousness" tasks us to question, to "read the world," and to then take action to transform it (Freire 1993). Like Freire, bell hooks's pedagogy views literacy as the "practice of freedom" (hooks 1994, 2000). The quest for freedom and the journey north to find it is a prevalent theme in African American literature, as was the actual quest for literacy (the two are often intertwined). Knowing this—along with the historical reality that enslaved people of African descent were denied access to literacy, citizenship, and their very humanity under slavery, and then were subjected to Jim Crow—made the theoretical tangible even before I encountered critical pedagogy.

As I write this, I can't help but recall one student who was fully engaged in a project. She was a strong writer from the start, although she seemed content to earn Bs on her papers. It wasn't until she was assigned an ethnographic paper of sorts that I saw a rather startling shift in her level of engagement. She was to investigate the current state of her neighborhood, including its socioeconomic and cultural makeup. Suddenly, this student was anticipating the final product. She began to envision the interviews she would conduct and the questions she wanted to ask. She was anticipating difficulties as well as solutions to problems that might arise in amassing the information she wanted to compile. I was curious about her avid interest and asked about the subjects she liked—I probably should have already known this—and found out she was engrossed because it was a chance to learn about her family's history of migrating to Brooklyn, New York, in the Fort Green area and buying a house there. That history became important to her because she recognized that the early impact of gentrification in her neighborhood occurred in ways that weren't all positive.

In another instance, a student was quite jazzed because his assignment allowed him a choice of a social issue to investigate. However, his enthusiasm waned once he started to describe what he needed to accomplish in the paper; he literally seemed to shrink in his chair. Confused by his changing demeanor but thinking he was concerned about his actual ability to write the paper, I asked what was wrong. After a moment of reflection, he stated, "There's no way I could do all that." Actually, he was right. His thinking and topic needed to be narrowed—which we did by brainstorming his topic—to fit the parameters of the assignment. This paper was especially important it seemed because he had always wanted to know why Black men were so often the victims of racism and of police brutality. He also informed me he would have to present his paper in class. It was going to be his very first presentation; he was sure he was going to be able to do it, but only if he had "really good information." Secretly, I hoped he would do well so he could maintain the level of enthusiasm he brought to this assignment to his work generally. I hadn't seen this level of engagement and interest from him in all our previous sessions. As he predicted, James aced his presentation (he did have the gift of gab). He mentioned that he was able to answer all the questions asked of him. However, he struggled with the paper, earning a C on the first draft and a B on the second.

Students like these have helped me understand the transformative power of education and knowledge when we engage students in useful and meaningful work (inquiry and writing in this context). These two students made me realize that having students become active participants in composing their essays is a key ingredient to helping them find their voices. Both students felt they were contributing to the discourse since they were made to ponder the audience—one his class and the other her family—including themselves. In addition, they were both being asked to take ownership and responsibility for their work, also key ingredients in facilitating student learning. Optimally, learners must be able to make connections between their own being and lived experiences and the constructed *reality*. These students illustrate that the process of becoming critically literate often takes us on a path to analyzing the ways we exist in the world, the ways in which that awareness shapes our actions and beliefs, and the governing systems that maintain those conditions.

I don't think I ever really shared my thinking about language and writing with students in the writing center, even though my writing center experience definitely shaped my teaching pedagogy and my approach to the teaching of composition. I should probably note that most of my tutees were working-class people of color, primarily African American, as am I. This is significant primarily because my pedagogy around writing and the teaching of writing is heavily influenced by the African-centered praxis of functionality as well as the pedagogy of W. E. B. DuBois, Carter G. Woodson, Paulo Freire, and bell hooks, who all offer liberatory education pedagogical approaches that link knowledge with action and argue against the notion that the mere imparting of information is education. DuBois (1995) argues that knowledge must itself be functional, and pedagogy "must root itself in group life and afterwards apply its knowledge and culture to actual living" (72). Woodson's (2008) *The Mis-Education of the Negro* is concerned about the miseducation and cultural indoctrination that occurs when education is focused on socializing people into modes of thinking and being rather than on promoting agency (a hypothesis similar to Freire's banking concept of education). For Freire (1993), the world must be understood from the perspective of one's own experience, circumstance, and needs and therefore must be approached as a phenomenon to be understood by the efforts and agency of learners themselves.

If we truly view classrooms as microcosms of the real world and as "radical spaces of possibilities," as hooks (1994, 12) describes, we must heed Baldwin's (1979) warning when dealing with diversity, difference, and Othering. In the 1979 *New York Times* article mentioned earlier, Baldwin maintains that "a child cannot be taught by anyone whose demand, essentially, is that the child repudiate his experience, and all that gives him sustenance, and enter a limbo in which he will no longer be black, and in which he knows that he can never be white." This quotation is especially relevant because one could insert the difference marker into the sentence (replacing "black") to contextualize the situation. Real learning and growth as writers requires metacognition, critical thinking, and reflection. A major objective of mine is to get students present on their pages and empowered enough to dare to write their thoughts and themselves into being (a risky proposition for sure). Helping students to develop voice, to participate in the discourse of the day, and to become active participants in their communities and society at large is a tall order, especially when writing competes with the demands of everyday life and education is viewed as a commodity. Yet it is through education—real learning—that one gains the power that lies in self-knowledge to become one's own agent in the world.

PART I: RACE
Review

As evidenced by existing controversy surrounding the Black Lives Matter movement, racism thrives in the United States in large part because talking about race often emerges as such a challenge for even the most progressive citizens of the globe. Part 1 of this collection offers narratives from women and men of color—graduate and undergraduate tutors, faculty, and writing center directors—to inform ongoing conversations about writing center practice and to help writing center practitioners start new conversations about race and racism that will enrich both research and practice in the field. While such works as Harry Denny's 2010 *Facing the Center*, Laura Greenfield and Karen Rowan's 2011 *Writing Centers and the New Racism*, Frankie Condon's 2012 *I Hope I Join the Band*, and, most recently, Frankie Condon and Vershawn Ashanti Young's *Performing Antiracist Pedagogy in Rhetoric, Writing, and Communication* have paved a path for discussions on inclusion, the stories in this collection renew a challenge to our readers as we continue to ask, do we truly understand lived realities of people of color and how those experiences impact writing center practice? Moreover, the accounts we include push on existing conversations by addressing the ways in which race intersects with other identity features. For instance, in chapter 2, "A Touching Place: Womanist Approaches to the Center," Alexandria Lockett explores the intersection of race and gender, discussing the way in which a Black female body in the writing center serves as an ideal starting point for highlighting other intersections such as those between race and class, geography, education, and socioeconomic privilege.

And though these accounts are methodically cataloged in one section entitled "Race," readers can recognize how each narrative easily fits into others found in this collection. For instance, though both Richard Sévère's "Black Male Bodies in the Center" and Talisha Haltiwanger Morrison's "Being Seen and Not Seen: A Black Female Body in the Writing Center" address issues of race, a critical conversation between the two chapters also invokes the idea of privilege, as Richard speaks as an administrator, faculty member, and Black male in contrast to Talisha,

DOI: 10.7330/9781607327837.p001

whose voice represents a Black, female graduate-student tutor. Likewise, Allia Abdullah-Matta in chapter 4, "Bodies In Space: His, Hers, and My Race," and Rochell Isaac in chapter 5, "Sacred Pages: Writing as a Discursive Political Act," are bonded by various similar experiences, including teaching writing in the classroom and tutoring in a writing center at the community college, yet we are still shown differing perspectives, as each author is influenced by her positionality within the institution. It is through these narratives that we encourage individuals in the field to reflect on how intersectionality informs the many facets of writing center work.

Moreover, the authors write from a space in which they inherently embody difference, unable to negotiate immutable traits that are systematically, politically, and socially coded. Talisha Haltiwanger Morrison's tutoring session with an Asian international student writing about Black women and the natural-hair movement is valuable for discussions about how cultural identity is perceived and received both in and out of the writing center. In such voices, we are confronted with what it means to be Black and in the center—a perspective that has been unequivocally silent for far too long in the writing center field.

We also hear the perspectives of a graduate student who speaks to negotiating agency as a woman of color and consumer of education while trying to maintain an identity in the writing center and the academy. Haltiwanger Morrison's experience of feelings of physical and emotional discomfort demonstrates the ways in which tutors' identities inherently converge. Most important, what can be said of the work done in the writing center when tutors are called to negotiate between their moral and professional obligations? We recognize that thinking about the ways tutors' many identities, in this case graduate student and woman of color, impact the work they do in the center requires significant investment in working through the ways we enact the student-to-professional trajectory. As many serve in the mentoring or faculty role, we must question how much consideration has been put into the notion that both in and out of the classroom, as stated by Charisse Jones and Kumea Shorter-Gooden's (2003) *Shifting*, "Black women are constantly assessing the bias and prejudices that they're facing and pondering the best way to respond. . . . They make split-second decisions on whether to challenge an opinion, on whether to work overtime. . . . They are exceedingly alert to their own behavior and vigilant about what's happening around them" (Jones and Shorter-Gooden 2003, 70–71).

Also present in this part are the raced experiences of the Black male academic and Black male tutors whose bodies are equally subject to racial microaggressions in the public space, the classroom, and ultimately in the writing center. Working against the distorted image of the "Black male as unruly, violent and uneducable" (Johnson and Bryan 2017, 166), these voices, like the others, engage in their own counterstorytelling. Their stories can be seen as by-products of a social epidemic in which Black male bodies are assaulted and murdered. As these lived accounts demonstrate, these bodies are forced to navigate public and private spaces under constant duress given that the Black male body, as Richard Sévère's chapter points out, "is a symbol of intimidation, aggression, and perceived anger—a body that speaks without an utterance" (43). Under such circumstances, we better understand these narratives when read alongside Lamar Johnson and Nathaniel Bryan (2017), who point out that "the misreading of Black males transfers into how they are treated in classrooms and often leads to how Black males are ultimately treated in the academy and society-writ-large" (164).

This section is firmly grounded in several aspects of critical race theory, feminist theory, and social identity politics, all of which can be useful for tutor training, professional development, and further research. The authors speak of navigating dominant cultural and political ideologies in ways that are counter, yet equally significant and powerful, to other perspectives articulated in this collection. Collectively, the authors utilize *critical race methodology* as a gateway for critical and intellectual interchange. Critical race methodology, as expressed by Daniel G. Solórzano and Tara J. Yosso, is "a theoretically grounded approach to research that foregrounds race and racism . . . and one that focuses on the racialized, gendered, and classed experiences of *students* [people] of color" (Solórzano and Yosso 2002, 23). Specifically, we see the use of counterstorytelling—"a method of telling stories of those people whose experiences are not often told" (i.e., those on the margins of society). Solórzano and Yosso offer three aspects of counterstories: "personal narratives, other people's narrative, and composite narratives that build community between those who are marginalized, resists and challenges the epistemology of those at the center, and helps individuals and groups to develop our understanding of reality and possibility" (quoted in Johnson and Bryan 2017, 169).

In using counterstories to focus on the aspects of the Black male and female body in the writing center, the authors provide perspectives that demonstrate profound understanding and awareness of how their bodies are viewed, identified, interrogated, challenged, admired, fetishized, and damaged. In chapter 2, Alexandria Lockett acknowledges that in educational settings, she can expect that her body will be surveilled and scrutinized, thus attesting to Carla L. Peterson's (2001) claim that "to the dominant culture, the black body was often both invisible and hypervisible" (xi). In this section, the authors' exploration of their marked and visible bodies demonstrates how intersectionality, inherent to identity politics, doesn't suggest a false equivalence between the forms of difference and oppression into which the writers speak. This spatial positioning of race reinforces and also colludes with the historical construction(s) of Black bodies in mainstream society.

The authors' use of counterstories provides a framework for future research and dialogue in writing center work. Counterstories in this collection serve as powerful modes of resisting what it means to be a tutor or an academic of color. More important, these perspectives demonstrate that race does not stand alone in conversations about disempowerment and marginalization—naturally, issues of gender, class, education, and socioeconomic status coalesce—thereby allowing for a broader and more critical examination of the complexity and density of writing center practices. As Allia Abdullah-Matta points out in chapter 4, race is ubiquitous whether we choose to consciously acknowledge it or not. Thus, the counterstory must become a tool for exposing, analyzing, and challenging the majoritarian stories of racial privilege given that "counter-stories can shatter complacency, challenge the dominant discourse on race, and further the struggle for racial reform" (Solórzano and Yosso 2002, 32). Aja Y. Martinez's chapter, "A Plea for Critical Race Theory Counterstory," in Condon and Young (2017) provides a concrete starting point and rationale for using counterstories as a theoretical framework by pointing out that "it is thus crucial to use a narrative methodology that counters other methods that seek to dismiss or decenter racism and those whose lives are daily affected by it" (65).

Moreover, there is much to be gained in hearing these perspectives as we consider tutor education and writing center practices. Consequently, this part also asks readers to think about the connections between different sorts of academic arenas and how oppression becomes a lived experienced for those who move throughout institutional spaces as teachers, as tutors, as students, and as administrators. For instance, Rochelle Isaac in chapter 5 focuses on language and bias in both the classroom and the writing center. Channeling Vershawn Ashanti Young's work, *Should Writers Use They Own English?*, Isaac demonstrates the copious ways in which writing centers, classrooms, and institutions of higher learning aren't impervious to public opinion and partiality. We are confronted every day with individuals' truths that serve as reminders that the center is not immune to the biased practices that affect all who occupy and enter the space. In fact, the authors in this part ask us to rethink the practices in our center and to reconsider tutor education because this space far too often mirrors racist, sexist, and classist practices of higher education. We envision directors using these narratives at staff meetings and/or professional-development workshops where participants can critically reflect on the narratives and provide their own perspectives and experiences. In doing so, we hope the field will take up larger inquiries that critically examine how we encourage tutors and writing center professionals to share their own narratives, their counterstories, in our centers.

Ultimately, the chapters in part 1 implore reflection and deliberate action. The manner in which the field utilizes these counternarratives and the voices represented in this section and text (overall) becomes a conversation of sustainability and effectiveness. In what ways is cultural competency truly a part of preparing future tutors, writing center practitioners, and even writers? Inevitably, through this theoretical methodology, as Harry Denny argues, the writers out themselves, disclosing moments of vulnerability, frustration, anger, and, at times, fear. How do we as a field use these moments didactically, not intermittently but as part of established curricula? As the narratives explore important topics such as embodiment and space, we urge readers to guide conversations on critical race theory and body politics in staff education. As editors of this collection, we envision writing center staff starting to write and share their own counterstories as ways to understand lived experience and thereby create truer senses of community. And, as previously mentioned, these narratives show how much more work is needed in the field on race. These stories must be analyzed and discussed in order for research to be conducted on issues of systemic racism in the writing center. Central to making our centers inclusive in meaningful ways is recruiting people of color to work in our spaces; outreach to those who may not feel as if they belong in the center; and encouragement to explore research pertinent to the everyday work and experiences of people of color. Now is the time that we, in our centers and in the field, affirm that Black Lives do matter and show this through tutor recruitment, education, research, and outreach.

PART II

Multilingualism

6

ON LETTING THE BROWN BODIES SPEAK (AND WRITE)

Nancy Alvarez

When I began tutoring at Bronx Community College (BCC) in 2011, I found myself tutoring in both English and Spanish, as BCC is a Hispanic-serving institution (HSI). According to the US Department of Education (2014), an HSI is an institution of higher education where at least 25 percent of the undergraduate, full-time students enrolled are Hispanic. At BCC, over 60 percent of the student body identifies as Hispanic/Latinx. Spanish and English are heard throughout the college on a regular basis. Although bilingual tutoring was not part of the job description, I fell into the rhythm of bilingual tutoring naturally, and I used the skills I had been taught through observing peer tutors and from reading tutor handbooks. Regardless of whether the session was in English, Spanish, or a mixture of both, I began each tutoring session by asking the student questions about their assignment and what their goals were for our session. We would scribble out a plan of action based on the student's needs, and then the student would get to writing—in English.

One day, one of the students I tutored regularly came in and sat at my table, sighed heavily, shoved some papers in front of me, and said, "It's a stew." I asked her what she meant. She said she had all these ideas for what she wanted to write, but she didn't know how to get her ideas in order, so she just put everything in her essay—like what you do when you're making a stew. What I thought was funny about this conversation was that it was in Spanish, so she didn't use the word *stew* but instead used the word *sancocho*. In my head, her sentences started to look like pieces of vegetables and meat, all simmering in a thick stock. Nothing wrong with that! I explained to her that it's supposed to be a sancocho, the really good kind that if you took anything out, the rest wouldn't taste as good. That made her smile, so she eased up and we rearranged her sancocho just a little bit, putting the potatoes next to the carrots, adding

DOI: 10.7330/9781607327837.c006

a bit of salt, and taking out just some of the onions (they added flavor but we didn't need them anymore).

After that session, I decided to use the sancocho metaphor with other students. One described her head as a sancocho. All the words and sentences were in her head, but she couldn't get the words down on paper because she worried her English wasn't good enough. She feared she'd drown in her stew if she wrote things down. I decided we should brainstorm in Spanish to prevent any drowning. I asked her, "What is it that you want to say?," and I took some quick notes down as she spoke. When she was done, I showed her the stew she had cooked up, written in English, and that made the stew look appealing to her, as if she wouldn't drown in it. She took the notes I had jotted down and turned them into an essay.

That's the thing about tutoring in Spanish: some might think that by tutoring in Spanish and writing in English, the line between collaboration, appropriation, and plagiarism becomes fuzzy. It can happen. If someone wants to use the word *head* but you think the word *brain* would be better, well, you could just ask them which word they want to use—*cabeza* or *cerebro* and let them decide. With ideas, it gets trickier. You don't want to say, "I know you're saying this, but what about saying this instead?" If you wouldn't say that in English, why would you say that in a different language? And some might think handing a student a Spanish/English dictionary is a way to empower them, but how many of us have looked up a synonym for a word we want to use and have found none of the synonyms really say what we mean to say? I've used a dictionary with the students I've tutored, but then we talk about the various words that come up with each definition. I find that online dictionaries sometimes work better than paper dictionaries because they offer more examples and explanations.

Hearing the different voices and languages at the writing center made the students at the BCC writing center feel as if their languages—various forms of English, Spanish, French, Urdu, Bangla, and others—weren't strange or out of the ordinary. Coming to the writing center made these multilingual students of color feel as if they belonged somewhere on campus as normal students, not as *ESL* students. In the writing center, they were all writers seeking to improve their writing . . . and their English-language skills.

In September 2011, I began my doctoral studies in English at St. John's University (SJU). During that fall semester, I didn't tutor at the writing center, but I tried studying there. The SJU writing center is really beautiful, with lots of tables, couches, and big windows, but I couldn't stand being in that space. I didn't feel comfortable sitting there as a thirty-year-old brown woman. Everyone looked so young and white to me. And every time I walked into the writing center, the consultants asked me if I was there for a tutoring session, which I soon became very sensitive to, as I feared they were judging my writing and academic skills based on my last name and complexion. For reference, St. John's University is located in Queens, New York, which is the most culturally diverse borough of New York City. There are over 130 languages spoken in Queens. In 2011, at SJUs Institute for Writing Studies, only English was spoken. For some reason this surprised me, but it made sense. It was silly of me to expect that what goes on in a two-year community college in the Bronx was going to be the same as what goes on in a four-year private, Catholic university in suburban Queens. And yet, it bothered me that our writing center was an English-only space filled with white tutors. There were some consultants of color at SJU (more so in 2017 than in 2011), but after I taught in Harlem, lived in the Bronx, and rode the subway all day long every day, the white consultants at the writing center stood out to me more than any of the *other* consultants. I wondered how the students I tutored at BCC would feel upon walking into SJU's writing center. Working with peer tutors who resemble most university faculty across the country probably wouldn't feel safe for students who are used to being judged by their English-language abilities by white humans—faculty and nonfaculty alike. The National Center for Education Statistics (NCES) (2016) report has provided the following analysis:

> In fall 2013, of all full-time faculty at degree-granting postsecondary institutions, 43 percent were White males, 35 percent were White females, 3 percent were Black males, 3 percent were Black females, 2 percent were Hispanic males, 2 percent were Hispanic females, 6 percent were Asian/Pacific Islander males, and 4 percent were Asian/Pacific Islander females. Making up less than 1 percent each were full-time faculty who were American Indian/Alaska Native and of Two or more races. (NCES 2016)

When there is such a wide disproportion between the hiring of white faculty versus the hiring of faculty of color, it's easy for students of *all* colors to assume incorrectly that faculty of color aren't being hired because they're not qualified enough. This idea trickles down into the writing center when the majority of tutoring staff and administrators are also white. Students of color are then held up to white standards and are led to believe these are the only *standards* that matter.

During the spring 2012 semester, I began tutoring at the SJU writing center and started my "fireside chats" with its director. It was a relief to hear the writing center wasn't an English-only center . . . officially. It just happened to be that way because no one tutored in any language other than English. In 2012, 44 percent of the twenty-one thousand students were white, and about 70 percent of the writing center staff of seventy students were White. During one chat with Harry Denny, he asked me what I would do if he wanted me to tutor in English only. I said I'd tutor in Spanish if needed, no matter what. He smiled at me and nodded. His response made feel as if we both had just passed a test. It was important for me to know the director of my writing center would not punish me for wanting to tutor in a language other than English.

My main concern about having a monoculture and monolingual tutoring staff that privileges white students who are fluent in only English is that these privileged tutors might have different concepts about what is considered *good writing*, and that affects how multicultural and multilingual *minority* students feel about their writing and their capability to do college work. Do writing center administrators instruct their tutoring staff during tutor training that all students have a right to their own language because of the National Council of Teachers of English's (NCTE) 1974 Resolution on the Students' Right to Their Own Language? Members of NCTE acknowledged that there are linguistic differences and we should all learn about them and accept them. Below, you will find the resolution:

> Afirmamos los estudiantes derecho a sus propios patrones y variedades de la lengua—los dialectos de su crianza o cualquier dialectos en que se encuentran su propia identidad y estilo. Los estudiosos de la lengua hace tiempo negaron que el mito de un dialecto estándar americano tiene toda validez. La afirmación de que cualquier dialecto es inaceptable equivale a un intento de un grupo social para ejercer su dominio sobre el otro. Tal afirmación lleva a falsos consejos para los oradores y escritores y asesoramiento inmoral para los seres humanos. Una nación orgullosa de su patrimonio y su variedad cultural y racial preservará su patrimonio de dialectos. Afirmamos enérgicamente que los maestros deben tener la experiencia y formación que les permitan respetar la diversidad y defender el derecho de los estudiantes en su propio idioma. (translation mine)

> [We affirm students' right to their own patterns and varieties of language—the dialects of their upbringing or any dialects in which they find their own identity and style. Language scholars have long denied that the myth of a standard American dialect is valid. The assertion that any dialect is unacceptable amounts to an attempt by one social group to exercise its dominion over the other. Such a statement leads to false advice for speakers and writers and immoral counseling for humans. A nation proud of its heritage and its cultural and racial variety will preserve its heritage of dialects. We strongly affirm that teachers must have the experience and

training that will enable them to respect diversity and defend the right of students in their own language]. (NCTE 1974, 1)

If you're comfortable reading in Spanish, you'll understand the first version of the resolution above. If this resolution were handed to a college student in a language they didn't understand or in one they were struggling with, would they find it significant? Would they feel safe or protected as a college student? Would it make them feel wanted and welcomed as a college writer? Probably not. So the resolution primarily protects those who are capable of understanding the language it was written in and would therefore protect those who don't need protection. The fact is that multilingual students are often unaware such a thing as language rights exists, maybe because the resolution only comes written in Standard English, and this makes me think the Resolution on the Students' Right to Their Own Language was not meant to protect multilingual students but rather only Standard English speakers who gain nothing from the resolution (NCTE 1974).

Writing centers must serve as agents for students, instead of as agents for institutions by serving as *fix-it* shops for professors and as places to acculturate marginalized students (Jacoby 1983; Land and Whitley 2006; Olson 2013; Wilson 2012). Anis Bawarshi and Stephanie Pelkowski write about what is gained and lost when marginalized writers in higher education are asked/forced/expected to write in academic English. They insist that the thought process is changed with writing; a person can't simply translate thoughts from one discourse to another without a change occurring. Many times, the change that occurs is a form of colonization (students begin to write in "academic English" without understanding the political and social ramifications of such a change), and writing centers should assist in fighting colonization instead of embracing it and vouching for it (Bawarshi and Pelkowski 1999, 41–59). Nancy Effinger Wilson (2012) declares, "When professors across the university campus believe that no language is wrong or invalid in and of itself, I will know that those diversity statements that appear on nearly every U.S. university website are more than mere words" (7). Wilson is calling out universities on their hypocritical practices, such as websites showing smiling students of color while hiding the high attrition rate of multicultural/multilingual students because of racist ideologies. Bawarshi and Pelkowski (1999) say, "What we are suggesting, finally, is that the writing center, in addition to helping marginalized students function within academic discourses, should also make explicit how these discourses affect them—how these discourses rhetorically and socially function" (53). They appear to be calling out for transparency in tutoring and in tutor-training sessions. Through transparency, writing center clients can make decisions about the discourse they want to write and think about with their tutors instead of letting the university decide what discourse is acceptable. But considering the ways in which writing centers across the country currently function, there is a persistent and ever-growing belief that speaking and writing in Standard English is the only way to have one common language that unites instead of divides. Enforcing Standard English in academia creates a mythic concept of easy-to-read writing *anyone* can understand, as if a piece of writing could ever have one universal way of being read (Greenfield and Rowan 2011a). The tutor's perception of Standard English (belief or disbelief in there being a "standard") and overall conscious or unconscious racist agenda can make or break a session but also make or break a client's perception of the writing center and even their feeling of belonging in college. The writing center either accepts multicultural/multilingual writers or it doesn't; there's no space for a weak stance for protecting the language rights of multicultural/multilingual tutors and writers.

My experiences as a tutor working at BCC and at SJU encouraged me to take up the work of access, equity, and language acceptance within writing centers. My focus is currently on tutor recruitment and hiring practices because I strongly believe that writing centers are fertile grounds for nurturing confidence in writers and that tutors are responsible for creating that space for *all* students. A tutor's job is more than just *fixing* a student's paper. Tutors can be allies for multilingual/multicultural students by providing agency. Tutors are often seen as *insiders* who can provide valuable information about the English language and academic norms to students who feel like *outsiders* because of their language, name, educational background, socioeconomic status, and/or skin color. But tutors shouldn't confuse their insider status with permission to push assimilation. It is essential that tutor training include discussion on NCTEs (1974) Resolution on the Students Rights to Their Own Language so tutors acknowledge and understand how important it is for them to foster a safe space for multilingual/multicultural students.

Writing centers can be complicit in nurturing Standard English and assimilation with promises that these ideas are for the good of the multicultural/multilingual student. It doesn't take much to convince a multicultural/multilingual student that becoming fluent in Standard English can *fix* all their problems. These students are easily convinced by their professors and writing center tutors that learning Standard English is the only way they will succeed in their classes, graduate from college, and land good, well-paying jobs. We need to work actively with our students, tutors, and the students who visit the writing center to not buy into the Standard English myth. We must reassure all students, tutors, and clients that they all belong in the writing center and that their contribution to *the university* and everything it represents is valuable and needed. What can writing center administrators and staff do to make sure all languages are accepted and respected in their writing centers?

7

NANEUN HANGUG SALAM-IBNIDA
Writing Centers and the Mixed-Raced Experience

Tammy S. Conard-Salvo

"What are you working on? What's your topic? What do you want to focus on?" I don't remember the student's responses, but I remember feeling a heightened sense of awareness that this student was Korean because his name, accent, and appearance were all familiar to me as a child of a Korean mother.

But I didn't initially disclose my identity to the student because the session wasn't about me—or so I thought at the time. I thought, like many tutors do, that the session was only about the student and his needs. The student expressed frustration with the writing assignment and the first-year writing course, and like so many other students, he just wanted to get through the required class. I was inexperienced at the time: a novice tutor who didn't go beyond the standard questions about the paper, so I didn't think about integrating my own identity as part of the rapport-building process. I certainly didn't consider, as Jay D. Sloan (2003) does, the necessary intellectual and rhetorical impact tutors have when they out themselves and help students (in his case) encounter difference (68).

We only had thirty minutes to discuss the essay, so we got down to business. One of us needed to read the essay aloud and figure out whether the student was fulfilling the assignment requirements and using strong rhetorical strategies to present an argument. We began discussing the essay, and we reached an impasse. As I tried to explain a concept and help the student work through some ideas, he didn't get it. So I did something I haven't done in a session since this one: I switched to speaking Korean, ever so briefly, to explain that I understood his frustration and to provide some vocabulary and examples. The tutorial took a positive turn. The student began to relax, and after the discussion was over, he made another appointment to see me.

DOI: 10.7330/9781607327837.c007

In the next and final tutorial with this student a few days later, we discussed his paper in English. He was comfortable enough working with me that he revealed his frustrations with going to school as well as his plans to go into the army. I remember telling him that while he was in school, he needed to concentrate on his studies and do his best to get through his writing course and that he might not be in the army forever. This might be an atypical response for a writing tutor, and I don't know that I would advise my own tutors to think and respond this way because of the parental nature of my comment. But for someone who understands the Korean cultural attitude toward a constant focus on education and a preference for directive pedagogy, a response like this is completely normal and expected. The student was not surprised. He nodded and took my statements in stride, and we finished the session.

At the time of these tutorials, Lady Falls Brown, the Texas Tech University Writing Center director, encouraged me to write about this experience, but I didn't know how to begin or why anyone else would be interested. Sure, there's the novelty of speaking in a language other than English during a writing tutorial, and our field has taken an interest in periodically questioning the ethics and efficacy of tutoring in other languages and exploring a number of related questions: Is using a language other than English forbidden in a tutorial session? Aren't we better at helping students when we can overcome the language barrier and have a productive conversation about writing? Are we hampering students who need to learn English in order to be successful at their institutions? Writing studies has addressed these questions in various ways, with the Conference on College Composition and Communication (CCCC) going so far as to issue a very strongly worded position statement, the National Council of Teachers of English's (NCTE) Resolution on the Students' Right to Their Own Language, as early as 1974. These topics and questions occasionally appear on the WCenter listserv when nervous administrators question the best practices for tutoring in languages other than English, and the writing centers at Dickinson College and elsewhere proudly offer multilingual tutorial sessions.

As a field, we haven't come to a consensus about the answers to these questions, and our unique institutional contexts often determine how best to address language in our writing centers. Narratives about bilingualism and translingualism in the writing center remain elusive and exoticized, but when they emerge, they reveal, according to Kerri Jordan, Steve Price, and Michele Eodice (2016), "that much of our current work in writing center theory and practice suggests that we are transitioning from writing coaches toward literacy sponsors in writing center spaces. When we start looking at things like translingual students' self advocacy and persistence, it behooves us to (re)consider our roles in their educational landscape." Conversations about privilege in writing centers continue to emerge, and scholars like Nancy Grimm (2011) urge all of us to "look more closely at ourselves and instead of others, particularly to examine the extent to which our writing center was based upon assumptions of language, literacy, and learning that privileged white mainstream students" (75).

Of course, I had no idea about my role and my unintentional activism during that tutorial twenty years ago. I spoke in Korean to the student only when communication became too difficult to continue the session, and I waited to *out* myself as a mixed-race Korean until the moment I code switched. Although I had a practical reason for switching to Korean, I engaged in an inner turmoil about the implications of code switching at that exact moment because I was acutely aware of not being immediately perceived as Korean, and in thinking back on that experience, I realize I am less interested in exploring the practicality of tutoring in another language and more interested in considering how my Korean, mixed-race identity influenced my interactions with the Korean student those many years ago—and how my identity has impacted my work in writing centers since then.

Only now, years later, can I see that my identity as a mixed-race person complicated the tutorial with the Korean student and contributed to my inability to write about the session when it happened. My growing awareness of my in-betweenness peaked during this time in graduate school in a way that wasn't possible growing up. As a child, I enjoyed a diverse upbringing in military communities surrounded by peers and classmates with similar backgrounds. Most of my friends were either mixed-race Koreans, mixed-race Asians, or multiracial in other ways. However, I attended an undergraduate institution that was *overwhelmingly* Caucasian. Until my university began an international exchange program, I was one of only two students of Asian descent on campus, often serving as the lone voice for Asians and Asian Americans, let alone for mixed-raced individuals. Although graduate school was more diverse, I needed to learn how to be comfortable in my own skin again. My academic focus on Asian American identity connected to my emerging personal narrative. This was public work, and I was proud of it. However, my use of the Korean language was private, even in a public space like the writing center. I wasn't ready to share this experience or to play the spokesperson role, especially after attending such a homogeneous undergraduate university.

Furthermore, outing myself was no easy decision, as my half-Korean identity could be met with a positive response or not, depending on the situation and context. Texas Tech University didn't have a very large Asian or Asian American student population at the time, and some Koreans welcomed me because a critical mass of Koreans didn't exist. Once other Koreans recognized I was familiar with the language and culture—that my mother was Korean—I was accepted . . . to a point. However, the barrier to even partial acceptance lay in the fact that my physical looks did not provide insight into my identity. Like many mixed-race people, I don't fit neatly into categories based on looks or behavior. I can fit into both US and Korean culture, and I fit into neither, caught between these cultures in a category of my own. Both Asian and non-Asians have openly questioned my background, and I have witnessed surreptitious stares as people try to figure out what I am. Or who I am. Or whether I belong.

****

Years later, looking through old report cards and educational records at my parents' house, I noticed a questionnaire accompanying some test results. One particular question asked, "Does your child hear a language(s) other than English spoken in the home?" My father had answered "yes" and listed "Korean." The test results indicated no linguistic intervention, such as a bilingual classroom, was needed. Strange, I thought. Why would I need language testing in third or fourth grade? I had been attending an English-speaking school since kindergarten, and none of my educational records showed any problems speaking or reading in English. My father clearly listed English as my preferred language and the one spoken most often at home. Could that one honest response about my bilingual household have been enough to mobilize teachers and administrators to administer the Oral Language Dominance Measure developed by El Paso Public Schools circa 1979? Why the assumption that my English language skills would be negatively affected if another language was spoken in my home? This school district *Othered* me simply because of my perceived (lack of) language skills.

Ironically, even though my mother spoke Korean at home, I didn't become fluent in Korean until the fifth grade, when my father was stationed in Uijeongbu for a US Army tour of duty. I met extended family and learned to communicate with them in their native language; most of my relatives could not speak English—even cousins who had studied English in school. My communication with my mother changed once I learned Korean, and I frequently used it to keep my conversation with her private. When Korean visitors came to the house, my mother intentionally addressed me in English, even though my mother's friends knew I understood Korean. She used English as a means of separating her conversation with friends from her conversation with family. Yet when we were in public, my mother spoke to me in Korean when she didn't want English speakers to eavesdrop.

Korean is the language of surprise for me: Koreans are often surprised to hear me speak *their* language because I don't look Korean to some people and no one assumes I am fluent and able to address them in the correct honorific. Honorifics recognize one's place in the culture. Using the correct titles acknowledges one's place in the family as well as the community and recognizes power and kinship. Anyone learning Korean can attest to the challenge of remembering multiple names for every person. Keeping the honorifics straight is more than choosing the right vocabulary: mother's aunt, father's brother, and so forth. Sometimes the response is pleasant; others respond kindly, replying in Korean and addressing me with respect. Sometimes the response is in English, a clear marker of rejection of my outsider status.

Code switching feels natural to many multiracial people. We have been doing it as long as we have been conscious. The rhetorical choice about using Korean or English for advantage is one of few empowering strategies I have available in a culture that marginalizes people who look like me and those who can transform themselves to fit in many different linguistically fraught situations. Code switching is also physical, allowing people like me to slip into and out of cultures and races—shape-shifting identities. Even though code switching is not easy, it becomes intuitive as a learned response to subtle and not-so-subtle signals. Only recently have we been given the option of selecting more than one race on official documents and forms such as the US Federal Census, as if multiracial identity could be neatly categorized in this box or that box. Although I feel relief at being able to fully represent my identity, I am still learning to be comfortable in my mixed-race skin after years of being forced to check only one box.

Maybe code switching—whether linguistic, cultural, or physical—is why I feel such affinity for "Multi-Cultural Voices: Peer Tutoring and Critical Reflection in the Writing Center," a *Writing Center Journal* piece written by Gail Y. Okawa, Thomas Fox, Lucy J. Y. Chang, Shana R. Windsor, Frank Bella Chevez, and Hayes LaGuan (1991). My undergraduate tutors in training read this essay every year because I want them to consider what happens when the academy polices language and writing; when students are expected to deny a part of themselves in order to assimilate; and when personal narratives are suppressed because they fit outside cultural norms. My novice tutors support acceptance of different identities and cultures, but they rarely know how to incorporate advocacy into their work as tutors. Okawa and her colleagues remind us that "one major consideration, especially in a multi-cultural writing center, is this: both tutors and students come to each tutoring session with experience and expectations that are culturally based" (Okawa et al. 1991, 14). Tutors (and directors) can easily forget that each participant in a tutorial session brings something distinct and valuable to the table because the dominant culture seeks to erase difference or requires conformity to a homogenous set of values.

Some of my tutors have only begun considering their culturally based expectations and experiences, and they must negotiate these differences with the writers with whom they work. When I tutored the Korean student, I was keenly aware that I could participate in a cultural and linguistic conversation my colleagues could not, yet I was not confident in the power of my cultural cachet and knowledge base. I am also reminded of Marian Yee's (1991) experience of meeting each new class of students who questioned her role as teacher because of her racial and cultural identity. My tutors do not question my role as an experienced writing center administrator, yet my anxieties about acceptance and difference have recently pushed me to help my students "recognize and read the dominant cultural narratives that construct their identities and their views of the world;" this approach is "a way to help them rethink writing . . . to help them to create narratives in which their differences need not be obliterated, but instead recognized and respected" (Yee 1991, 29). The only way I can help tutors rewrite and establish these new narratives is to consider my own identity and the role I play in reshaping the writing center.

As a tutor and now as an administrator, I bring with me not only different identities and values but also my anxieties over acceptance that haven't disappeared just because I'm now in a greater position of power than when I was a student. I still live a life of paradox not uncommon with multiracial, multicultural individuals: although I'm used to being the model minority, following instructions and being quiet and selfless, I'm also the assertive boss lady, not a stereotypical Asian American, not demure or petite. I take charge and can call a class or meeting to order by easily projecting my voice. Now I'm a writing center administrator thinking about language, access, and communication. Purdue University has a large and growing population of undergraduate international students who are primarily from China but also from Korea, India, and South America. I find myself with outsider status once again, witnessing students who don't have to look very far to find linguistically and culturally similar friends. Students who themselves are a part of a critical mass of people who look just like them, who must negotiate a Caucasian American, middle-class dominant culture that expects them to speak and write with native-like fluency. But these students may not see me as an advocate, a potential ally, as someone who can be empathetic about code switching and assimilation and help them navigate unfamiliar environments, because I am part of the establishment.

****

Recently I attended an open house for Purdue's new Asian American and Asian Resource and Cultural Center (AAARC). We have several other centers on campus for other underrepresented groups, and this was my first opportunity to see the long-overdue space designed specifically for Asian American and Asian members of the campus community. Purdue has plenty of programs for both students and faculty, and I wanted to know how the AAARC could support a mixed-race administrative staff member who is nervous about belonging.

The interim director described services and programming, and I was too shy to ask questions while others were present. Later, during a private moment, I outed myself as Asian American. A thousand anxious voices clamored for attention, and I tried not to sound desperate. Me, me, I'm one of you, too. I may not look like it, but I am. The conversation turned to controversy about the word *hapa* (half), and I volunteered to discuss this further at a later date, indicating my openness to offer feedback and ideas about programming for mixed-race issues. Suddenly, I extended myself beyond the reaches of the writing lab into territory I've visited only in private, in a galaxy far, far away. I'm a writing center administrator. I'm hired to train tutors and manage daily operations of the writing lab. What business do I having bringing my personal agenda into someone else's space? Wait, isn't this my space, too? But shouldn't I stick to writing center work? Wait, aren't outreach and cultural identity also part of writing center work?

Too often we limit writing center work to just talking about the paper, but how can we talk about a writer's document, how can we even address rhetorical concerns such as audience and purpose, without considering not only what writers say but also whom we represent in our writing center spaces? How can we not think about reflecting and accepting, even with conflict and discomfort, the campuses we have and hope to have? And so we've whitewashed writing centers and created "safe spaces" that only truly feel safe for a small segment of the population. We avoid uncomfortable conversations because we don't want to offend, and in the process, we've rendered underrepresented populations even more invisible and powerless. The reality, however, is that safe spaces do not exist, and as Jackie Grutsch McKinney (2013) in *Peripheral Visions for Writing Centers* states, "Cozy homes . . . can certainly make us feel good. . . . [but] homes are culturally marked" (25). I implicate myself in this critique because for so long (and even now), I hesitated to consider my own personal and relevant agenda in my professional work. For so long, I failed to raise diversity discussions in my tutor-training courses, and when I did, I kept my own multiracial voice quiet for fear of making my prospective tutors uncomfortable. Until recently, I did not out myself as half Korean, nevermind the other half that includes Native American ancestry. I avoided sharing anything about myself, a mistake in hindsight because I compartmentalized my personal interests from my professional work. Even now when sharing my identity and mixing the personal with the professional, I become anxious. I feel exposed and vulnerable to rejection, keenly aware that multiracial voices remain virtually nonexistent in the academy and within writing centers.

Mixed-race folk like myself have often confronted identity crises and pressure to either conform or to choose one racial or ethnic identity. This history, this reality, can be difficult to explain to a largely homogenous academy, and writing centers are no exception, despite the progress we've made in diversifying our spaces and in both acknowledging and reflecting the rich, varied, multicultural, and multilingual campuses where we are housed. But much of our attention in these areas focuses on clients, who are often, but not always, students.

My reality is one of constant conflict with the personal and the professional and with the public and the private. My husband and I are in the midst of a very public domestic infant adoption process, and colleagues and friends around the world have witnessed as we've shared our adoption story and blurred the boundaries of work and home lives. We've juggled our various personas through online profiles and social media as we hope for an expectant mother to choose us. Not only have I experienced the angst and crisis of wanting and being denied parenthood, I have felt challenged to describe and make public my ethnic identity in a sea of other prospective adoptive parents, the vast majority of whom are Caucasian. In a particularly difficult moment of reevaluating the pictures we've used in our profile, it was noted that I am not smiling in many of the pictures. I look serious. I've heard this characterization many times before, with friends and photographers complaining when I didn't present a large, toothy grin on command. And when I do smile, my eyes turn into crescent-moon slivers that give the impression of closed eyes. "Open your eyes," I'm commanded. And so it's become a funny-but-not-funny joke that a photographer should double check to make sure my eyes are open.

I called the one person I thought would understand, my sister. I thought she would sympathize and commiserate, but she gave me no solace or comfort because her own exhaustion—the entire country's exhaustion—with identity issues has boiled over into anger over political correctness and the constant state of offense in which everyone is mired. She is tired of walking on eggshells and of worrying whether or not someone will misunderstand a comment or joke. The nation is tired of confronting issues it thought it had already resolved. I am tired, too, of many things. Of having to explain who I am. Of worrying about *passing*. Of wondering how I will be received once I've outed myself. Of not only national but also global regression. Of people like me being erased, pigeonholed, whitewashed, or worse, feeling or being unsafe. And of being less than whole, unwanted, un-American.

As much as I'm tied to my Korean culture, I am separated from it. When my mother died thirteen years ago, I lost a sense of cultural legitimacy, my one and only authentic tie to Korea. Or so I have thought these days. Others would tell me I'm being ridiculous, that of course I am Korean *enough*, whatever that might mean. But that argument was easy to make when my mother was alive and serving as a bridge to that part of my heritage. Feeling secure in one's identity is a feeling born out of privilege, an argument made by those who have never had to question their cultural legitimacy. Now I am afraid and adrift, unable to travel the thousands of miles to see family who still live in South Korea, family who would undoubtedly welcome me. My self-consciousness and imposter syndrome keep me from doing so. As I struggle to remember a Korean word or phrase because I am very much out of practice, I am reminded, again and again, that I don't belong.

Of course, my professional communities would say they welcome me, but our discussions of race and identity do not always include mixed-race identities. We value differences, but we don't always know what to do with hybridity—either obvious, intentional fusion or subtle, undetectable negotiation of multiple identities and communities.

PART II: MULTILINGUALISM
Review

Nancy's and Tammy's essays obviously cannot capture the totality of the multilingual experience in writing centers, nor those of all the writers, tutors, and other staff that work, teach, and learn within them. And that wasn't our intention. Nancy (chapter 6) and Tammy (chapter 7) might fit well in other parts of this collection based on their narratives, so we invite readers to understand that the boundaries throughout their pieces are permeable. Nancy's and Tammy's bodies are no less racialized than those about which our colleagues in section 1 on race testify; they just have different histories, different material consequences, and different realities. As cisgender, straight-identified women, Nancy and Tammy are also subject to the tensions and privilege of gender and sexuality the following section 3 takes up. They can never step outside the institutional, systemic nature of patriarchy that enacts double standards, polices their bodies, and values their work differently than that of male colleagues. Still, the privilege of heterosexuality and its hegemonic practices imprint on them and their interactions with the world. As academics, their cultural capital confers a level of distinction that makes them relatively elite, even if their economic standing isn't on par with the corporatized sectors in our society. For Nancy, being a graduate student and adjunct instructor in New York City has its own parallels with the classed experiences Elizabeth addresses in her chapter 14 essay, and Tammy possesses the economic and professional security of a full-time administrator. In the caste system of academia, both occupy positions that reinscribe a degree of occupational marginality.

These intersectional factors that cut across the language experiences and politics about which Nancy and Tammy write exist in a larger array of conversations about multilingualism and writing centers as well as in writing studies more broadly. Carol Severino's (1993a) article on how tutors might avoid appropriation offers classic advice and discussion material for writing center curricula (181–201). Ilona Leki's (1992) *Understanding ESL Writers*, Dana R. Ferris and John S. Hedgcock's (1998) *Teaching ESL Composition*, and Ferris's (2003) *Response to Student Writing*

DOI: 10.7330/9781607327837.p002

provide foundational scholarship that can guide tutors and writing instructors alike on effective response and feedback for multilingual writers. Muriel Harris and Tony Silva's early scholarship has influenced how tutors understand and approach ESL writers (Harris and Silva 1993, 525–37), though Shanti Bruce and Ben Rafoth's editions of *ESL Writers* (Bruce and Rafoth 2004, 2009), as well as their *Tutoring Second Language Writers*, has been especially helpful as the transfer of multilingual and linguistic research into writing centers has grown more and more complex (Bruce and Rafoth 2016). In a review of Bruce and Rafoth's 2016 edition, Vicki R. Kennell and Beth A. Towle note a shift from a more expansive discussion of multilingual writers to one that has a far narrower focus on the needs of urban, coastal multilingual writers and gives less attention to the transitory international writer research-extensive universities have seen (Kennell and Towle 2016, 227–30). In that vein, Paul Matsuda, Christina Ortmeier-Hooper, and Xiaoye You's collection, *The Politics of Second Language Writing*, pushes us to think more critically about our understanding of and practices toward multilingual writers (Matsuda, Ortmeier-Hooper, and You 2006). Similarly, an older collection, *Generation 1.5 Meets College Composition*, edited by Linda Harklau, Kay M. Losey, and Meryl Siegal (1999), invites readers to complicate the ever-shifting landscape of multilingual students in US educational institutions and those institutions' policies and pedagogical practices.

More recent scholarship pushes us to think differently about multilingual writers altogether. Vershawn Ashanti Young's (2011) "Should Writers Use They Own English?," Young, Aja Y. Martinez, and the National Council of Teachers of English's (2011) *Code-Meshing as World English*, and A. Suresh Canagarajah's (2006) article "The Place of World Englishes in Composition: Pluralization Continued" help us imagine the tutoring and teaching of writing not as a false choice between one privileged code over all others but as a space where writers can grapple with the rhetorical impact of switching in and out of or even meshing codes. Students and tutors alike can come to recognize the hybridity and malleability of language in and beyond the academy and disciplines. In "Language Difference in Writing: Toward a Translingual Approach," Bruce Horner, Min-Zhan Lu, Jacqueline Jones Royster, and John Trimbur (2011) suggest that "the long-standing aim of traditional writing instruction has been to reduce 'interference,' excising what appears to show difference [in writing]" (303). In place of conformity and uniformity, they call for "a new paradigm: a translingual approach" that "sees difference in language not as a barrier to overcome or as a problem to manage, but as a resource for producing meaning in writing, speaking, reading, and listening" (Horner et al. 2011, 303). As the essays of our multilingualism section suggest, our writing centers might exist as spaces through which to organize for meaning making through translingualism because writing center consultants sustain varieties of multiple languages and are well equipped to reflect on their language differences as strengths. They are thereby equipped to use their consultations to undercut monolingual hegemony by moving between language varieties with both monolingual and multilingual student writers. Tutors can invite one another and other writers to respect the language backgrounds they bring with them—to see the ways in which writing is always already a negotiation with academic English because it exists as an ever-moving target and because nonacademic vernaculars of English have great value in that they shape writers' identities and histories. Consultants can also invite one another as well as other writers to reflect on the real pressures that keep academic English in a position of power even though the standard form often functions to devalue diverse identities.

Research on multilingualism in writing centers has a rich history and a potential impact on writing centers that engage it. While critical and narrative research has tended to dominate, scholarship remains to be done on a host of empirical fronts, from quantitative and qualitative studies of the impact and experiences of these writers and their tutors in sessions to quasi-experimental or hybrid designs that seek to target specific variables and to triangulate insight. Nearly every writing center "bean counts," as Neal Lerner (1997, 2001) notes, yet too little aggregation is happening across institutional types and locations. We fail to ask, on a systematic basis, what sorts of multilingual writers we are seeing, for what purposes, and with what impact. Writing centers at large research institutions have seen transformation in their use by multilingual writers, mirroring international admissions practices, yet the multilingualism experienced in coastal, urban areas is quite different. How are those differences significant? What do they portend for tutor training? What are the language politics and dynamics of a student or staff member who is a permanent resident or an undocumented citizen as opposed to undergraduate or graduate students temporarily in the United States? How can writing centers influence and impact campus conversations and research inquiry around multilingualism? How might we raise consciousness about the politics of accent and linguistics?

Aside from the inquiry multilingual writers and tutors invite us to consider, we invite readers to consider their implications on the everyday practice and education that happens in writing centers. To what degree should (or do) our values around multilingual writers imprint on the recruiting and selection of tutors, regardless of level or status? How do we create curricula for either credit-bearing or ongoing training that make space for tutors and administrators alike to gain educational and research capital based on the needs of multilingual writers? Nancy and Tammy push us to have conversations about the differences among tolerance, acceptance, and even celebration of the politics of accent in writing centers, whether in or beyond sessions. Tammy's narrative challenges all of us to think about the unique tensions and pressures writing center administrators must contend with, especially when not operating from the relative privilege of student or faculty positions, both of which possess considerable support networks. Nancy's narrative also speaks to a vulnerability those of us with privileged positions and unmarked bodies or voices might not think about deeply: how do we resist the temptation to offer up assimilation as the only tenable choice for multilingual learners and workers in our spaces?

Too often, we in writing centers are privileged with tacit knowledge of the rules the game of academic success requires, and we withhold them, or just as problematically, we dole out that knowledge uncritically, with well-meaning intentions. For students who lack the linguistic or rhetorical privilege of codes and conventions of academic English (or even specific disciplinary knowledge), access to it isn't either/or—it's material, it has real-world consequences. Instead, we must think about the situation as one for gentle activism of *both/and*, helping students understand they can make strategic decisions about *both* code switching *and* advancing discourses that mesh codes, accents, and vernaculars. Such practices empower students to teach back to one another, tutors, professors, and administrators about the multiplicity of voices all of us inhabit. That said, for those of us whose bodies and voices signify and perform the very privilege Nancy and Tammy are writing into, especially in writing centers, we must leverage those very advantages to ensure we are, and our spaces are, always complicating the dynamics by continually interrogating how we reenact an ostracizing teaching and learning environment when we fail to think about linguistic and ethnic diversity. How do we make space whenever or wherever possible for students, clients, tutors, administrators, and faculty alike to speak back to (or against) the dominant vernacular operative in the college or university? As Victor Villanueva Jr. (2003) asks, how do we teach those with privilege to be silent and hear and those without to speak and be heard? We encourage writing centers to have sustained, perhaps even difficult, dialogues about the administration of language and its consequences so everyone learns and internalizes the reality of a polyvocal discursive world that's accented, affected, and challenged.

PART III

Gender and Sexuality

8

EVERYDAY TRUTHS
Reflections from a Woman Writing Center Professional

Anna Sicari

Five and a half years ago, I was a twenty-two-year-old woman who had just started working in a writing center as I entered a graduate program. I did not think much about the everyday work I did as a tutor—except that I enjoyed the work, I thought it was good work, and I appreciated helping students with their concerns with writing. I certainly did not think about any theory grounding the work I did (as a literature student, theory was still abstract to me, to be used when applying it to a paper) or about issues of identity. One particular session that stood out to me then was when I was working with a young female student who was struggling with a paper about abortion—this paper was for a Christian-living type course (I work at a Catholic institution). Her professor—male, and a conservative Catholic—seemed to encourage his students to write about the evils of abortion. She herself—Catholic, and a woman—seemed reluctant to write about this. Not sure where she stood on the issue, she wanted to receive a good grade on the paper and felt she would not achieve the A she sought if she chose to complicate the topic of abortion, writing on reasons as to why a woman might choose to have an abortion and larger issues of reproductive rights, feminism, and what it is like to be a woman living in a patriarchal world.

This conversation between the student and me took place just shortly after Rush Limbaugh called Sandra Fluke "a slut" and later suggested she should let us (the United States, I assume) watch videos of her having sex in lieu of paying for birth control. While my client and I did not discuss this public controversy in our session, I still felt Rush Limbaugh's presence in our session—the conservative white male was policing our language and the freedom to express ourselves as women.

Reflection. As an instructor and writing center professional, I encourage the students who enter these writing spaces to reflect on their work and, later, to reflect on their reflections and to rethink their writing

DOI: 10.7330/9781607327837.c008

after time has passed. A few years after this session, I wrote about it. This session was one of the many sessions I have had that formed the foundations of my current research project, which stems from my dissertation. I presented a paper on this session at CCCCs a few years ago, along with my fellow editors of this collection, believing this session to be an example of the everyday activist work we do in writing centers: listen in order to understand and learn from one another, explore why issues may bother us, and examine what this might mean with our students in order for change to occur. While the client and I did not necessarily discuss Rush Limbaugh, we did discuss issues of authority, power, language, and what it means when we write. This dialogue, I told the audience, this pedagogy that embraces rhetorical listening, is the type of feminist work we perform every day at the writing center. This pedagogy is why writing centers are important, why the work we do is so difficult, and why examining and theorizing identity politics in our everyday praxis must be explored more thoroughly.

A year and a half later, I again reflected on this situation, and now I reflect on my reflection. Slightly naïve and idealistic, I still strongly believe in the everyday work we do in a writing center. But—with time, insight, and experience—my belief about this everyday work and its value is now complicated with institutional forces I still believe stem from the patriarchal system of the academy. This chapter explores how gender intersects with leadership as well as the everyday navigations of a woman writing center tutor and professional.

"BUT I'M SMARTER THAN HIM."

This was a mantra I developed during a particularly difficult time in my academic career. During my first year of doctoral school, I had several experiences in which I felt my gender: of being policed by women; of having moments in which I felt the physicality of my body; and of moments of being silenced. My mantra of "being smarter than him" was my own way of navigating doctoral school. It helped give me the authority and confidence needed to succeed. I was twenty-five years old when I entered my doctoral program in hopes of one day directing a writing center. That same year, I accepted a leadership position at a writing center at another institution. As a doctoral student with three years of writing center experience, I had earned some degree of authority while still being a relatively young (certainly by academia's standards) woman. I was eager to work with the writing center director at this institution—I was entering a brand-new space and, while I had a wonderful and supportive relationship with the male writing center director at my doctoral program's center, I was excited to work with a female writing center director. I imagined collaborating with her on different projects, discussing writing center theory and pedagogy and how it informs our everyday practices, and sharing with her the struggles of being a woman of authority in an academic space. More specifically, I looked forward to sharing with her the struggles of being a female writing center professional (WCP)—a position I believe to be feminized—and the daily obstacles one faces as both a woman and a WCP.

Eagerness quickly grew into disappointment, as I found myself questioned and undermined by her in a way that was entirely new to me. I went from being a confident tutor and leader at one center to being apprehensive and nervous at the other center. As the only female of the three professional staff members at that writing center, I started noticing that the leadership responsibilities I once had were gradually being removed from me and given to my two male colleagues. I began to feel the long stares my boss, the woman I had hoped would be a mentor, gave me when I entered the space, and there were even moments I was nervous about taking off my jacket. Was my outfit somehow inappropriate? I felt the physicality of my body in ways I never had before. The way I interacted with students, something for which I had always been praised, was not appreciated in this space—she was quick to let me know each and every time. It was a long and exhausting semester of working with this woman. By the end of it, I started internalizing the comments, stares, and e-mails I received from her. I was not the confident woman I wanted to become; instead, I was insecure. In reflection on my experience with this woman, I think now of the backlash Hillary Clinton received during her 2016 presidential campaign and Madeleine Albright's requoting her own famous saying, "There is a special place in hell for women who don't help other women." I myself rolled my eyes when I saw that on the news—upset with both Hillary Clinton and Madeleine Albright for sending me to hell.

This research project focuses on the public and how it intersects with the private, or the everyday. I want to turn a little to Hillary Clinton and Madeleine Albright and offer my thoughts on how I see this moment in my experience with the woman writing center director (even though the Clinton/Albright controversy occurred three years after the fact). While I want to condemn this woman—there is a special place in hell for WCPs who don't help other WCPs—I can also see how easy it is for women to perpetuate the patriarchal systems in place. Women police women. And while I certainly believe my boss policed me in ways she did not police my two male colleagues, my gender played a major role in my everyday struggles. I also believe *she* was policed in an institution that did not value her. And so I cannot help but think about Hillary Clinton and Madeleine Albright—two women in the patriarchal system of politics and government. Might there be a special place in hell for women who don't help other women? There is power in reflection and in recognizing one's own complicity in patriarchy.

To return to my earlier mantra, I laugh, as this line is not one that would readily come out of my mouth. That is not my voice. "This is the oppressor's language / yet I need it to talk to you" (Rich 50). This is not my language, and yet it is the language I am mimicking; I am calling it my own in order to express myself. It was what I told myself, time and time again, when I saw male colleagues being recognized in ways I was not, given the leadership roles I wanted, and earning authority so *easily*, as easy as stepping inside the room.

When I think of my mantra, I am reminded of bell hooks's (2000) *Feminism Is for Everybody* and her claim on how to fight against patriarchy, and I firmly agree with her when she states, "To end patriarchy (another way of naming institutionalized sexism) we need to be clear that we are all participants in perpetuating sexism until we change our minds and our hearts, until we let go of sexist thought and action and replace it with feminist thought and action" (hooks 2000, ix). This mantra—"but I'm smarter than him"—though it helped me during a difficult time, did not necessarily stem from feminist thought and action. I believe that to examine my mantra, to look at the phrase I told myself daily, with the emphasis on the word *him*, I need to turn to Adrienne Rich's 1972 essay "When We Dead Awaken: Writing as Revision." Rich claims,

> Until we can understand the assumptions in which we are drenched we cannot know ourselves. And this drive to self-knowledge, for women, is more than a search for identity: it is part of our refusal of the self-destructiveness of male-dominated society. (Rich 1972, 18)

My mantra was my own "drive to self-knowledge," and it certainly was more than just a search for my identity; it was allowing me to understand the implications behind this woman's choices and decisions that demonstrated she valued my male counterpart's abilities over mine (and my own complicit behavior in these experiences). It made me realize the powerful system we are all living under and that we are all wholly affected by. Rich (1972) uses the word "drenched," a word I love in this essay. Soaked, covered, saturated—we are all drenched with patriarchy. I could not direct my anger at the men in the situations I faced; their behaviors and their assumptions are not entirely their fault. We are all drenched in patriarchal assumptions. Women included.

My mantra was my own attempt at destroying these assumptions, making sure they did not take a hold of me—refusing to quit, refusing to doubt or else I, too, would be covered in the self-hatred sexism wants me to be covered in. Drenched. I go to this word again because drenched does not bring connotations of hopelessness with it; I can clean up something that is drenched. I can absorb it. I can wipe it clean. *I am smarter than him.* My refusal to be destroyed. My bit in cleaning up the mess that was created. My wiping down of the patriarchal oppression these moments have created. This mantra was not directed at a person or at a single event or any particular moment in time. This mantra was addressed to hatred, to oppression, to sexism, to violence. These words, which were not mine, were used to understand the situation I was put in (perhaps worse still, by fellow women). Again, I think back to Adrienne Rich (1994) and her poem "Diving into the Wreck." She writes,

> I came to explore the wreck
> The words are purposes
> The words are maps
> I came to see the damage that was done and the treasures that prevail (Rich 1994, 52–55).

The mantra is what drove me to carry on and continue. However, these words are not words that can create the peace that can end sexism and oppression. This mantra values superiority, subverting the ideology of man over woman, and this is not what feminism is about. However, this clash must happen in order for any true attempt against sexism to take place. There must be a conversation, perhaps even a fight: contact zones must occur. We must get into it.

> We circle silently
> about the wreck
> we dive into the hold / I am she: I am he. (Rich 1994, 74–77).

Although I am speaking from a personal space of past memories and current trials, I know these are gendered experiences all professional academic women face; these experiences are created for us and can make women in the academy feel inferior, intimidated, and isolated. My particular focus and interest lies in the gendered moments female tutors and writing center directors experience daily; I am also interested in how the work and research of writing centers are continually denounced, to this day, as not academic or not important, and this problematic thinking is certainly steeped in sexism. Writing center scholarship, though often theoretical, still focuses on daily, lived experiences; this scholarship studies the importance of collaboration and is often written collaboratively, and it is often focused on students and their narratives. This work is viewed as "feminine," and I argue that writing center scholarship and studies are not taken as seriously as are other fields in the academy because they are so heavily feminine. Across the country, most writing centers are heavily female staffed (as tutors and administrators) and are still seen as supplementary to the classroom.

One of the most influential writing center essays, an essay that still gets cited and one I argue is a starting point for much WC scholarship today, "Collaboration, Control, and the Idea of the Writing Center," written by a woman, Andrea Lunsford (1991), discusses the importance of collaboration while simultaneously recognizing how this type of work is often deemed as unimportant and trivial; all serious work is independent and isolated, as many other disciplines emphasize. Lunsford writes, "In spite of the very real risks involved, we need to embrace the idea of writing centers as . . . centers for collaboration. . . . Such a center would place control, power, and authority not in the tutor or staff, not in the individual student, but in the negotiating group" (Lunsford, 1991, 8). Writing centers are powerful sites of collaboration in which tutors and directors alike are very aware of power and authority and are taught to think about these issues as they consult with writers. Lunsford's (1991) plea for collaboration as a site that attempts to disperse power to all is powerful and Foucauldian—it is calling forth a radical pedagogy that places power in all. And yet, I fear these powerful pleas are often only heard by and through the writing center community, this community being particularly more isolated than composition or literary studies. And this isolation, I argue, is because of how feminized writing centers are—so much so that they are primarily represented by women.

Writing center pedagogy and practice embraces silence, renegotiation, disruption, and moments that transform identity. Writing center ideals and practices ask those who participate in such pedagogy to question hegemonic discourse and to value ideals that go against heteronormative behavior and thought. In *The Everyday Writing Center*, Anne Ellen Geller, Michele Eodice, Frankie Condon, Meg Carroll, and Elizabeth H. Boquet (2007) claim, "When we are able to pursue the broken silence rather than turn away from it in fear or shame, then we may begin both to participate more fully in the (re)negotiation of meaning (especially around identity) and to invest more fully in that (re)negotiation of the principles we espouse and the responsibility we believe we bear" (Geller et al. 2007, 19). Silence is often gendered as feminine—it is often seen as weak and inarticulate, ignored and isolated. This view or use of silence is a female condition, and I can speak to moments of silence that have rendered me weak and inarticulate—not confident enough, not dominant. Through years of tutoring, I came to value my silence, to appreciate my patience, to recognize that, often, less is more in helping someone come to terms with their voice and their identity. My silence, my encouragement, my nondirective approach are some of my best assets as a tutor and teacher, though too often, these are recognized as character faults—career blockers. "You have to act more like a leader; take control!" or "Encouragement is not necessarily the best way to tutor, sometimes it helps to be more direct" are comments I've heard regularly throughout my academic career.

Yet, my writing center experience teaches me otherwise. It tells me that sometimes a lack of control is the best way to navigate difficult situations and to allow for critical thinking. Tutoring makes me recognize that silence is often powerful, that allowing space for questioning and reflecting is crucial to the student in finding their own voice. Geller et al. (2007) write, "We are concerned that tutors and directors, facing multiple pressures, may rely too heavily (as all of us do on occasion) on technical approaches . . . these mindsets may actually discourage tutors from admitting or even noticing that on-the-ground practices contradict implicit or explicit writing center 'policy'" (Geller et al. 2007, 21). This type of approach to writing center pedagogy, a focus on "technical approaches," or a rigid policy of best practices without thinking of the individual, does not focus on the whole person and is one way in which writing center studies is often complicit in regulating students, limiting their voices, and failing to recognize that the work we do is empowering and educational. Rather, feminist rhet/comp scholars have taught me there is power in silence and there is much to learn from rhetorical listening (Glenn and Ratcliffe 2011). As a woman WCP and former tutor, I recognize the everyday challenges of being both a woman and a writing center professional. I believe that in silence, in listening to learn, in reflection, I can navigate successfully in the hyperfeminized space of the writing center and capture the empowering and important work I do.

I'm far from saying anything new or outrageous in my claim of the feminization of writing centers (and that this feminization devalues the work of the writing center in the patriarchal setting of the academy). Harry Denny (2010) writes in his work *Facing the Center*, "I learned that . . . this notion of feminization . . . cuts any number of ways . . . served to marginalize and diminish the work of individuals, collectives, and units. . . . If as [Susan] Miller speculates, composition studies programs have become the potty trainers of novice writers' work, what must that bode for writing centers, frequently positioned as the sites for . . . discursive remediation" (Denny 2010, 91). This claim is certainly one I think about regularly as a person who sees the power of writing centers and the transformative work and space they take up; I firmly believe writing centers can be (or are) more transforming in shaping a student's identity than any classroom, and it is precisely because of this (what some call *feminized* or *subservient*) space the writing center takes up. The writing center is not the academic classroom—the writing center does not have to be a site of policing and grading. The writing center is created for the student (not for the teacher). The gendering politics (although there are many different variables at play, this project primarily focuses on gender) that infiltrate and dominate writing centers and their space in the academy are there for a reason; this is another form of policing the student, making sure all spaces (even spaces seen as only for students) correctly police any citizen in the academy and transform their language, their bodies, their identities into the proper, standard codes. If writing centers are to continue to be seen as subservient, I argue that writing centers should do so subversively. If writing centers are feminized, writing centers should truly embrace and explore feminist pedagogy and be spaces for collaboration and mentorship, spaces that embrace a love for people and allow for students to find their identities. As a subversive site, as a feminized site, writing centers can be transformative spaces, influencing and creating new pedagogies for classrooms and professors, thus shifting the power dynamic by having writing centers and professors and university administrators work together. This, too, would put writing center studies at the forefront of the academy—and pleas for the radical pedagogy writing centers advocate for would be read by a wider audience.

While I truly believe writing centers can and will be seen as powerful and transformative sites (through using their "feminized" place in the academy), and I continue in my own professional career to be part of this transformation, I am firmly aware of how difficult the process is and will be. Small steps must be taken, conversations must take place, written-work scholarship must be disseminated and read. To push on Jackie Grutsch McKinney's idea of the "writing center grand narrative"—writing centers as "cozy homes"—I think many women tutors and writing center professionals can think of many times in which the writing center was anything but cozy (Grutsch McKinney 2013, 3, 22). Moments of being harassed, undermined, or ignored by students, faculty, and administrators—these are moments, too, that take place in our "cozy homes," in our writing centers. And these are the narratives, the stories, and the experiences we need to talk about—to start with our centers to bring about institutional change. And because I truly believe women must push back on certain writing center narratives that continue to dominate the field, I am happy to be one of the many voices in this collection who *do* push back. Intersectionality and the importance of true inclusivity is what true feminist thought and action is about. In a March 7, 2016, *Writing Center Journal Blog* post, Karen Keaton Jackson writes about the lack of communication and understanding between HBCUs and PWIs and the need for dialogue at a broader level. I wholeheartedly agree with Jackson in this assertion and believe the field of writing centers must start entering into a real dialogue—one that consists not only of talking but also of learning to listen, to understand, and to change.

Women WCPs and tutors must speak out and discuss moments in which they see and feel their gender policing them and the work they do. Female tutors also must talk about moments in which they have felt violated or quieted because of their bodies. Female students who enter the writing center for guidance must express their thoughts on how their papers impede their language and how perhaps writing sessions have transformed their discourse into something other than who they are. I urge women tutors and WCPs to start speaking their daily truths of what it is like entering the writing center. This concept of women and their truth, and the importance of telling their truth, has been addressed by women writers and feminists. And, a woman's truth must continually be addressed until change occurs. Adrienne Rich (1977) writes in her essay "Women and Honor: Some Notes on Lying," "When a woman tells the truth she is creating the possibility for more truth around her" (4). This chapter is about women WCPs, their truths, and the hope for more truth in the academy—creating possibilities for all women that do not yet exist. And we can start from the center, a little bit more in unison. Only once these conversations happen can change begin. And while it is crucial for women to start telling their truths, it is important that all people on the margins start speaking about their daily experiences and struggles in the institution.

Reflection. While I want to end on the importance of dialogue—of telling our everyday truths in the center—I really want to emphasize the importance of reflection. Stories and truth telling can only go so far if no one is listening. At CCCCs this past year, I was on a panel with women I deeply admired—Michele Eodice, Melissa Nicolas, Elizabeth Boquet, Cheryl Glenn, Roxanne Mountford, and Krista Ratcliffe. The panel's title had the word *feminist* in it. The crowd, with the exception of two or three, consisted of only women. The room, though full, was not packed the way these rooms can be for "superstar" academics. Cheryl Glenn made a comment that struck out to me—if *feminist* had not been in the title, would more people have been in the room? More specifically, would there have been more men attending? While I walked away thinking our panel was special—that we all did some good work that day—I did wonder, "Who was listening?" Telling our truths only gets us so far. We must listen in order to learn, we must read, and we must take the time to think. We need that critical space of silence and understanding. To reflect.

9

OF QUEERS, JEERS, AND FEARS
Writing Centers as (Im)Possible Safe Spaces

Harry Denny

SCENE 1: Early on in my tenure at a private, urban, religious-affiliated institution, my faculty mentor spirited me away one afternoon for a discreet conversation in the lunchroom of its law school. In those first years, I coveted my time with this colleague, a straight white man who shared behind-the-scenes gossip or who sought out counsel as we collaborated to grow our larger writing studies unit. Those meetings were exhilarating, a kind of interiority to the club of academic seniority, power, planning, and deliberation for which writing center directors everywhere yearn. Except this time he needed to tell me a gay male coworker had made a complaint about me to our institutional equity and compliance office. The coworker had shared e-mails and described encounters in which, by his view, I had made him uncomfortable and the workplace, by extension, difficult. Years later, I remember that conversation vividly: the sheer humiliation of it—the shame of a public naming of private transgression, the fear of my academic and public reputation ruined, and the anger that I had no recourse or ability for redress. It was also a transformative moment because I became a different director, teacher, mentor, and activist. I learned in the most personal terms possible that what I intended didn't matter but rather that how my actions are taken up or interpreted are what matters. I couldn't own how another perceived my actions. And I had to accept another's truth, even if it wasn't my own. I had come up on the wrong side of a game of identity politics.

From that moment, my relationships with peers, coworkers, students, and others involved a level of wariness, a measure of caution, or a degree of calculation I hadn't exercised before. I had lost a presumption of privilege that had enabled me to plod through life up to that point unexamined, uncritical, and unaware. As a man, I hadn't experienced what it must be like to be a woman, subject to unilateral sexual objectification wherever she goes; as a white guy, I didn't know what it was like

DOI: 10.7330/9781607327837.c009

to be a person of color, subject to the presumption of racial harassment, often as pretext for unwarranted oppression, unprovoked violence. And as a generally assimilationist gay man, I hadn't encountered the everyday antipathy to queer people, subject to stereotypes that we are sexual predators and opportunists. I realized I now signified as a cliché, one I abhorred and one I had enabled. I was no longer safe, I didn't feel safe anymore, and the writing center would never again be a place free of risk for me, even though intellectually I had known danger was ubiquitous. I had had the luxury of experiencing it, up to that point, as generally abstract and exterior, an experience for other people out there. I was naïve and an easy target. After the complaint was disclosed, I no longer opened my house to queer students in need or met with male students behind closed doors; my office became a site of threat, rife with the potential for recrimination and suspicion; and I became reluctant to share rides alone or hotel rooms at conferences. Mentoring relationships with men became fraught, and I avoided them with few exceptions. I worried about how close I sat next to a male student I was tutoring or another with whom I was meeting during office hours. I reread and parsed messages, concerned I was being too encouraging or too supportive (will he misread what I'm saying as flirting?). I looked across that writing center and saw my heterosexual and queer female colleagues have same-sex intellectual, professional, and collegial relationships I both craved and now feared. I was scarred by the experience and now go forward with a certain armor that's not unique to most who are both privileged and objects of oppression. My guard is always up because I know now my queer identity and its stereotypes can always be used to marginalize me (used against me) despite whatever power and privilege I simultaneously carry with me into any interaction.

SCENE 2: Late in my time at the same institution, a graduate student who had taken a couple of my classes found himself caught up in a world of trouble on campus. For a creative writing course, the instructor had invited students to write a fiction piece imagining the most horrific experience or moment possible. The male student apparently obliged, and what he shared for the creative writing workshop sufficiently disturbed students that they advocated that my colleague contact campus security. Evidently his piece portended a campus shooting spree in which he was the agent. Campus security contacted the NYPD, who in turn referred the matter to the Joint Terrorism Task Force, a partnership of local, state, and federal police. When the student next returned to campus, parking just beyond its walls, he was tackled, taken into custody, and brought to a precinct station where he was questioned about his intentions. Another colleague from the English department told me what had gone down and shared that he had taken it upon himself to be an advocate for the student. From the picture he painted (and what I'm sharing here), the student, to me, had been unfairly treated, targeted because he was perceived to be an awkward, odd student. When he showed up at my going-away party at that institution, I encouraged him to think about taking legal action against the institution. No too long after my smug advice, another colleague shared that the alarming writing fantasized about targeting me for the shooting, that he wanted to kill me. That realization left me reeling. To this day, I'm still not certain which was more disconcerting: being the object of violence in the student's fantasy, or nobody telling me about it except in an accidental, fumbling sort of way.

This moment was the perfect bookend to my experience at that institution. I told my partner on learning of the backstory that I could think of no better sign that my decision to leave that school was prescient. Like the first scene I described, it upended my complacency about the relative safety of space, even in writing centers. It also represented another extreme in the range of violence (or potential for violence) queer people encounter and for which we develop strategies to resist when entering the public domain. Such risk is everywhere and nowhere, forcing us to be on physical, mental, and rhetorical guard at all times. We never know when the next fag comment or punch might happen. Such ubiquity and randomness of violence was ironic considering I lived at the time in a post-9/11 New York City, where collective experience with trauma is intertwined with a civic identity. Even the mass shooting at the Pulse nightclub in Orlando, Florida, demonstrated that marginally "safe" community spaces were illusory. The relative security I've experienced for most of my life is more a testament to the privilege I enjoy as a white middle-class gay man. For the many others who don't share my position in society, violence—whatever form it takes—is ubiquitous to their reality and life with systemic oppression. Whether violence comes in the form of hateful rhetoric, mediated discourse, physical blows, or even a horrific massacre, we can no longer allow ourselves to imagine a world where social problems are rendered external or exterior, as if our own realities and everyday lives aren't imprinted with all the very relations of domination we consume as spectacles beyond us.

My own experiences, searing as they are, don't rise to the level of horrific when compared to what that might have been, what has happened in other places beyond my frame of reference, but they're still stronger than the everyday slights or cuts that accumulate for most marginalized peoples in any workplace, in almost any public. By sharing them, I'm not seeking sympathy or pity; rather, I hope to point out that working, learning, and teaching in a writing center is fraught for anyone, whether client, tutor, faculty, or administrator. Given much time in any writing center, conflict, whether directly experienced or shared by proxy, is endemic, but training and education almost never prepare the uniniti- ated for it. And that risk comes in many forms even as its incidence may be, for most, rare. We don't go to work expecting harassment about who we are; we don't tutor expecting challenges to our cred based on how our bodies signify; clients don't seek out help with the expectation of having their performance read alongside stereotypes rooted in identity formations. As I've written in *Facing the Center*, helping writers doesn't involve just supporting the formation of that identity in isolation from all the others that make up who we are and the communities with which we identify or that we aspire to join. All of who we are commingles and spurs each of our identities in parallel and divergent ways. For faculty, administration, or tutors in writing centers, we too are growing and being shaped by multiple forces within, outside, and across us. Who we are is an amalgam of past, present, and future. These forces are critical, yet we rarely have the language or occasion to speak into and interrogate them.

When our televisions flash the images of the Pulse nightclub, and when we learn about the victims of the madness that happens in spaces like that, in those moments, we bear witness to a sort of collective trauma. They represent a spectacle that's deeply pedagogical—we're being taught on so many levels: that despite our social and cultural progress, a small minority still view queer folks as a threat that needs elimination; that queer people must be invisible so we don't offend the hegemony of heteronormative performativity; that violence against queers is political fodder for appropriation to advance nativist mindsets (that the attack wasn't against/about gay people but against America and democracy, that it advances some anti-Muslim movement). But the public revulsion, the consensus that what happens in a mass shooting when a group is targeted for violence is wrong, redirects attention from another reality, a coexisting one that violence comes in more usual forms that garner less, if any, attention. Left unexamined is why other, smaller-scale violence against queers is not prosecuted or why a growing number of businesses can choose to deny public accommodation to queers. Unchallenged is whether a person of color can move across cam- pus or town without being subject to police harassment. Unquestioned is whether one's citizenship status warrants harassment and threats of deportation. These occasions occupy a middle ground between the vulgar and spectacular performance of oppression and violence and its everyday companion. This latter experience with oppression happens when queer people or anyone marginalized through common interaction is policed into a state of compliance, silence, complacency, or even invisibility. It's about a boss asking someone to check queer identity at the door to the workplace. It's about stereotyped notions of queer folk being used to marginalize someone's status in public. It's about whispers and rumors in the air that contaminate reputations. In writing centers, where trust, intimate sharing of thoughts and words, and physical proximity are part and parcel of what we do, systemic moves to make interaction toxic render a space unsafe; as Beth Boquet (2004) suggests, faith in space as intrinsically secure is illusory, perhaps naïve.

Writing centers, of course, don't exist in a vacuum; the wider world seeps in, whether through the mindsets of those working there, the assignments writers bring with them, or interaction that forces interpersonal dynamics that might not otherwise happen. Some might argue our business is exclusive to the teaching and mentoring of writers, that we ought to save the world on our own time, as Stanley Fish (2003) once claimed. The reality is that writers and writing exist in a social world involving communicative transactions among people who represent complex dynamics, histories, and identities. The interaction intrinsic to the everyday teaching and learning in writing centers requires negotiation, and that negotiation invites conflict that must be owned and mitigated, if possible. Writing centers exist in institutions and in a sociocultural context in which tensions must be navigated; they are of this world and must exist in it. Writing centers are contact zones, as Mary Louise Pratt (1991) imagined, yet as spaces where discourse communities bump up against one another, such collisions aren't always benign, nor do they always have the potential for malevolent outcomes. Routine or not, the dynamic is messy and awkward, especially as individuals learn to negotiate one another and unfamiliar interpersonal and institutional dynamics or conventions. Most often, those of us who embody and perform privilege need to slow down, shut up, and listen, and we'll begin to hear, if we can train ourselves to be silent and to listen. Incident after incident after incident of daily microaggressions, even macroaggressions, that our students and consultants, maybe even our professors, encounter in the everyday make teaching and learning an exercise of violence, the avoidance of violence, that leaves them as survivors of education as a traumatic experience.

It'd be naïve, if not a tad narcissistic, for me to think my own traumas are unique. Instead, they are part and parcel of a litany of others, many of which the other writers in this collection have taken up. Together, they make possible a system that inscribes and enforces marginality and white supremacy. I think of Michael, an African American man who as an English major also worked in one of my former writing centers throughout his undergraduate years. As a junior, he participated in our writing fellows program that partnered him with a colleague from English who was teaching an upper-level course dominated by seniors, most of whom were also writing consultants themselves. Those very peers refused to work with him because as English majors, they didn't "need" the writing center. Besides, many said, they were stronger writers, by their own estimation, than he was. When Michael himself was a senior, he was in the writing center out of sight of, but still close enough to overhear, two white women who were his peers gossip about his getting into a top-tier law school. They demurred, "Well, you know, affirmative action." Thinking and speaking about one's superiority to another because of their identity is the core of a performance of oppression and racism. What do we do when these sorts of microaggressions are happening in our spaces? How do we act as allies? Under what circumstances is that kind of activism appropriate? Welcomed? And how do we make for change and teaching moments, usually from the privileged position of not being the object of everyday oppression?

Whether in my other life on a New York City campus or today on a major research-university campus, microaggressions are endemic to interaction. Sometimes, such everyday oppression presenting itself as a byproduct of traffic from multilingual writers has been and continues to be a bone of contention among tutors. They often preface descriptions of session problems with the catch phrase, almost whispered, "Well, you know, they're ESL." The consultants themselves aren't alone in stereotyping, if not generalizing, about multilingual learners. On another occasion, as my consultants and I were prepping for a regional writing center conference, I walked in on heated discussion in our breakroom. Lexi was retelling the story of an experience she'd just had in a session, during which a Korean student told her, "You're pretty smart for a black girl." Lexi and another consultant, who is also a woman of color, were nonplussed by the exchange, but the white consultants in the breakroom were outraged and wanted the student banned from the center, or at least told that sort of discourse isn't permissible. Lexi and Joselin had the mindset that this sort of interaction happens to them all the time as consultants. Striking to me was how quickly and intensely an international student can learn and internalize common social and cultural stereotypes most people "native" to the United States act on (and sometime resist) as birthright. Existing-while-being-a-person-of-color is really no different that the presumed suspiciousness that gets a carload of tutors of color en route to a writing center conference pulled over not once, but twice, by staties.

For each of these occasions, the politics of identity are legible, material, and felt. And most important, moments like these find themselves at the core of conversations in writing centers. We can't dodge conflict about identity, sequestering the work of sessions to the arenas of rhetoric, language, and grammar by supposing they each aren't always already implicated in those very forces that constitute who we are and how we communicate to others. How might a queer person be out and work or tutor without a cloud of sexual doubt and recrimination hanging over them? How might a person of color enter into dialogue in a conference without the pre-text that their presence is dubious or unwarranted? How might a working-class student learn the rules of the academic game if access to it and mentoring are delayed, deferred, or deterred? Our politics of race always intersect with the complicated dynamics of class, and our fissures around class can never be separated from the sociocultural dynamics of our sexed and gendered identities. But if we can't talk, often in the uncomfortable moment of realization of our own privilege or marginalization, we are, I'm afraid, lost. We must do the active work of creating the spaces to hear and deeply listen to one another and to perform the work of challenging the inertia of the status quo and moving toward a commonplace interrogation of the hegemonic practices of domination in our everyday lives, teaching, and learning.

At a recent IWCA special-interest group meeting for the LGBTQ+ community, which happened right on the cusp of the 2016 election, participants were understandably fearful of what might happen should Donald Trump get elected. Discussion took a curious turn when people began to make arguments for regulating behavior or offering codes of conduct for working with tutors. In order to protect our corners of the world from hostile outsiders, to make spaces "safe" for queers and other marginalized people, the temptation to control the conditions under which tutoring happens and the people for whom tutoring is happening is an understandable response, a collective attempt at "self-care" that's ultimately ill-conceived because no place or person is ever entirely safe. We must find theories and practices that enable workable tutoring and mentoring, a pedagogy that coexists in an environment for sustainable advocacy. One such example comes from the University of Washington (UW) Tacoma, where Asao Inuoe and his staff developed an antiracist and social justice statement to guide their work (Kaletka 2017). The statement provides an awareness of the institutional and systemic nature of oppression and how it gets reinscribed through everyday teaching and learning practices than happen in and around spaces like writing centers. The beauty of the UW Tacoma's statement comes in its collaborative creation but also its promise to provide everyone in the space a common language for taking up and challenging the literacy practices of education itself.

Such smart implementation of critical pedagogy is a benchmark to which more writing centers should aspire. Just as important, statements like the one at the UW Tacoma writing center provide an active, ongoing discussion; they embrace the inherent conflict that comes with challenging orthodoxy ("standard" English) while providing everyone in the space a way to push back at and push through those very institutional structures and systems that police what's "normal" and accepted in literacy practices across campus (Kaletka 2017). Does that mean Inuoe and his staff are unilaterally setting standards aside? Of course not. They are making one another and the folks who use the space understand the ideological and material consequences of the choices everyone makes around language and rhetoric and empowering them to make informed choices. This gentle activism happening on so many levels—from a unit's shared vision to its execution in sessions—is a model for what all writing centers should be doing to contest oppression, all the while making sure our units follow through on our mission. Rather than retreat into bubbles of common political, economic, social, and cultural identities and beliefs, we must be more aggressive about our engagement, both as individuals and as collectives or communities. Individually, perhaps we need rhetorical readiness and "street-smart" awareness to guide our interactions with the unknown. Collectively, perhaps we need more collective work, actively processing through and developing shared awareness of ownership for issues to which we are never innocent bystanders.

I bring myself back to the stories with which I began. Being a visible, out queer person necessarily involves risk, even as spaces and communities strive toward inclusion and diversity. We are going to get burned, sometimes by our own doing, sometimes by our own people, or sometimes by any number of combinations. Our eyes, our thoughts, and our energies too often are turned to preventing or reacting to negative forces. Contemporary culture seems to thrive on the spectacle. If I could go back with lessons learned across a number of writing centers and the passage of life, I likely would not change most actions; instead, I'd make sure the lessons I learn make me ever more emboldened to stay true to a core faith rooted in the practice of every writing center session:

To meet writers where they are. To be in the moment and embrace the endless possibilities of the relationships and learning we build working with writers or preparing tutors to engage them. If we grant that no space can ever be safe and that all learning requires some discomfort, then perhaps the ideal of the writing center and those who work in it is, instead, a notion of brave(r) questioning, of playful inquiry toward orthodoxy, and of continuous challenging of assumptions, both those offered and those engrained in ourselves.

Writing centers don't appear to be going anywhere, even as our positioning and status vary from institution to institution, but we remain a contact zone of immense complexity that confers on each of us a responsibility of privilege and expertise we could do well to use strategically to continue to advocate for change. That is, we must continue to push and problem pose just as gently or aggressively as we might in a session, as must our wider institutions. Every question or raised eyebrow spurs a deepened engagement that can perpetuate a journey toward improvement.

10

THE POLITICS OF "I GOT IT"
Intersections, Performances, and Rhetorics of Masculinities in the Center

Robert Mundy

Sunday is a popular day for the writing center. Something about these evenings is frightening, a reminder of the week to come, work that hasn't begun, and assignments past due. If Friday signals a closing of the week—some sense of victory, a notion of endless weekend possibility—Sunday functions as a cold reminder of reality, the here and now, the responsibilities we have yet to fulfill, and the work that must get done. Needless to say, our satellite writing center, a tiny space nestled on the first floor of our newly constructed residence hall, can become rather busy. And given the hours, those who arrive on Sunday nights are often more anxious than our usual clients, as the clock, which seems to be always lurking just beneath the surface, stands prominently at the forefront.

Jack entered the writing center on one of those Sunday evenings. As an alumnus, he was not as visually stressed as our other students, having none of the telltale signs evident—the pajamas that have been worn for quite possibly the entire weekend, the unshaven face or unkempt hair that signals a forgoing of overall cleanliness for time in front of the computer. Having been through the rigors of an undergraduate degree, he read as being quite seasoned. His graduate attire, equal parts slovenly and trendy, suggested he was a young man who was aware of what the writing center offered and the support he could find there. His session that evening was to discuss the academic step he was preparing to take. As a recent graduate who was passionate about continuing his education, he had meticulously drafted his graduate dossier. All was in order, his transcripts accounted for, work experience noted, and letters of recommendation signed. With the exception of his personal statement, the goal of our session, his proverbial ducks were in a row. Having spoken with him via e-mail, as well as with his undergraduate academic advisor,

DOI: 10.7330/9781607327837.c010

the latter a colleague who suggested Jack and I work together because of our similar pasts and academic trajectories, I had expected to meet a student who was, perhaps, at his wits end, looking for an outlet—any outlet, seeing as he was struggling with putting pen to paper or, in his case, fingers to keyboard.

Initially, the manner in which he carried himself signaled otherwise. His air suggested confidence, an *I got it* attitude, that regardless of his struggles, he had it all under control, that his inability to complete a sound draft was only a momentary hiccup. He was by no means cocky—slightly overconfident perhaps, but not bombastic; however, his outward affect was not in line with what I soon learned was his internal strife. Turning to his draft, his initial ease seemed to evaporate within moments. The stress of pending writing appeared heavy on his mind, and his slumped posture suggested defeat, imminently if not in the moment. Scribbled on a sheet of paper was his first attempt, writing he held close to his chest, work that by his own admission was not indicative of himself as a student, a writer, or a man. And in hearing him speak, I could see his assertion was correct: what he had written was somehow outside who he was, prose that came across as contrived and writing that could never cross the threshold of the corporeal into the soul. Only a few minutes into the session, we both understood one thing—that he didn't *have it*—that his confidence was artificial, regardless of how earnest he felt such a depiction of himself to be. I knew this because Jack and I were one and the same; our walk and talk, our overall outward presentation of ourselves, suggested we *had it all together*, but such posturing only concealed the simple truth that we did not.

In that moment, I thought of Steve, my dearest friend, and the night we spent writing that same statement years ago, the one that fumbled out my first attempt at verbalizing who I was and what set me apart from other applicants. I could recall painstakingly trying to impress a group of readers I knew nothing about with a writerly identity and individual sense of self I had not yet begun to craft, much less understand, drafting a story of conjecture and pretense rather than of intimacy and experience. I also meditated on my time in graduate school, my struggles to perform as a pedigreed professional and not a working-class male, the moments when I, like Jack, first came to embody the maxim *I got it*. To cover for such deficiencies, I soon adopted this mantra, a spoken discursive maneuver that signaled autonomy and self-assuredness, regardless of whether or not I felt comfortable with what I was taxed with accomplishing. Jack and I both invoked such phrasing to avoid suspicion, to save face, and to maintain the integrity we purportedly should leverage as men. However, embedded in such language was a sense of machismo, an air of entitle-ment and male privilege in great tension with our classed past. *I got it* was vernacular, a placeholder, for *I have agency; you don't need to explain it to me.* Our collective use of the locution signaled a choreographed act, a socially innate response to our missteps and a mechanism we both used to hide our uncertainties, insecurities, and flaws. This behavior, at times, is manifested in an inability to seek help and/or support, a socially con-structed but typical male trait, or a performative maneuver to signal pos-session of capital. In the simplest of terms, the phrase functions as a sort of shorthand for male training, the larger narrative of masculinity men have subscribed to for much of their lives truncated into a glib response.

What I saw in Jack was a mirror image of myself, two men who were in the midst of a struggle to comprehend the fraught nature of masculinity and class identity, guys who felt great discord between their public selves and private ruminations. Although our public affect and male perfor-mance may seem to contradict any notion of masculine conflict, Jack's experience as a student and my experiences in graduate school and later as a first-generation academic speak to an overwhelming sense of inter-nal tension. Quite often, my male identity reads as authoritative; how-ever, at the same time, my body, along with its subsequent performance, is coded as working class. In one moment I am highly representative of what Raewyn Connell (1987) has defined as the "hegemonic male," white, heterosexual, stoic, and physically imposing. Concurrently, given the space I inhabit, my male standing varies from complicit to marginal-ized, even subordinate (Connell 1995). As a graduate student, I learned firsthand of how "gender is done," a performance of self tethered to a specific context (West and Zimmerman 1987). I also learned that such masculine performativity is often inauthentic; it is "coerced," as Judith Butler (1990b) indicates, culturally manufactured to accrue capital or mask an internalized notion of self that may place the subject on the margin. As Donna LeCourt (2006) contends, class operates similarly: "A performative theory of class asserts that classed habitus is not continu-ally present, an unchanging way of seeing and valuing; instead, classed positions are continually iterated in response to specific social spaces" (38). Butler's (1990a) *Gender Trouble* also offers insight into the relation-ship between gender performativity and discourse: *I got it* functions linguistically to position the subject and shape presentation according to the prevailing social system and how subjects see themselves acting within such a paradigm (Butler 1990a). The phrase, therefore, under-girded a production of masculinity that my male body could not out-wardly sustain.

Knowing the expectations assigned to such writing and the steep hill Jack would have to climb to gain acceptance into some truly daunting programs, I wanted to shout out, to take his hand and forcefully direct his thoughts, emotions, and words. Hearing him stutter, I wanted to provide him diction. Watching his form contort, almost recede into itself, I wanted to prop him up, to not only be his support but also to become his proxy. In short, I nearly surrendered to gendered assumptions that research suggests play out in writing centers, that men should be "directive and dominant in tutoring sessions" (Neuleib and Scharton 1994, 62), reaffirming or normalizing problematic gender performances relevant to writing interactions and the asymmetrical power dynamics that take shape in these moments (Black 1998). In doing so, I would have been perpetuating male privilege, acting the part of the "authoritative father," as Elizabeth A. Flynn (1994, 178) writes, leveraging my newly minted standing in the middle class and the academy, thus falling in line with a decidedly gendered approach, one that is institutionally valued (Jarratt 2000; Miller 1991). And I am sure, given the extent to which his body had sunk into his seat, signaling impending defeat, and his constant reassurances that he could take whatever criticism I had to offer, that "he was *strong* enough to hear the truth," Jack would have gladly relinquished his agency, any agency, in a maneuver typical of the findings in Laurel Johnson Black's (1998) *Between Talk and Teaching*. He instead opted not to challenge my perceived male authority, further supporting the myth that male tutors are more "analytical," "straightforward," and thus highly effective (Hunzer 1997, 6).

Rather than taking up such a directive position, I again channeled my own experiences, particularly the days spent discussing my dissertation with Harry Denny, my director, a time in which he began to challenge the *I got it* persona I had crafted. Just hearing the words must have been maddening for him, as I went to them with great frequency. In truth, I remember little about the writing. Rather, what does come to mind are the conversations we had, the hours spent drinking wine or grabbing lunch away from the desk and keyboard. I was not ready to write; I needed to talk, to work through it all, to make sense of who I was and what I wanted to accomplish. In short, I learned patience, to revel in uncertainty, to be comfortable with *not getting it*. I learned to redirect my impulsivity, to temper my frenetic approach, to slow down and learn it, to process, to wrangle with my impetuousness, to understand what had compelled me to rush forward, and to consider the factors I was experiencing as a result of my male and classed identity. At that time and in the years that followed, he cautiously nudged me to unpack such articulation, to see my phrasing as something larger than simply an attempt to *get by*, and to unravel such thinking according to the conditions and expectations of higher education.

Jack did not write a single word that first evening. Instead, he told me his story, and, in time, I shared my own, just as Harry had done years before when he spoke to me about his working-class upbringing in Iowa, complete with a visual aid, a picture of him riding a tractor. At first, Jack's words did not come with great deftness. There were many starts and stops, typical accounts were told, experiences shared that somehow read as too perfect for a medical school application. After several Sunday evenings, we began to make progress and push past the "I was a sick kid, so I want to be a doctor" story and the Horatio Alger myth of being a self-made man in a meritocratic culture, that hard work is the answer to all that stands in one's way. This myth is reminiscent of the work of Donovan Hohn (1999) in "'The Me Experience': Composing as a Man"—that men relinquish "their own significance to narratives of the self-made man," thus finding value in "masculine individualism" and "individual identity" (293). At some unidentifiable moment during one of our final sessions, the clichés were left to the wayside. We were finally *outside the box* without having to make such a trite claim. His first draft was no longer in his hands or on the desk. It was gone, and in its place were Jack's experiences, his fears, his relationships, and his life's work.

Much of the conversation focused on his family, his stay-at-home mother and union-laborer father. He spoke of his father's working-class male narrative, his mother's supportive familial role, and his uncertainties of applying to and one day entering medical school. To be a working-class man and a graduate student seemed mutually exclusive to Jack, so much so that he, at times, muted the former's stories, electing to gloss over details so as to not offend his parents, particularly his father. To suggest that he was somehow deficient as a result of his upbringing was a conversation he was uncomfortable broaching. Regardless, he knew their stories quite well, and the words suddenly became available to him. I learned what it meant to be a man in his estimation, to put forth physical action for monetary gain, to be a man of working-class roots, as his father had been—one who returns home, hands callused from a day's labor to support a family. A man's labor was anything but the work of a graduate student, in Jack's estimation.

In a similar sense, I, along with my family, had also grappled with the economics of education. Although my mother and father did not by any means consider academic labor to have less merit than physical exertion, they were exceedingly aware of the high stakes and relatively low financial reward of such work. My parents, who had worked tirelessly to economically enter the middle class, still maintained a blue-collar mentality. In their eyes, for me to leave a secure job, one with a "great retirement plan," and attend graduate school was a substantial risk. "There is just so much uncertainty, Bobby," my mother would say, in terms of school and the dicey job market. And she was indeed correct; I was certainly putting much on the line, jumping headfirst into water much shallower than I even understood. Around that time, we talked about debt, a lot, a fear in her mind that somehow even eclipsed death. Mortality for my mother was inevitable, but to avoid being beholden to creditors was well within my grasp. Although they traversed economic class, my mother and father successfully orchestrated a life that avoided debt at all cost, and here I was consciously deciding to break with such logic.

Nevertheless, I decided to return to my studies, a commitment that was challenged immediately. I sat obediently that first night of graduate school alone in the assigned classroom, waiting for others to join me. Well past the official start time, I remained the only student. If some part of me worried I would be out of place back at school, this moment proved I was an outsider. I never moved—never looked for the class, a group that was meeting in the writing center per an e-mail I had missed. I couldn't move, as to do so would only underscore my novice status, the "imposter" Nancy Mack (2006) has described in her work. Better to miss class and later apologize than to enter late, to make a spectacle of myself, to highlight my apparent flaws. In my mind, to ask for support, to insinuate I was not ready and willing for whatever the task, was a mistake of immense proportions. In time, Harry, after reading his class roster and noting my absence, sent a fellow student out on a reconnaissance mission to find and retrieve me. I was eventually tracked down, but by no means did entering the proper classroom signal I had entered the academy.

Upon arrival on campus, some faces were welcoming, while others made me conscious of pedigree, or my apparent lack thereof. I soon became far more aware of my New York persona, my Long Island accent, one that was further exacerbated by my baritone voice. If my voice didn't give me away, my body, that which once afforded me great standing, had betrayed me, was now treasonous. My tattooed arms, which featured images similar to the ones my uncles and grandfathers—all navy men, cops, union laborers, and truck drivers—had pressed into their skin, marked me as other. My male form was of little value in this space; rather, it was deemed "'unacceptable' in academic contexts where mind is privileged over body" (LeCourt and Napoleone 2011, 81). Similar to

Kenji Yoshino (2007), who in *Covering* addresses the concept of "covering" as toning "down disfavored identity to fit into the mainstream" (ix), I learned, with some practice, to speak softer and slower, to translate my colloquial sensibility at a moment's notice into something that better resembled academic prose, to present a calm and cool demeanor that my masculinity affords and not the disarray of my classed standing. I purchased formal dress shirts to cover my pigmented, bare forearms in the hopes of distancing myself from my past. I wanted to be clean and proper, to relinquish who I was as a classed being, just as sociologists Richard Hoggart (1998), in *The Uses of Literacy*, and Paul Willis (1981), in *Learning to Labor*, describe in their respective writing that considers working-class identities and the "middle-class enterprise" (Bloom 1996) that is higher education. I tried, but I was more "barroom" than classroom, to borrow a line from Julie Lindquist (1999), more of a "non-gifted academic," as David Borkowski (2004) described himself to be in "Not Too Late to Take the Sanitation Test," than a "scholarship boy" (Rodriguez 1981), and I knew it. *I got it*, for me, came about out of necessity. I had no options. I had to *get it*. My psyche, career, and wallet dictated as much.

Jack and I never had the opportunity to debrief after our final meeting. Months later, in a tattered flannel jacket and his high school's wrestling t-shirt, he stopped by my office to inform me that he had been accepted into medical school. I thought to myself, *what a beautiful juxtaposition*. After that final meeting, we occasionally crossed paths in the English corridor, and each time, Jack made a point to say thank you. For what exactly remains uncertain, but pressing him would have seemed to ruin the relationship we had formed with ill-fitting sentiment. Each time he offered me his gratitude, I smiled and thanked him just the same. If nothing else, a dialogue was had that often goes unmentioned. In a sense, we quietly, in that nondescript classroom, entered our stories into the larger record of the writing center. I hope Jack saw the value in our chats and can now better understand the regulatory nature of gender, class, and discourse—the narratives he has grown accustomed to spinning and the ones he has yet to completely script, the stories he did not have the words to appropriately claim. I certainly walked away with greater insight as well. Our time together challenged me to consider my own understanding and presentation of working-class masculinity—to examine my own experiences as a man, the narratives I have crafted, and the ones I have capitulated to; the moments in which I have *had it*; the times I worked from a position of immense privilege; and the (many) times I feigned understanding, opting to cover and hide, outwardly articulating "I got it" when clearly I did not. Narratives are funny that way. We keep some in our back pocket, prepared and rehearsed, ready for immediate recitation. These are the stories we are conditioned to tell, the utterances that come as second nature given the sheer amount of times we have riffed on the central theme.

WHEN YOU ARE NOT YOURS ALONE

The locales and actors may have changed, but the junction of masculinity and class remains paramount during my workplace interactions, and I can speak with much sincerity to how my male identity shapes the spaces I inhabit and relationships I have forged. Just out of graduate school, in my first full-time position as an assistant writing center director, my male persona was again a focal point. Most likely a source of frustration for my former director, a woman I still consider a mentor and a friend to this day, my male performance gave me distinct privileges she was not afforded. Outside the talk of tutor hours and appointments, the day's script, we spoke candidly; she provided me with greater insight into her experiences at this particular school and in the larger academy, her many successes, her daily exasperations, the struggles many working in staff positions face. Given the politics in and about the writing center, historically and in regard to this specific college, I sensed she didn't get the recognition she deserved. In most cases, she was the smartest person in the room, well read and extremely articulate in her work; however, she was not on a tenure line and worked outside a department, an area of contention if we are to consider the writing of Anne Ellen Geller and Harry Denny (2013) that considers how writing center directors can feel displaced in the academy when they are not tethered to scholarship, the classroom, or a department.

For many, she was a woman who oversaw a *remedial* space, doing the work other academics would not, nurturing the *ill-prepared* students (Miller 1991), fussing tirelessly over the private space of the center like a "wife" (Olson and Ashton-Jones 1995, 51), and serving as a "handmaiden" for the larger institution (Grimm 1999, 82). Of course, the pejorative associations of feminist pedagogy, regardless of the strides such thinking has afforded our field, have complicated and continue to complicate the work we do day to day, but as a white, straight, educated man, I somehow get a pass, the sting is somewhat less severe on the grounds of my perceived identity. In the center, I benefited from my male privilege while interacting with faculty and conversing with students; I could say "I got it" or gesticulate accordingly and people were ready to buy in. If my former director did the same, the response from students and other faculty would have been less flattering, in some cases bordering on profane. Leadership for me in those early days was about an outward sense of certainty, one that would galvanize the room and make believers out of those men and women I was hired to direct. Rarely was my approach questioned, as I was staging administration in a culturally acceptable manner. I was the archetypical man who had all the answers. *I got it*, fulfilled the social script of leadership, although problematically. Our staff, the majority first-generation students, most women of color, deferred to me, seeing as I looked the part—dressed, spoke, and carried myself in such a way that evoked a sense of *having it*, so much so that students entering the center to make appointments often mistook me for the director, even if the director herself was standing next to me.

The authority I was assigned must have given the *real* director of the center fits. She was far too intelligent to believe I had any true power in this space, but I couldn't help feeling she saw many of my accomplishments as related to my male standing in one way or another, or that I got ahead in large part because of my masculine performance. She was always complimentary and without question my greatest supporter, but I couldn't help but wonder whether she speculated that my affect made me both more likeable and marketable, that perhaps I connected well with colleagues and students not because of who I was or who I wanted to be but rather because of my unmistakable maleness. Little did she know that the *I got it* persona, which constituted a perceived selling point for me, was also a deeply challenging element of my own self-definition. I immediately looked into a future and envisioned a caricature of my *authentic self* constantly being marshaled and hectored. And I didn't necessarily like what I saw. This image continues to weigh heavy on my mind, leaving me to wonder how I signify in the classroom, at the writing center, and among my colleagues. Do I come off as a chest bumpin', beer swillin', sports talkin' guy? Does my voice have an accent that marks me as such? What should I make of being read as a working-class guys' guy? To what degree am I being patronized, even marginalized, and what end does such a position serve when I work with students? If I am more approachable on class and gender grounds for some, how is my style read or taken up by others?

Today I sit in an enviable position, comfortably holding a tenure-track line. As a writing program administrator, I have had to take a hard look at myself—how I present and subsequently how I am read. I have put great effort into developing and maintaining an awareness of my privilege, checking myself at just about every turn to avoid leadership practices that problematically position me outside the larger group of my colleagues. Such awareness has helped me to support an inclusive writing program, one that continues to build from the bottom up rather than the top down, with all members, from all academic lines, acting as equal voices. Although I have worked to create equity within the program, my worth to the larger institution and its many stakeholders is often found in my former self. The male performance I have actively sought to avoid in the context of writing spaces is in fact desirable to the overarching culture of the academy.

At times, I have been asked to lead unilaterally, to take charge, to do the bidding of an administrative hierarchy that runs counter to the epistemological underpinnings of our field. As such, I have been assigned what I call the role of departmental *muscle*, being asked in several instances to *act the thug*, to settle disputes that take shape from time to time. On one such occasion a faculty member outside of the English department questioned the value and approach to one of the writing courses we offer. From the opposite side of the room, I was summoned over by a superior to take up the challenge, be the enforcer. Being placed in this role, I am positioned rather uncomfortably. Whereas being gruff, rough around the edges, and intimidating, as colleagues have described me, may appeal to upper administration, I am at the same time viewed as a caricature, complete with a guttural accent and affect, the lesser. I cringe in these moments, thinking that my work to sculpt an academic identity with great precision was for naught and that I have and always will be viewed as a presence rather than a peer. I am left to wonder, do I still emote a sense of my past self? Does my male body in its size, voice, posture, and disposition marginalize others? Regardless of my efforts, does my *I got it* persona bubble out from underneath the surface, pressing through the sutures that hold together my outward identity no matter how hard I try to keep such an identifier at bay?

There are also times when I question whether my positive interactions with students should be attributed more to my affectual presentation than my teaching acumen. As a writing program administrator, my role in the department is to oversee the writing courses and writing-enhanced program while maintaining a close relationship with the writing center. Given the dynamic of our department, I share many of the writing responsibilities and work in close proximity with the center's director. Similar in age, height, education, and even sense of humor, the director and I share much in common. What differentiates us is how we enact our masculinities. Recently, the director has started leading outreach writing workshops through the center. On a few occasions, he asked me to join, to help wrangle some unruly classes. His approach was passive, as the students paid little attention to the direction he was providing, and he did little to command their attention; rather, he provided only a prompt and then remained on the margins of the classroom. I, however, jumped right in, talking with students, particularly the ones who were not on task. After the session, we debriefed, and the director noted that he "was almost too gay for the students." He described his sexual orientation as a limiting factor to his teaching—what kept students at arm's length and the classrooms in a disorderly state. I too was troubled by how I was being read in these moments. Again, I came across as the muscle, perhaps more so at that time given our juxtaposed male performances. If the director was "too gay," by his own admission, I wondered if I was "too straight," gaining the students' trust or attention by simply acting as his foil, the *guy's guy* I mentioned earlier. That night, I returned to my most recent teaching evaluations and looked for passages that spoke to my performance of identity in the classroom. Over and over again, students offered up comments that spoke more to my class and gender than to my teaching. For the students of my classes, I was a "bro," "dude," and a "good guy."

PUBLIC MEN AND PUBLIC RHETORICS

Narratives such as these are not all that uncommon; we are the students who enter and the men who staff our writing centers. I do, however, wonder how often stories similar to the ones described in this chapter are addressed or even voiced in these spaces. In that sense, I am reminded of Jackie Grutsch McKinney's (2013) *Peripheral Visions for Writing Centers*, a text in which she challenges the prevailing narrative of writing centers, moments when the grand narrative reads as larger than the sum of its parts, clouding or trivializing the many gaps that await new stories to fill these voids by questioning, daring to break the embedded mold of the time-honored script. Grand narratives, just as they function in the context of the writing center, operate similarly within ourselves and in our culture. At times we speak them to show solidarity; at other times, we tell them in the hopes of finding comfort, to signal a sense of belonging and safety; sometimes, we recite them to cover, to hide the blemishes we know all too well and fear will become glaringly evident. As is the case with many narratives, we find ourselves simply in the midst of drafting a position, a voice in the larger conversation, trying with great desperation to be heard.

Robert J. Connors's (1996) scholarship in "Teaching and Learning as a Man" cuts at the heart of these conversations and attempts to locate what he sees as a damaged male narrative. Connors's interest in exploring the relationship between male identity formation and writing is indeed worth further introspection. However, his attempts at addressing the issues men face as teachers and learners are thwarted for several reasons, two of which lend themselves nicely to the experiences noted in this chapter. In short, Connors argues that the shift from antagonistic rhetoric to feminized composition has relegated men, all men, to positions of academic outsiders. In making such an essentialized claim, Connors never considers the many intersections that shape male identity. One glaring omission from his work is an exploration of working-class identities, the many first-generation male students who are entering the ranks of the academy and how their entrance is rife with complications. To resolve the hurt and loss men supposedly face today, Connors advocates for what best can be described as the teachings of Robert Bly's (1990) mythopoetic men's movement in *Iron John*, a call to locate a masculinity of the past and reestablish a male voice that has since been muted.

Connors's call for the return of past notions of masculinity resonates particularly well today with regard to the present political climate, evidenced in the stump speeches and pundit reflections of the most recent presidential election. Trump himself plays on similar notions of *insider* and *outsider* status, performing hegemonic masculinity on a global stage but doing so in the hopes of galvanizing his base supporters. Susan Faludi's (2000) *Stiffed* describes these blue-collar workers as being "stiffed" in a time that Hanna Rosin's (2012) work has coined as "the end of men," both noting globalization and the service economy as breaking the pact among men, country, and economy that ostensibly existed since industrialization. Trump has preyed upon this notion of *having it* or, in this case *getting it back*, telling men, particularly white working-class men, that their male birthright makes them deserving.

Margaret O. Tipper (1999), in "Real Men Don't Do Writing Centers," falls victim to similar mistakes Connors (1996) made with regard to addressing the needs of male writers. She does well to address the scholarship that considers what keeps men from using writing centers, and even, to an extent, riffs on the *I got it* language on which I have focused my attention. However, much of Tipper's article emphasizes how the center is perceived, but I am less inclined to be concerned with the optics of the space than I am with the work that goes on there. And to that end, Tipper does address solutions, such as directive tutoring practices, but again, such a one-size-fits-all approach is troubling. That being said, she too essentializes masculinity and creates a problematic gradation, positioning *real men* at the top. For Tipper, the men she is looking to capture in the center are jocks, guys who take on hegemonic male positions and who fail to consider how the building of a center to suit their distinct needs may keep other men, those with less social or economic capital, from entering the space. She states, "It has taken me longer than I like to admit to realize that rather than trying to change the boys, perhaps we should try changing some of our practices in the Writing Center, perhaps we have been too much lace and not enough locker room" (Tipper 1999, 32). I wonder how much thought she gave to drawing such a metaphor? This insinuation that locker rooms are for all men, and that the culture and politics of these spaces are inclusive, is problematic, if not naïve. Recently, over the din of cable news networks, a video from 2005 was released in which Trump spoke of his sexual exploits: "I don't even wait. And when you're a star, they let you do it. You can do anything . . . Grab 'em by the pussy" (*New York Times*, October 8, 2016). For many, such language was given a pass, explained away as "boys being boys" or simply as "locker-room" talk—what guys do and are supposed to do when with fellow members of the male tribe. The locker room, however, functions as a political space and thus provides a point of access for discussing how hegemony is constructed and disseminated in regional and local spheres.

These controversies and the ways in which we internalize them, whether in our own lives or out in the public, allow us to look into our private/public selves, how we are read and how we would like to be read, along with the discrepancies that exist between the two. They present an occasion to reflect on the pedagogy embedded in such events and the inscribing of codes of masculinity through our mentoring. I, like others in this collection, look to these public controversies as a means to provide context and to highlight the permeable boundaries that exist between the center, the larger institution, and the culture that envelops it all. Ready or not, men who *have it* are already among us and their numbers are growing rapidly. These working-class male students carry much with them into our centers, the expectations of home, the institution, and the larger culture that shape the manner in which they perform their masculine selves. As I noted earlier, I am not so much concerned with quick pedagogical fixes; instead, I opt for awareness. Success in providing entré will be determined by our awareness of and familiarity with the needs of these specific students. In time, we will all contend with, if we haven't already, the *I got it* identity of male students; however, what we make of this language will determine our effectiveness. Such perceived bravado may cause us to step back. It may incite anger or frustration. Reacting is inevitable; conversely, we must learn to temper our responses, as strong as they may be and as justified as such a response may feel. Instead, I ask that we work with students where they stand, as individuals and not as part of a larger conglomerate. To do so, we must be aware of our own biases and consider the countertransference that occurs when we come face to face with those very individuals who signify as counter or similar to ourselves. Rooted in such performance and/or discourse are masculinities, not a monolithic sense of masculinity. To understand this simple truth may be our greatest benefit. Whatever our gender, and whether we are a student, consultant, or instructor, we all have our stories to tell, moments when we covered, times in which stood on the margin, and instances in which we benefited from some sense of privilege. We must remember how these moments felt, what they looked and sounded like, and how we strode forward.

PART III: GENDER AND SEXUALITY
Review

In calling our centers *safe spaces*, a term that originated in relation to the LGBTQ+ community, many of us hope to emphasize that the writing center is a place for open dialogue and inclusivity for all regardless of race, class, gender, nationality, or identities beyond or between. Yet after reading chapters 8, 9, and 10 from part 3, "Gender and Sexuality," we must ask ourselves whether our centers are actually safe spaces for all gender identities and sexualities and whether a safe space can ever exist as something more than an idea. This section review asks readers to reflect on ways in which they have been policed or have policed gender and sexuality in the everyday bodies that enter our so-called safe spaces, regardless of whether this policing happens, for instance, in establishing dress codes to make sure female consultants cover their breasts, in tutors wondering how to handle a session in which the student has written a homophobic paper, or in asking jokingly what a fraternity brother is doing working in the writing center. These chapters remind us that our spaces are fraught with conflict, insecurity, and moments of exclusion because of our bodies and our sexualities. They remind us that we work in institutions that promote neoliberal and patriarchal practices in overt and covert ways. Queer theorists such as Eve Sedgwick and Judith Butler, in works such as *Epistemology of the Closet* and *Gender Trouble*, respectively, discuss the need for all people to investigate constructions of sexual identity and gender as they would benefit society instead of further reinforcing binary constructs of homo/hetero and male/female. These timely reflections speak to everyday realities in US society as government officials and everyday citizens alike work to undermine the work done by LGBTQ+ activists, feminist activists, and those committed to creating a more inclusive society as they fight for basic equality rights.

In the writing center community, we see conversations on bodies time and time again, sometimes in ways we perhaps do not even notice. For example, on the WCenter listserv, we often see concerned directors ask the larger community about dress-code policies, worried about the appearance of their tutors in a "professional" space. Margaret Weaver's

DOI: 10.7330/9781607327837.p003

2004 article "Censoring What Tutors' Clothing Says" is often the scholarship people recommend directors read when faced with issues of dress and performance, as she complicates the concepts of "safe house" and "contact zone" as directors attempt to create a community in their center while addressing tutors' perceptions of "professionalism." While this article is worthy of critical attention and discussion, it surprisingly offers little in the way of addressing gender and sexuality. Older scholarship in writing center studies, work such as Margaret Tipper's (1999) "Real Men Don't Do Writing Centers," Mary Trachsel's (1995) "Nurturant Ethics and Academic Ideals: Convergence in the Writing Center," and Lisa Birnbaum's (1995) article, "Toward a Gender-Balanced Staff in the Writing Center" suggest that the field was once concerned with gender and how it intersects with writing center work and the everyday issues that arise in our spaces. National studies on writing center administrators make note of gender (Balester and McDonald 1999; Denny and Geller 2013; Isaacs and Knight 2014), as women tend to dominate as administrators in the field, and yet there is not much recent literature that examines and interrogates gender.

Even more necessary is critical attention on the writing center's ability to handle moments of pain and trauma as society continues to marginalize bodies, as we can see in Jay Sloan and Andrew Rihn's analysis of the discussion on the WCenter listserv about Tyler Clementi's suicide in their article "Rainbows in the Past Were Gay: LGBTQ+IA in the WC." In this article, the authors write specifically on the silencing of the LGBTQ+ community: "Is it possible that we, the writing center scholarly community, have unwittingly overlooked a segment of the population? Have we been 'inoculated' by our best intentions? We believe this silence on LGBTQ+IA issues has plagued writing center scholarship for far too long, resulting in the marginalization of LGBTQ+IA communities through omission, exclusion, and invalidation" (4–5). In this article, they respond to Jonathan Alexander and David Wallace's 2009 article "The Queer Turn in Composition Studies: Reviewing and Assessing an Emerging Scholarship," as both works critique their disciplines for the lack of scholarship on queer bodies, gender identity, and sexuality. Part 3 of *Out in the Center* reveals that much work is needed in investigating gender and sexuality in writing center research and scholarship, as professionals, tutors, and students continue to be marginalized and excluded because of heteronormative institutional practices and policies.

Our bodies are narratives: they tell a story about gender and sexuality, a story we construct and then perform. The stories of the bodies in part 3 speak of the pain and suffering that comes from the necessary performances and scripts we feel we need to take on because we *put on* our gender, and a very real punishment exists when one does not perform one's gender well. In what ways does Rob's use of *I got it* reflect the same fear of his gendered narrative, or the narrative imposed on him, as Harry's deliberate use of physical space and his concern, as the "bad gay man," about ever sitting too close to a male-identified student. How does Anna perform gender in ways that are both helpful and harmful in her navigation of the academy—being seen as caring and compassionate, womanly, or being seen as too sexual, too personal, to be a rigorous academic. The chapters in part 3 do not give any steadfast solutions to everyday issues that arise in our centers nor do they give us practical strategies to incorporate into tutor education. We do not apologize for this omission, as these stories complicate simple solutions to problems we read on the WCenter listserv. Instead, we offer a list of possible questions to investigate and discuss, both in meetings and in our research. What happens when we enforce dress codes in the writing center? Who are we excluding and what bodies are we further marginalizing? Are we empowering the women who are in our centers and preparing them for leadership? What does male leadership look like and how do we respond to it? What scripts or performances do all our tutors subscribe to when they enter the center? How do we respond to moments of homophobia, heterosexism, and sexual prejudice in our center? How have we been complicit in policing sexualities and genders in our centers? How do we create an inclusive pedagogy for all genders and sexualities?

We want these questions to lead to research and informed discussions in the center, fully aware that they are difficult to have and perhaps leave us with more questions than answers. Harry's stories are not easy to discuss—how his sexuality can create moments of resistance and violence in the center, how his body is read by others, and how these experiences have impacted his own work as a director of a writing center. Yet these are the stories, this is the research the center, a place that consists of bodies attempting to understand, must address. We can imagine a center discussing the ways gender informs our work and the need for all of us, including white straight men who are inclined to say "I got it," to reflect on our experiences and share them in order to learn from difference. We invite readers to consider the everyday moments in which the dynamics our authors take up arise in unique contexts, whether in sessions, in staff meetings, on road trips to conferences, or at social events beyond the work that happens in our spaces.

These stories show the much-needed work to be done if we are to create socially just writing centers focused on advocacy and intersectionality. At the root of social justice work is rhetorical listening (Glenn and Ratcliffe 2011) and understanding. We must listen to our own practitioners' stories, as advised by Frankie Condon's 2017 Northeast Writing Centers Association keynote address "Writing in the Margins: Language, Labor, and Class." Narrative analysis (Chase 2005; Langellier 1989; Mischler 1995) uses the sharing and telling of stories as the method of research—in order to understand the state of the current world and make sense of it, we must acknowledge our stories and how we construct our realities. Counternarratives are extremely important in both critical race theory and queer theory, as we learn from bodies that have been and continue to be marginalized. We hear stories every day in our writing centers, make sense of those stories through research, and learn from the data. This part asks readers to make sense of the stories constructed through gender and sexuality and how they impact our spaces and then use these stories as foundations for our future education and research. We can imagine studies that investigate gender and contingent labor, as we see women dominate as writing center administrators, and while gendered leadership is becoming an important topic to explore in the field of rhetoric and composition, it is a topic writing center professionals have not done much research on. Scholarship that explores masculinity and investigates the performances done by those bodies who feel they do not belong in the writing center—whether they are bodies such as Michael's, the African American consultant Harry references in his chapter, or bodies of working-class white men such as Rob describes—is underinvestigated and necessary work. Qualitative studies on LGBTQ+ tutors, and the need to listen to and learn from their voices, are necessary if we are to attempt to queer our writing centers.

It takes far more than a rainbow sticker on our door or even an LGBTQ+ SIG at IWCA for us as a community to say we are inclusive of all sexualities and genders and that our writing centers are safe spaces. The chapters in part 3 indicate a real need for writing centers to take on research that interrogates sexuality and gender and for directors and tutors to collaborate and create a curriculum that does not just include LGBTQ+ scholarship but makes it central to their everyday work. And while we are not living in a safe world, and recognize that perhaps our centers may never be safe, we can and must discuss gender and sexuality with our staff and produce more scholarship on these topics in order to create the dialogue necessary to move us toward a socially just future.

PART IV

Religion

11

ON GUARD!

Sami Korgan

Courtney Bailey Parker (2014) observes that "we are quick to study writing centers' relationship to non-native English speakers, non-traditional students, and clients with diverse socio-economic and ethnic backgrounds, but few writing center practitioners have yet investigated how we can respect and negotiate faith traditions in a writing conference" (1). While I have found that the work that I do in the writing center causes me to question aspects of my identity, particularly my faith, more often than not, I agree that the challenges of respect negotiation are almost always at play. Questions arise: How do my faith and ethnicity as aspects of my identity make me guarded, and how does this influence my experience in the writing center? How does this necessity to choose either hiding or showing aspects of myself that aren't visible, but matter deeply, play out in sessions and with fellow consultants? How do I make this decision—how do I come to and process guarding who I am or choose when a moment necessitates coming out in faith? Finally, how do experiences within the writing center, the larger institution, and the public sphere complicate these moments?

In terms of religions and ethnic identity(ies), it is not easy to make a clear distinction between *coming out* and being *on guard*. Oftentimes, I find that the process by which I wrestle to find a space of comfort and confidence is continually in flux. Although my identity is not solely determined by my religion or my ethnicity, the intersection of these two aspects creates an unavoidable tension in my life—my work, my education, my interactions—that forces me to make a decision: come out in my identity, expose and share very personal parts of myself, or keep guarding it.

I was born and raised in Southern California. A suburban city, Corona had a casual reputation among its residents for its large number of parks and churches, and one of the major streets that runs through town was known as "church row" among the younger crowd, especially during

DOI: 10.7330/9781607327837.c011

my time in high school. During these four years specifically, church was more of a sociocultural experience than a religious practice. Every Wednesday evening, I was guaranteed to find my friends at Crossroads, the large Evangelical Christian megachurch (located conveniently on "church row"), even if they weren't Christian. Because of this mentality, I never felt I had to hide my religious beliefs growing up. Born and raised nondenominational Christian, I found a thriving community and became part of a close-knit group of friends through my youth group. Most of them attended my high school, and we never felt as if our faith was something to hide, lie about, or downplay—from each other or anyone else. In fact, it was something that should be shared and expressed. I was never a strong evangelical, one who was set on spreading the word and inviting people to church, but I cannot remember a time when I was ashamed of my faith, lied about it, or refused to share aspects of it.

This experience was really different than my fears and feelings about my ethnicity as I was growing up. My father is Persian, born and raised in Tabriz, Iran, and born and raised Muslim. However, whenever anyone asks about my Persian identity, I claim, "Yeah, I am, but I'm only half-Persian," as if there is something wrong with being just, or wholly, Persian. As I think about and reflect on why I was always so open about my religion growing up and more guarded with my ethnicity, I can't help but wonder if guarding my ethnicity was a way of protecting my faith. If people knew I was Persian, would they automatically assume I was Muslim too? Was I privileging one aspect of my identity over the other, or did I have to compromise my whole identity to protect the parts that mattered more to me at the time?

My time growing up in Corona was obviously not free of problems of identity confusion and rejection. Although I may have described it this way, I did so because I want to show how uncomplicated these experiences of faith in Corona, a primarily white and Hispanic, religion-practicing suburb, seem in comparison to my experiences at St. John's University (SJU)—a somewhat conservative (in practice) Catholic university where Catholics aren't necessarily the majority, at least not today.

About two years ago, I had a writing center session with an international student who was writing a paper for an Introduction to Theology class—a required course for all students at St. John's. During the session, the client began to ask me about my own faith and religious identity. He was persistent—expecting me to have all the answers, asking about why "we" pray to the Virgin Mary. I assume that by the word "we" he meant me and all the other White, American Catholics at St. John's, but also, by using "we," he seemed to be trying to find his place within this SJU

Catholic institution and *identity*. I didn't think telling him whether or not I was Catholic was relevant to the session, and I told my directors after the session that I thought disclosing the information was a violation of my personal space and privacy. I wasn't willing to open up to the client and say, "I'm Christian." I felt protective of my faith and identity.

This moment is really interesting for me because in the session, I was not only taken aback by the student's questioning but also annoyed and angry by his persistence. Looking back, what if I had used this moment as a *coming out* moment rather than a *guarded* moment? What turn would the session have taken? Perhaps I could have helped shift this student's outlook on what it means to be a student at St. John's, building a comradery on the possibility that maybe neither of us was Catholic, or learning from each other and our different faiths. It is clear he wasn't attacking me, so why was I so on guard?

Just a few months ago, I had another theology session in which, again, an international student writing a paper about the Bible asked me if I "knew about this stuff." I immediately responded "No," and the session proceeded—my answer was accepted. After the student left, I found one of our directors. I looked at her, and I told her, "I just lied to a client." I felt weird and guilty: to the client, to the space and what we do, and to myself and what I believe in. My reflex to immediately lie about my faith in the center isn't something that should go unexamined.

In Laura Rich's (2003) "When Theologies Conflict: Reflections on Role Issues in a Christian Writing Center," Rich highlights the unique way in which tutors have access to conversations about faith, particularly at a Christian university. She details a specific tutoring session she had: "As evidence of his religious preference conflicted with mine, I casually mentioned my beliefs, but chose instead to focus on my duties as a tutor. Perhaps I planted seeds of faith that would be harvested later, I decided. But as I struggled through this session, I began to question the priority of my roles. . . . This confusion of roles lies in the fact that I tutor at a faith-based university" (Rich 2003, 10). While I was also a consultant at a faith-based university, the challenge for me was not that I was a consultant at a faith-based institution and had responsibilities relating to our mission but that I felt alone in my faith among the tutor group with whom I wanted to fit in.

Our writing center, in general, is a pretty liberal space—there's really no denying that—at least among the consultants. It can be seen as a safe haven on an institutionally Catholic campus, as a space to talk about all sorts of issues that aren't talked about in other areas of the university, such as sexuality, race, and class, to name a few. However, sometimes this hyperliberal environment can outdo itself without realizing who it's hurting. Last year, during my final semester as an undergrad, I was sitting at one of the back tables with a group of some of my consultant friends, and we were talking about some of the new hires. One of the older consultants who had been around for a while made the comment, "If we ever hire a Republican, I'll quit!" Most everyone seemed to appreciate the comment and laughed. I share this not to point fingers or to say we cannot joke or have common opinions—that is one of the aspects that make us work really well together, and we hire each other because we know who will excel at the job. At the same time, for a space that claims to be open and liberal, open-mindedness sometimes seems to go in only one direction. As Parker (2014) reminds us, "In pursuit of connection across cultural, ethnic, economic, and social borders in the writing center, we must not diminish the reality that faith tradition often stretches across these boundaries, simultaneously transcending and complicating the neat categories we would like to assign to our research" (6). We cannot ignore the reality of faith in our students, in our tutors, and in our centers.

Another example of this issue was with a student, Mitch. Mitch was my year, an English major/prelaw student, who was smart and always expressed an interest in working at the writing center. However, Mitch was very, very Catholic, very open about his religion and his conservative views, views that often turned the other consultants off or rubbed them the wrong way. I know a few consultants had classes with Mitch and simply thought he wouldn't fit in at the center. Sadly for Mitch, I felt the same—I too was turned off by his hyperconservative views and how open he was about them. I was also left wondering what this says about our mentality as group of consultants who say the space is welcoming but don't always practice this same judgment-free attitude. Instead are we practicing what Harry Denny (2010) in his *Facing the Center* calls a "clubhouse mentality," in which only certain types of thinkers fit in, leading to exclusionary practices among tutors (148).

This is not to say that as a writing center, we aren't trying to be a group that's aware of identity politics. But awareness and activism are two different movements. We talk about race and sexuality (often during our monthly meetings), but we talk about these issues under the assumption that most of us are in agreement about them. And, if one of us isn't in agreement, would we really verbalize it? Isn't college as much about fitting in as it is about finding yourself? Liberals are more *open*—right? We agree collectively that racism is wrong and won't be tolerated and we will be open to homosexuality, but what about religion? What about

Mitch? We don't talk enough about religion and how to approach different beliefs in the writing center, yet it is so crucial. We talk about all these really important issues like race, sex, and class, but we rarely talk about faith, and maybe it's because this aspect seems to be all around us at our Catholic institution. Being on a faith-based campus where the faith it's based on isn't in the majority should really draw our attention to conversations of religious differences and acceptance.

So, as much as the writing center advertises itself as an open space, my faith is something I feel I can't, at least not at this time, be open about in the center. I believe that, even if I'm not the same as Mitch (I am not a conservative Catholic), I won't be accepted. I won't be seen as a *cool Christian* or anything like that, and I don't want to compromise something personal to me. I feel as if my faith will be judged, and that's not worth it to me.

My relationship to my faith took a complete turn in college, and in the writing center especially, from not giving it a second thought in Corona to being hyperaware of my choices at St. John's, and so did the way I approach my ethnicity—from hiding it and being unsure of what I wanted people to know to learning to be open about it. As much as I feel my faith doesn't belong in the center (although I hope for a change in this view in the future in terms of ongoing dialogue, openness, and an awareness that turns toward an activist mentality), I feel the writing center is the closest I can get to that space of comfort and confidence in my identity. This open, liberal space, the writing center, has allowed me to have conversations about my ethnicity, even learn about it, in ways that aren't possible in Corona, in ways that can only happen on a college campus. The number of intelligent, interesting, and passion-charged conversations I have had about the Middle East, Iran, and current politics goes beyond my scope of knowledge, and it feels good to know my fellow consultants find it "super awesome" that I am Persian. Now, when I explain I am half Persian, I no longer feel satisfied with trying to guard who I am, but rather, I feel excited when my classmates and fellow consultants respond, "Yeah, but that's still so interesting." And it is.

My hope is that I can have similar conversations about my faith, that when someone asks about it, I won't feel ashamed or as if I have to defend it. I truly believe this can happen through more awareness, dialogue, and activism. In a writing center, I think it is crucial that we continue to learn not only about the students we are working with at our institution but also about our fellow consultants, directors, and administrators. As Deborah Brandt, Ellen Cushman, Anne Ruggles Gere, Anne Herrington, Richard E. Miller, Victor Villanueva, Min-Zhan

Lu, and Gesa Kirsch (2001) note, "Because discussions of religion have been essentially off-limits in higher education, we have failed to develop sophisticated and nuanced theoretical discourses to articulate spirituality" (46). Once we create a space for discourse about different faiths as aspects of identity, whether it be in staff meetings or with online staff discussion boards, for example, we can hope to begin to have more important, meaningful coming-out moments.

12

COMING OUT AS JEWISH AT A CATHOLIC UNIVERSITY

Ella Leviyeva

"So Ella, I have a Jewish question I've been meaning to ask you." My peers snicker collectively and look up from their work, eager to learn another miscellaneous fact from their designated Jewish friend. A consultant at a neighboring table leans back in his chair and shouts, "You're Jewish? Wow, that is so cool!" My peers expect me to appease their curiosity and educate them on a culture so otherworldly to them.

Surrounded by people from my cultural background throughout my entire life, I saw difference all around me, but I never felt different. It was not until I entered St. John's University, one of the most diverse campuses in the nation, that I truly felt as Jewish as I am perceived. What was before just a part of my identity soon became my identifying factor—it became my label. Through my work as a St. John's Writing Center (WC) consultant, it has become clear to me, a Russian Jewish immigrant, that although this is my story, my immigrant narrative, it is not my identity. At the very least, it is not my perceived identity.

Though I am part of an ethnic and religious minority, I appear to be simply white on the surface. The markings of my minority status are not obvious aspects of my being, such as my speech or dress. Thus, I walk through diverse campuses such as ours essentially *passing* as the "norm," and it is through this perplexing body that I realize I am, and always have been, still a member of the *Other*. With every passing day, I learn more about being an outsider, culturally and religiously, and I know now that this contributes to the fallacious perception and subsequent formation of my identity.

So if my identity is not explicitly apparent to others—what gives it away? Well, I do. I often feel as though I need to *reveal* myself to others, as if being Jewish is a truth I must tell new friends upon meeting them or else I am pretending to fit in. Though this concept of *fitting in* at such a culturally and religiously diverse school seems perplexing, it is

DOI: 10.7330/9781607327837.c012

a reality that plays out in all my interactions. That includes my sessions with clients at the university writing center. But there is a difference in the way I *reveal* myself in each unique encounter. When I tell my friends I am Jewish, an immigrant, or a nonnative English speaker, I am shy and meek—nearly embarrassed at our differences. If, and only if, I tell my clients I am Jewish, an immigrant, or a nonnative speaker, I do so as a tool with students of similar backgrounds or journeys to make the sessions more relaxed, relatable, and productive. In the social sense, my identity is highlighted through difference, but in a session at the writing center, it is highlighted through similarity.

The reason I choose to reveal my identity in these two different manners is because I have the luxury of doing so through my ability to blend in because of my outward appearance. I am well aware of the fact that if I had a thick Russian accent or dressed according to strict Orthodox Jewish laws or even had a more foreign-sounding name, I would not have this option to *reveal* my identity and that it would be forced upon me. So in a session in which a student is talking in detail about a biblical verse, my asking them for a brief summary as I take notes would be viewed as cultural ignorance rather than just great listening skills. In a session in which I am asked for my opinion on a religious matter to kickstart their brainstorming, my Socratic method of questioning would be seen as nervous subject aversion rather than an effective and stimulating dialogue. Though I use the same techniques and approach sessions with the same writing center theories as the other consultants use, my personal identity and my lack of physical markings play a big role in how I am received.

Asserting my identity is especially challenging in the hegemonic Catholic university that is St. John's, where theology courses are part of the core curriculum and a cross is nailed above every doorway. The theology requirements in each college of the institution send a mix of religious and nonreligious students to the writing center, all struggling to grapple with the intersection between faith and its expression through writing. We cannot take on the role of teaching religion and must focus on our goal of teaching students to be better writers. As consultants, this is a distinction we must grasp and convey to our clients.

Through experience, I have learned that the sessions in which I feel most comfortable and in my element are with multilingual students. I feel more at home with fellow foreigners than I do with my curious peers, as there is a difference in the level of understanding. Perhaps it is because I identify with them, or they with me, but I really feel a sense of responsibility to engage with and enrich these international students. A big part of my interaction with my clients is this moment of *coming out* as a multilingual, immigrant student myself. This is where my differences feel most positive—my multilingual peers feel a greater connection to me as a WC consultant when they simply see me as Ella, the former ESL student who is now an English major. In these instances, my identity is my strength, my secret tool that most others do not have the ability to throw out there. It is through the writing center that I was able to come to terms with my identity as unique and empowering on campus.

13
FLOATING ON QUICKSAND
Negotiating Academe While Tutoring as a Muslim

Hadi Banat

Religion remains invisible in writing centers, and opportunities to perform religious identities are limited or even rare. Christianity is deeply rooted in the community, but apart from the sound of ringing church bells near campus, a group of students offering free Bibles, and preachers giving public performances about heaven and hell, it is not visibly existent in our writing classrooms and writing center tutorial sessions at Purdue University. Phillip P. Marzluf (2011) describes the intricacies of religious expression in academic institutions as a literacy conflict that resembles "clashes between the religious and the secular, between emotion and reason, or between competing rhetorical stances" that represent the conflicting points of view and literacy values demarcating the identities performed by fundamentalist Christian students and secular faculty and instructors (268–69).

Researchers such as Jeannette M. Lindholm (2000), Priscilla Perkins (2001), Amy Goodburn (1998), and Elizabeth Vander Lei and Lauren Fitzgerald (2007) believe religious faith is a significant dimension of identity as powerful as its other components. Harry Denny's (2010) *Facing the Center* exposes the politics of writing center tutorials influenced by identity markers such as race, ethnicity, social class, gender, sexuality, and nationality; however, religious faith is persistently bracketed in writing center scholarship as an additional marker that can further complicate writers' and tutors' personas. Marzluf (2011) complains about the incessant marginalization and rejection of religious students' literacy practices and beliefs in writing classrooms, despite the cautionary emphasis composition theories place on resisting normative judgments about language and identity. The exclusion of religion, however, cannot endure amid the current rhetoric that highlights President Trump's administration's stance in favor of the Muslim ban, in addition to the media's persistent narratives on religious extremism, Islamophobic

DOI: 10.7330/9781607327837.c013

incidents, and terrorist bombings of religious sites in different parts of the world. Celebrating the multireligious and multicultural nature of US society is currently interrogated and cannot be restricted to spaces outside academia. If writing classrooms and writing centers do not invite and trigger the *coming out* of diverse religious identities and faces, writers will continue to struggle with the hegemony of standardization and the denunciation of their own religious repertoires, thus "disconnecting formal education from many of the traditions that give meaning to human existence" (Lindholm 2000, 55). In this chapter, I deconstruct my reality and multiple belongings as I share my narratives inside and outside the writing centers of three institutions in Lebanon, the United Arab Emirates, and the United States.

MY CONFLICTING IDENTITIES

My notion of identity gets more nuanced with the passage of time, with the evolution of events, with every change, with every promotion, and with every step forward. My sense of identity has been complicated by the accumulation of my memories, by the value systems and beliefs I have encountered in every new setting, and by the places I have visited and the people I have met. Understanding who I am and where I belong was not a conscious pursuit. I never intended to articulate my precise sense of belonging because I was always distracted by the vibrant combat among forces in my contact zones. Mary Louise Pratt (1991) defines contact zones as "social spaces where cultures meet, clash, and grapple with each other, often in contexts of highly asymmetrical relations of power, such as colonialism, slavery, or their aftermaths as they are lived out in many parts of the world today" (34). Thinking about our multiple identities and the circumstances in which they may have clashed with one another is intriguing but deadly, as Amin Maalouf's (2010) *In the Name of Identity* describes it, clarifying that the search for self is not deadly, but being pushed to reduce your identity to a single belonging by xenophobes and fanatics constitutes an illustration of extreme bigotry.

Denny (2010) explains the concept of face in writing centers by highlighting the importance of asking questions about "who we are, and how we come to know and present identity" (2). The question that motivates discussion and invites debate is whether identity lies in a coherent and unified reality or in a multifaceted and dynamic existence and persona. My story started in the United Arab Emirates, where I took a teaching job at an international school in Abu Dhabi in 2006. The school was predominantly staffed by Palestinian teachers, and their very first impression about me, which they carefully translated through their comments, their body language, and their hushed conversations in staff rooms, did not make my transition easier. Being Palestinian myself, I expected to find a more inviting community who would help me get in touch with my roots, with my heritage, and with my culture. However, what I failed to understand at the time was that your position in a community has to do with how you present yourself to the participants in that community and also highly depends on the discourse you use. Reflecting upon my past made me wonder why my expectations were high. My first memories of people, places, and spaces were in Lebanon. My parents, who were first cousins, left Palestine as four-year-old children during the 1948 exodus. When Professor JoAnn Phillion read "The Trail of Tears," a poem written by Brian Childers (1998), in our Multicultural Education seminar, I experienced sensations and emotions of solidarity. Such events awaken in us the complexity of reality and of the power of rhetoric because shared narratives make the unfamiliar familiar and the specific universal. Getting introduced to Native American narratives made me empathize with my great-grandparents, grandparents, and my own parents, who walked from Palestine to Beirut carrying tins of gold they deemed sufficient to sustain a good life until they could return to their spacious lots of land and farms. Since then, we have been fighting for our right of return because according to the United Nations' (1948) *Universal Declaration of Human Rights*, Palestinians have the right to return to their country of origin: "Everyone has the right to leave any country, including his own, and to return to his country" (United Nations 1948). The United Nations' 1951 Refugee Convention relating to the status of refugees, on the other hand, prohibits the return of individuals to a country where they face serious threats to their life or freedom (United Nations 1951). If the 1951 Refugee Convention is the alibi used to deprive us of our right of return, the whole world is one funny joke. I do not think the Middle East I grew up in is safer than Palestine. I do not believe all the restrictions that have been enforced on Palestinian refugees in Lebanon have made them freer than they would be living in Occupied Palestine. What is home and where is home?

Denny (2010) exposes the dynamics of nationality when they become visible in writing center tutorials. Claiming citizenship is straightforward when you hold a document that proves your belonging to a certain place confined within geographical boundaries, to a specific country on a map. Denny (2010) shares illuminating narratives about what remains unsaid in tutorial sessions, about what unites a tutor and tutee who look like each other but have completely different realities, thus showcasing the nuanced reality for Generation 1.5 immigrants in the United States. It becomes harder when your country of origin does not exist on a map and when common and universal knowledge does not offer you access to claim your origin. It gets more complex when you are born in a country for which you cannot hold a passport. My parents grew up in a camp for Palestinian refugees in Beirut, the capital city of Lebanon. My great-grandfather had been the mayor of a small town in Akka (Acre) called Sheikh Dawood. The transition from living an affluent lifestyle to experiencing the lifelong, painful reality of being powerless refugees who are not allowed to have a legal job, to own property, or to pass on inheritance in Lebanon was probably the significant reason my parents wanted us to assimilate within the Lebanese culture. In Lebanon, they were first-generation college students. They got engaged and went to Beirut Arab University to pursue their education while working for the schools of the United Nations Relief and Works Agency (UNRWA). Their dream was big, and I have to say I lived a privileged life in comparison to the scarce opportunities many Palestinians had access to in Lebanon. My mother finished her BA degree in psychology, while my father graduated with a degree in history. They bought an apartment outside the camp and got married. The apartment has not been legally registered to this day. When they talk about their past, they usually refer to proud memories, to New Year's parties, Christmas trees, a trip to Hungary, picnics, nice cars, decent jobs, and a happy life. These are the stories my parents narrated in the basement of our building to distract us from the noise of bombs and explosions that were the daily theme during the Israeli occupation of Lebanon and the many civil wars that lasted from 1975 to 1991. It was not until later in life that I was told that my mother used to wake up at 5 a.m. when she was a teenager to fill iron tanks of water and to carry them home before every school day. It was not until later that I learned that my father used to chase cigarette butts in the sandy fields with his friends when they could not afford buying a pack of cigarettes. It was not until later that I discovered the Lebanese army took my father as a hostage for twenty-two nights, and my mother counted the nights with trepidation while hiding behind the curtains of her bedroom. My parents lived in poverty as kids and in fear as adults. They were afraid of losing each other because of fanatics. They were afraid of losing their children on the daily bus trip to school during war. They were afraid of losing their jobs because they would not be able to find alternative jobs in Lebanon. They were afraid of a multitude of facts that made them forget about their roots and their responsibility of passing Palestinian heritage to their children.

Living in a neighborhood full of Lebanese people, going to an expensive private school, traveling abroad, and having nice possessions were affordances my parents granted us. For them, an education is the only means of survival for Palestinian refugees, and that is one principle they lived by very persistently. They were offering us a lifestyle they did not have as young people. For that, I shall remain forever grateful. Growing up in a non-Palestinian community made me speak a different dialect of Arabic, have different affiliations, share different affinities, set different priorities, experience different social spheres, and interact with a different entourage. I am one example of a group of people whose national identity was muted and erased. Denny (2010) relies on Kenji Yoshino's (2007) *Covering* for an explanation of identity politics to highlight the myth of the melting pot in US culture. To become a US resident means to discard what is intrinsic, human ties to race and ethnicity. Because my parents attempted to *Lebanize* us and encourage us to melt within the Lebanese culture, the way I presented myself to the Palestinian staff at the school in Abu Dhabi was an image foreign to them. I did not project any symbol that represented the Palestinian culture, thus making me an outsider in my own alleged community.

That incident marked the impetus of my search for self, my search for my identity, for a home, for a culture, and for a community to which I could belong. I felt literally naked without a definition. I did not want to be defined by my education, my path of life, my own preferences, my values, my hobbies, my interests, my social class, my sexual orientation, and my religion. I wanted to be defined and marked by a geographical location, by a nationality, and by a passport I still do not have. I wanted to assimilate within a community and create a public face that makes me indistinguishable from Palestinians who have experienced the same exigencyof living dual realities.

Denny (2010) sees in permanent residents' and international students' visits to writing centers an agenda to assimilate by conforming to standardization and correctness. Their worries about "broken English" and an accented style in writing push them to ask for editing, proofreading, and correctness in tutorials. Sometimes their requests are turned down aggressively due to writing center policies against editing. I believe this population of tutees is not ignorant of writing center practices. Their frequent encounters in tutorials have been sufficient to showcase how sessions operate and what kind of assistance and mentoring writing centers provide. However, their traumatizing experiences outside the writing center, either through conversations with faculty or harsh feedback comments, create a stinging urge to avoid stigma. In a different setting, I also wanted to resist marginalization every time I attempted to call Lebanon *home*; however, the frowns I received when I incessantly tried to snatch all the ties and connections I have been building all my life. My affiliation with Lebanon is continuously obstructed by constant reminders—on the surface they are gentle, yet they are vicious and bigoted deep down. These reminders are made by Lebanese neighbors, friends, teachers, and classmates. They never fail to make the most direct remarks, and they never miss an opportunity to highlight the fact that Lebanon is not my country. These are the same hypocrites who obtain foreign citizenship by either immigration or marriage and then find a valid rationale for announcing a new sense of belonging to a place they have not lived in for more than five years. However, having been born in Lebanon and lived all of my life there is not sufficient to make me Lebanese, according to their biased minds. What does it mean to belong to a country?

In *Imagined Communities*, Benedict Anderson (1991) connects nationality to cultural practices that enable citizens to become insiders, and he does not confine nationality to geographical borders but highlights shared ways of knowing, doing, and being as prerequisites for understanding nationality. My affiliation with the Palestinian community in the United Arab Emirates grew stronger with time, at least as a figment of my imagination. I wanted to belong. I decided to belong. I chose my country of existence because nobody can deny the fact that I am Palestinian. When I realized there is a general consensus about a connection between our sense of belonging and our nationality, I felt I had achieved a milestone. I felt that by allocating my starting point, the other destinations were contexts that added to my repertoire. In every new context, there is a point of reference to share with people when they ask questions such as, what do you really feel you are?

While living in the United Arab Emirates, I started observing my Palestinian community. I wanted to learn as fast as I could. I started looking for Palestinian friends. I spent more time with my extended family who live in the Emirates. I found every opportunity to immerse myself in the Palestinian culture. When I projected such an image, my Palestinian community started to take me seriously. Their facial expressions became milder, their smiles warmer, and their hushed conversations behind closed doors ceased. I started getting invitations to dinner parties, BBQ picnics, baby showers, weddings, and birthday parties. I felt happier, and my sensation of comfort and trust was connected to my Palestinian community that was growing bigger and also to the United

Arab Emirates, which gave me access to my cultural origin. As a result, my ties have become stronger. My contract with the school was for only two years and did not get renewed, and my aspirations became higher when I defended my thesis and obtained an MA degree in English. Since going back to Lebanon was no longer an option on my agenda, I looked for university lecturer positions in the United Arab Emirates.

I moved to Sharjah, where I started teaching at a public university owned by the ruler of Sharjah, His Highness Sheikh Sultan Bin Mohammed Al Qasimi. Being a successful university lecturer, a reliable colleague, and an active participant devoted to community and university service constructed a persona that was different from that of a middle-school English teacher. The developments I had experienced in building my career and in finding my cultural ties made me happier, more comfortable, and more secure. When asked about my origin, I confidently referred to my Palestinian nationality. Questions that followed sounded more like requests for further information than investigative interrogations. In my scenario, being Palestinian is not enough. People want to know if you are a Palestinian from the West Bank or Gaza or among the refugees that fled to Lebanon, Syria, Egypt, and Jordan. I did not mind the questions that followed because my right for existence was no longer denied. It has become evident that the connection between a person's nationality and their origin is closely intertwined with a perception about their sense of belonging. This revelation has become the truth, my truth. This realization has made me understand better the concept of identity I have read about in works by Amin Maalouf (2010) and Orhan Pamuk (2007), who tackle questions of belonging through their experiences with a new land, country of origin, ownership, and family. I felt better when I discovered a solution for a problem that had previously triggered a sense of identity crisis. Whether I am considered a person who surrendered to what the general public believes in or a person who gave up on their path of life, I honestly do not care because deep down I am aware that my multiple opposed identities constantly meet, clash, and grapple with each other, thus manufacturing a mediator with a privileged role. All the heartbreaking choices I have made during my life, all the successes I have achieved, and all the extra hours of toil I have spent proving myself were worth it. My overachiever persona fits within Eric Liu's (1999) framework in *The Accidental Asian* of the "model minority," which describes how marginalized people are keen on overcompensating for their difference through industrious investments (128). My challenging experiences have equipped me with skills to build bonds, resolve conflicts, and moderate misunderstandings. They have prepared me to communicate with different communities of people, to survive in different cultures, and to overcome stressful situations.

However, these skills have not made matters simpler. When I thought life was getting better, my identity was on the verge of becoming more complex with the intricacies of new places, new ventures, new titles, new aspirations, and new communities. At a time when everyone thought I was happily moving to the United States to live the dream of pursuing my PhD studies, I was worried about how to situate myself in the new culture. I was not worried about my academic persona; I was more concerned about my new status as a US permanent resident, a status I acquired through my mother, who became a US citizen by naturalization. Ilona Leki's (1992) *Understanding ESL Writers* discusses the difficulties both international and immigrant second language (L2) students experience when moving to the United States, highlighting the comprehensive cultural differences that make integrating with US students challenging if not implausible. My realization that my sense of belonging is connected to a document that announces my nationality has ceased to give me any sense of comfort or consolation. If I want to rely on this assumption I have reached, I should consider myself American too. As much as this development eliminates all the obstacles I have encountered all my life, it will add new and different complexities I have not yet figured out how to sort out.

I will no longer need a portfolio of corroborating evidence to convince an embassy to grant me a tourist visa. I will be able to buy an apartment in Lebanon and register it. I will be able to pass on my inheritance one day. I will be able to work legally in Lebanon as a US citizen. I will be able to contact my embassy at times of conflict and emergency. I will be able to obtain the first passport I will have ever had. I will be able to move freely in the world without any restrictions. I will be able to visit Palestine, the country of my ancestors and an imaginary home I constructed through my pursuit of finding the deep roots of my true identity. On the other hand, will I be able to connect with US culture? Will I be able to find myself amid the chaos and messiness of my new reality? Will I be able to acculturate within my new context? How can I acclimate with all the new developments? These are troubling questions that might take me a while to answer. I am confronted with a new set of complexities that evolved because of my newly acquired status.

The marginalization during my past has helped me look for myself, reflect upon my identity, and redeem a cultural heritage my parents wanted to keep in the closet. The privileges of the present are giving me access to unlimited opportunities of comfort, security, representation, and authority. Between these two conditions, I find myself in a vicious circle. I am returning to the starting point. I am in a vast culture full of different communities, and I am not quite sure if my sense of belonging matters to my US audience. At Purdue, I am a domestic student on paper, but in reality I am international. I am from the Middle East. I am Arab, and I am Muslim. These affinities are part of my identity. These spheres are part of my existence. These affiliations represent a system of values and beliefs advertised and publicized by media agencies, which do not miss a chance to misrepresent the Middle East.

The demographics of students in US institutions have been changing radically, and composition studies have been empowering African American and Latin voices. When multiculturalism is addressed in composition studies, discourse including African American and Latin student populations is the predominant focus (Silva and Leki 2004). However, international and other language-minority students are not included. Despite the emphasis second language studies have placed on international students, the field has prevalently addressed identity issues of L2 writers in relation to writing challenges, L2 proficiency, and demarcating between international and Generation 1.5 immigrant students; however, the nuance of acculturation and integration beyond language proficiency has not been highlighted. Identity is a multifaceted concept, as Denny (2010) projects, and it poses unique challenges that vary from one population to another. For example, at the age of thirty-three, I do not feel I am ready to embark upon a new discovery, conduct a new experiment of existence, or bet on a new sense of belonging. Furthermore, I do not feel the slightest obligation to convey what the Middle East is. I do not feel I can spend more time and exert more effort in proving myself to anyone. I do not desire to participate in a political battle. I do not want to be tarnished by the friction that exists in the fragmented world in which we live. However, I want to continue educating my students about other cultures. I want to use my classroom and my education to defy all the efforts exerted by the media to misrepresent and stereotype whole nations and cultures. I want to rely on civility and courtesy to educate the youth. I want to utilize the dynamic complexity of my identity to spot and work with the sensitivities, fears, and doubts I encounter in tutorial sessions. I do not want to find a new *home* in the United States. I am from the Middle East. I am Palestinian, whether typical or atypical. My sense of uniqueness relates to my choices and decisions, to a journey that prepared me to stand out in a competitive environment. Denny (2010) relies on Carol Severino's (2006) description of the assimilationist goal of L2 learning to describe the dynamics involving the push to pass or cover in new discourse communities in order to avoid social stigma. Earlier, in previous scholarship, Severino (1993b) described the politics of English as a second language (ESL) programs designed for refugees to encourage "cultural and economic assimilation" (183), and James W. Tollefson's (1989) *Alien Winds* examined ESL programs designed for refugees that promote the ideology of "accepting the principle of starting at the bottom of the employment ladder" (57), thus surfacing the charged identities among the L2 population of new immigrants. However, the population of immigrants and refugees (permanent-resident students) has become increasingly diverse and dynamic; taking into consideration the current and latest international events, a prepackaged ESL support program can no longer be considered a one-size-fits-all program. Through my reality and many others, we expose new narratives that shed light on different needs not necessarily connected to L2 proficiency or writing ability, needs that require further research in writing center scholarship, composition, and second language studies.

IN THE CENTER

Dissecting myself and figuring out my different components has been a healthy exercise to reflect on my practices as a tutor in the writing center. I sometimes feel I am carrying the heavy weight of high expectations and humongous responsibilities. I feel my complex path of life and conflicting identities should make it possible for me to delineate my tutees' identities in the writing center. However, the places I have worked in are different in terms of culture and audience. The ticking of the clock remains the common factor that sometimes obstructs my ability to decipher the identities of my tutees amid the ashes of grammatical problems, inaccurate citation practices, chaotic organization of content, and other challenges in their writing.

Unlike the classroom, the twenty-five to fifty-minute orphan encounters do not sufficiently allow time for you to make a humanistic connection with your tutees. The clock is ticking from the moment you smile, introduce yourself, and lead them to your work station. You want to achieve as much as possible. You must meet the expected agenda set by your tutee. You must fill in a report, smile, say your goodbyes, and then move to the second client. It is a pretty automatic process if you focus on the tasks only. It becomes somehow mechanical when you distract yourself from noticing the anxiety, fear, worry, confusion, excitement, and/or relief in your tutees' behaviors. And yet you sometimes get surprised.

IN THE UNITED ARAB EMIRATES

One day I was getting ready for my appointment when a student entered the room with a smile I could not interpret. The face was familiar, the scent of perfume was identifiable, the handshake was firm yet gentle, but the smile this time was a paradox of anticipation and hesitation. He was a student I had taught in Communicative English the previous spring semester. He politely greeted me and asked about my summer holiday, and so I reciprocated. I asked how I could be of help and what he wanted to work on for that particular session. He was not carrying any pens or books with him . . . just his mobile phone. I was preparing my scratch paper and pencil when he asked if he could close the door. That day, I was the only tutor in the room. It was a small office on the men's campus of this institution, and for a moment I felt perplexed. I did not want to close the door, but at the same time I did not want to shut him out. In the back of my mind, I remembered he was a decent student with impeccable manners. He was studying law and keen on becoming a judge. I confidently smiled, avoiding confrontation, and said we could on the condition we place a paper on the door for the other students having appointments after his. After he closed the door and sat down, he made two big announcements.

"I am gay and I am on drugs." His short sentence rationalized the anticipation and hesitation I had witnessed in his smile. For a moment, a swarm of ideas were buzzing in my head. I was very aware of my context. For the sake of his well-being and comfort, I could not act as if I were shocked. I could not disclose such information to any other person at that institution. I could not make the student regret the very brave step he made. We were in Sharjah, a very conservative emirate and a city that has been elected twice as the capital of Islamic culture. I did not want to scare him or push him away with any hasty reaction that might be deemed inappropriate, insensitive, or inconsiderate. I was also concerned that my liberal views might be echoed outside the vicinity of that small office and reach upper management; if that happened, the very next thing on the agenda would probably be a termination of my work contract and a one-way ticket to Beirut. I was in a fuzzy and difficult situation, but I decided to be a human and to care less about the intricacies of my work environment and the risk I was taking and more about the student.

I smiled and said, "There is nothing wrong with being gay. Do you have a boyfriend?"

I felt that his hesitation was resolved and his anticipation was satisfied. He calmed down. In a later conversation, I asked about the reasons he exposed two delicate secrets to me in a context very sensitive to a count-less list of taboos. His answer was predictable.

"You are Lebanese and liberal. You seem pretty cool."

I am not sure whether he wanted to say more, but the power dynam-ics were obstructing him from expressing all his views and articulating all his reasons, observations, and perceptions. Unfortunately, this stu-dent could not *come out* to any other person in his community, and his opinion about my liberal views encouraged him to mark his identity in a safe place. Denny (2010) discusses "the automatic functioning of mainstream gender and sexual identity politics [explaining] that as we mark who we are, we signify the operation of social and cultural forces on us" (88). My student chose the writing center as a space to come out rather than the classroom. The writing center is a small office on the men's campus whose location does not invite much traffic, and consid-ering the patriarchal context of the United Arab Emirates, the writing center might not be the ideal place for men to visit. The classroom, on the other hand, has other male students—UAE citizens and citizens of other neighboring countries and cultures; thus, it cannot be the most suitable context for coming out, taking into consideration all the societal and cultural constraints that limit the honesty of conversations despite our presence in an all-male environment. Being queer would be considered contradictory with masculinity, a trait highly regarded in typical Arab societies. My student would most certainly pass for being straight, which contradicts the societal norms and expectations about queer men. Therefore, my student's approach was unique in that con-text within those boundaries, and I could not ignore this exceptional coming-out moment and steer my tutee's direction into another typical writing center agenda. As Denny (2010) suggests, there is no set of pro-tocols and prescriptions we can use for such moments; we must rely on our intuition and be flexible to respond to identity issues and faces that come out of the dark because "gender and sexuality are central to who we are and provide a register of what's possible" (89).

I said, "I am pretty cool with you being attracted to men, and you can tell me more about your boyfriend in a minute. However, I do not think you should be doing drugs. Are you on drugs because you are gay?"

The last question I asked was very complicated because the answer would not be straightforward. When I considered all the factors that drove him to his drug addiction, being gay was the least significant if rel-evant. That first tutoring session with him did not include any grammar instruction, content development, or rhetorical organization advice. It was purely an opportunity for a tutee to come out to the only person he could talk to about such issues. It was not the only session during which I sat and listened attentively and tried to pass my guidance to him, but we shifted the setting from the writing center to my office. He approached me because he knew I would not try to *cure* him of his gayness and because he was sure I would not call the counseling center to disclose any information about his drug addiction. In the latter case, the counseling center would contact special authorities outside the institution that would put him under surveillance. I was in a dilemma, but I decided to comfort his anxieties and talk him out of his drug addiction, or so I hoped.

I am not quite sure whether I succeeded, but the last thing I knew was that he graduated with a degree in law and is currently pursuing judicial studies. He broke up with his boyfriend, who was torn between his true identity and the cultural expectations of their society. He met a more assertive guy he began dating. He reported that his drug addiction was on and off, assuring me that he could control it. I left the United Arab Emirates with many rich experiences that added complicated but inspiring narratives to my repertoire and trained me to sense the gentleness underneath a firm handshake.

I do not think such a scenario would have happened had this student been only my tutee at the writing center. My relationship with him in a classroom setting for one whole semester provided him an adequate overview of my background and thus enabled him to make that call. I wonder if in a tutoring session in the United States or Lebanon, I would have such an intense encounter.

IN LEBANON

The Lebanese context is of a different nature. In a country that coped with British and French colonization, with the presence of multiple religions, with the acknowledgment of various religious sects, with the constant struggle of different political groups, with a spoken and written repertoire of three languages, and with a balance in religious demographics and representation, I would expect my tutees to acknowledge my differences, and they would expect me to reciprocate. I would not anticipate students outing themselves to me in a context in which being gay is accepted in certain parts of the country, in certain places, in certain social spaces, and in certain families. I would not expect a student to expose his drug addiction in a context in which taking drugs is not legalized but not uncommon. I am not the only liberal representative of that culture, but I might be the only Muslim tutor in an all-Christian institution. My mother always wondered why the contexts I worked in were rather unconventional or not always compatible with the different components of my identity. But I could never limit my career choices in a country where Palestinians are not legally allowed to work. I applied for jobs in Lebanon and tried to work at any institution that opened its door. I also never agreed with my mother that I could be only one thing, have only one identity, celebrate only one component of myself, and thereby limit myself to one particular prescripted context.

When Gebran Tueni, a Christian Lebanese journalist and politician, was assassinated on December 12, 2005, I was afraid to attend my tutoring shift at the institution where I worked. All students, faculty, and staff were Christian Lebanese, and I was the only Palestinian Muslim. It was a small private institution that offered me a teaching job just because I was a graduate from the American University of Beirut, the most prestigious educational institution in the Middle East. But when I awakened that morning, I found no excuse not to go.

At the writing center, I did not know whether I had to replace my usual greetings with apologies and condolences. Such a swing was relevant to the occasion but not to the context of our work in the writing center unless some students looked really angry. But my fears and worries were unfounded; my tutees attended their sessions and worked on their agendas just like any other day. One student worked on grammar, the other on punctuation, and a third on thesis statements and topic sentences. In a country where the Sunni Muslim Prime Minister Rafic Hariri had been assassinated exactly ten months prior to the car bombing of Gebran Tueni, I believe my tutees were able to acknowledge that I could be a tutor and a Muslim at the same time. I could fit in both categories on one day even when their feelings were running high amid political and emotional unrest.

In Lebanon, I can celebrate all my conflicting identities. I am not reduced to one because people are trained to spot the conflicts and differences that exist in each and every individual. The only component they might have a problem with would be my Lebanese citizenship. As long as I acknowledge my Palestinian nationality, which I have become aware of, they can tolerate all the other spaces and bubbles I navigate.

IN THE UNITED STATES

In a melting pot or a salad bowl, my differences become privileges. At the writing center, I am a graduate student in second language studies, an Arab, a Muslim, a Middle Easterner, and an ESL user. I have more than ten years of teaching and tutoring experience in different professional contexts that have endowed me with expertise and rhetorical confidence when dealing with writing center faculty, staff, administrators, tutors, and peers. The very first two days at the writing center, I gazed at the empty slots in the online scheduler and wondered whether I would have had some traffic had my name been James, John, or Mike. I was concerned because I was one of very few nonnative speakers working as a writing tutor. How does a demographic change influence traffic? I asked my wise mentor, who was the writing center director, that fearless question, and he advised me to be patient and wait. My worries and fears subsided by the third day of the semester when the number of filled slots in my online scheduler increased significantly.

Outside the Writing Center

I once engaged in a weird conversation initiated by an international student in my program in a computer lab on the second floor of Heavilon Hall. That day, the computer lab was inundated with white Americans. As I was making myself comfortable in my chair and logging onto my computer, she surprised me with a strange question, which was out of context.

"Do you eat meat?"

I was certain it was an opening for a conversation/interrogation that would lead to a discussion about ISIS. Living in a war zone, where Palestinians were slaughtered every day during the Lebanese civil war, equipped me with ammunition to tone down the intentions of bigoted individuals trying to attack me for who I am and what I represent. I was thus trained to answer any question and to shield myself from any potential attack.

I said, "Yes, I love meat."

"Do you eat all kinds of meat?"

With a big confident smile, I said, "Except pork."

Nobody stirred in the room because her question was an obvious invasion of privacy in a public sphere.

With a facial expression announcing confusion, she persisted: "But why?"

I said, "For religious reasons . . . I am a Muslim, and in Islam we do not eat pork."

She rose from her chair and got closer to me and with a smile asked, "So . . . are these stories in the news about Islam true?"

I left the keyboard and turned toward her: "Which ones?"

"You know . . . ISIS and what they are doing to Christians."

I sarcastically answered because I was running out of patience. I was quite sure a PhD student should be exposed a bit or have the least of critical thinking skills to demarcate violence and terrorism from religious faith.

I said, "Members of ISIS do not represent Islam. We do not consider them Muslims. Do you take for granted every accusation made by certain news agencies? You should know better. There are many misrepresentations of people from your country in the news that I never took for granted."

At that point, she was clearly embarrassed after an attempt to shame me. This conversation was the strangest event that has taken place for me at Purdue.

Back to the Center

In the writing center, I feel comfortable with my tutees. This sense of comfort stems from their persistence to work on their writing. Their interest in becoming better writers allows them to acknowledge that the tutor of their session can have other realities that would not intervene to make the tutoring experience less fruitful or less rewarding. My different realities make me more sensitive to the hidden identities behind the façade of textual features and writing concerns.

I could see in my Japanese tutee a writer with a voice that rationalizes the struggles she encounters in her teaching, communication, and writing. I could find in a Chinese tutee an aspiring researcher who mistakenly thought correcting all her grammatical mistakes would guarantee her a conference publication. I also met in another Chinese graduate student, a critical business analyst and a writer with a systematic way of reasoning. I also encountered an African American student whom I encouraged to express her voice about the imbalance between experiencing racism in one's country due to white supremacy and encountering racism in a foreign country due to international political tensions. I met several domestic students who wanted to discuss rhetoric and learn more about the elements of visual design, and there were those other students who were uncomfortable with their command of grammar.

It is not a perfect place because you still meet some students who are playing the system to get by and graduate. You have sessions in which students want to automatically work on their citation practices and leave. You meet some tutees who still see the writing center as a fix-it-all laundromat. And yes, amid the constraints of session duration, the very ambitious agendas set by tutees, the background noises, the different shapes and colors, and the negotiation we participate in, we sometimes do fail to be in touch with the identities of our tutees and the faces they hide.

A wise question I might not find an answer to was addressed by my professor and mentor Harry Denny: "What do you make of identities that aren't embodied or must be disclosed? Do they have a place, might they come up?" Until they come up in tutorial sessions, we aspire to become better tutors, more sensitive to the needs of our students, wiser at evaluation and assessment, more pragmatic about running our sessions, more compassionate in our conversations, and more transparent and welcoming when the opportunity arises.

PART IV: RELIGION
Review

Perhaps in large part because the terrorist attacks of 9/11 ushered in the twenty-first century by bringing religious difference to the forefront of public dialogue, many contemporary conversations about social identity inevitably address, in subtle or overt ways, the differences between belief systems and believers of different kinds. As Sharon Crowley (2006) suggests in *Toward a Civil Discourse*, a work that explores contemporary fundamentalist and liberal rhetoric, "Most of the major disagreements that currently circulate in American political discourse arise from conflicts between liberal and apocalyptist approaches to argument" (23). According to Crowley, "Liberal pluralism harbors the hope that difference can be erased if only everyone will just be reasonable—which means something like 'think as we do'" (41). And fundamentalists seek a similar sort of uniformity of thinking. Crowley (2006) observes that "there is no way to prove to a believer that she is wrong. Arguments from complexity or nuance suggest only that those who make them are confused. And for believers the sower of confusion, the agent of complexity, is Satan" (147). As a result, liberals who shun faith for enlightenment-era reason and fundamentalists of different religious heritages exist in a dialogic impasse with one another. They speak at cross-purposes because they value different kinds of evidence and different ways of arguing.

Crowley's (2006) work serves as an example of a relatively developed body of scholarship that examines the rhetorical practices of religious believers, and this body of scholarship includes, for instance, William FitzGerald's (2012) book, *Spiritual Modalities*, and David S. Cunningham's (1991) *Theological Studies* article, "Theology as Rhetoric." But less scholarship exists on the everyday conflicts that involve faith in the writing classroom. Book-length works such as Elizabeth Vander Lei and Bonnie Lenore Kyburz's *Negotiating Religious Faith in the Composition Classroom*, or articles such as Elizabeth Vander Lei and Lauren Fitzgerald's (2007) "What in God's Name? Administering the Conflicts of Religious Belief in Writing Programs," or Phillip P. Marzluf's (2011) "Religion in U.S. Writing Classes: Challenging the Conflict Narrative" begin conversations

DOI: 10.7330/9781607327837.p004

about what it means for students in writing courses to write about faith and for their instructors to respond to that writing ethically and effectively. These works speak to the reality that perhaps creates a relative void in the scholarship about religion and writing program or center work: that writing instructors and writing program administrators alike "find talking about religion difficult," to appropriate Vander Lei and Fitzgerald's 2007 words (186). And even less scholarship exists on writing centers and religion or religious difference, despite the turn to social identity and identity politics that a work such as Harry Denny's (2010) *Facing the Center* represents. Notably, Denny's (2010) field-changing work includes chapters on race, class, gender, and nationality, and it certainly makes mention of religion, most notably in the chapter on gender, but it lacks the sort of full exploration of faith and writing center work that the field needs in an age in which religious difference continually comes to the fore of public controversies and private struggles.

The authors Sami Korgan, Ella Leviyeva, and Hadi Banat (chapters 11–13), included in this collection's part IV on faith, begin the process of filling this noteworthy void in writing center scholarship, and through the stories they tell, the authors of these chapters push on the limits of Crowley's framework in ways that echo Liliana M. Naydan's 2016 analysis of religious impasses in *Rhetorics of Religion in American Fiction*. By exploring ways in which their identities as religious believers intersect with other features of their identities, they show ways in which tensions involving religious faith transcend the liberal/fundamentalist binary. For them, the United States on the whole and writing centers in particular exist as contact zones with dialogic impasses that certainly may emerge between fundamentalists and liberals but that may also emerge between less polarized kinds of believers and nonbelievers and in less expected ways. For instance, these dialogic impasses come to exist between believers of different kinds, be they of fundamentalist or nonfundamentalist varieties, be they evangelical Christians such as Korgan (chapter 11), Russian Jews such as Leviyeva (chapter 12), Palestinian Muslims such as Banat (chapter 13), or of faiths beyond the ones on which the mainstream media fixate. Moreover, these impasses come to exist within believers' and nonbelievers' own bodies because of intersectionality, most notably when believers have nationalities, races, ethnicities, or other identity features that defy popular expectations for believers of a particular variety. As but one example, the intersection between ethnicity and religion in Korgan's identity speaks to the problem of expectations Americans might have for believers of different kinds. Korgan's Persian ethnicity may run counter to popular US expectations of what constitutes an evangelical Christian because Americans have conceived of evangelical Christianity through the lens of white westerners such as Billy Graham, Jimmy Carter, or George W. Bush—even though evangelical believers in reality come from a range of ethnicities.

Furthermore, the authors of part 4 create a foundation for writing center staff-meeting conversations about religious belief and the everyday challenges of writing center conversations that resonate with religiously charged national or international conversations or issues. Whether writing center employees work at Catholic colleges such as St. John's University, which both Korgan and Leviyeva mention, at secular public institutions such as the one Banat mentions, or at institutions with other religious affiliations in the United States or abroad, religious belief emerges as a subtext to writing center conversations because everyone, be they atheist, fundamentalist, or somewhere between on the spectrum of faithlessness and faith, sustains a belief system that might come into conflict with someone else's. And most religious believers in the modern world likely negotiate conflicts within themselves as well because approaches to religious devotion and practice inevitably transform and face social challenges as history rolls forward, while religious texts that serve as blueprints for religious ways of thinking and being remain precariously stagnant. Hence, as the old adage goes, we shouldn't talk about religion or politics if we seek polite conversation because there is no way to have a benign conversation about faith or faithlessness.

Given that conflict seems inevitable when talking about faith and faithlessness, tutor-education initiatives in writing centers might preface conversations about religion with staff members and writing center administrators by articulating a commitment to what Sonja K. Foss and Cindy L. Griffin (1996) call an *invitational rhetoric* in "Beyond Persuasion: A Proposal for an Invitational Rhetoric." In short, they might articulate a commitment to a mode of discourse that prioritizes and most values understanding one another as opposed to winning an argument or persuading listeners to think in different ways (Foss and Griffin 1996, 2–18). Likewise, staff-meeting conversations might foster understanding by underscoring the ways in which religion intersects with features of social identity that writing center professionals perhaps feel somewhat more accustomed to exploring. This suggestion in no way intimates that a conversation about a subject such as race, for instance, is an easy one to have at a writing center staff meeting. But the abundance of conference panels, workshops, and roundtables on race at the International Writing Centers Association Conference or at the National Conference on Peer Tutoring has equipped writing center professionals to talk about race in ways they have not yet been equipped to talk about religion and faith. And, as this edited collection on the whole intimates, to talk about religion and faith is to talk about race and ethnicity—and an array of other identity features—especially in a twenty-first-century United States that has a living history of conflating Arab identity with Islamic belief. These complex intersections might even shape the direction of future writing center scholarship about faith.

Questions that might produce a useful staff-meeting discussion as well as the foundation for future research on religion and writing centers include the following: Who are you as a believer or nonbeliever? What religious beliefs do you value or oppose? From where do your ideas about different belief systems come? How do or don't you fit with extant orthodoxies that set the terms for belief systems, be they religious or secular? In what ways does your belief or secularism intersect with other aspects or features of your identity? When has religious belief emerged as the focus of a writing center consultation or as the subtext of that conversation because of the subject about which a student is writing, be that a subject involving access to healthcare, access to US citizenship, or subjects beyond or between? How have you revealed or concealed your identity as a believer or nonbeliever in a writing center consultation? How have you revealed or concealed your discomfort in encounters with believers of different sorts in writing centers? How have you explored differences in belief systems in writing center consultations in order to attain an understanding of values that differ from your own? What have you learned from your writing center practice about belief systems or specific beliefs? What do you still want to learn and how might you learn it? How have you worked to help others attain an understanding of belief systems that differ from their own? What do you think they've learned about belief systems or specific beliefs from their writing center consultation or consultations? And, finally and most important, how might you handle a situation involving differences in belief systems differently in the future based on your reflections on your past experiences?

PART V

Class

14

AN ADJUNCT AMONG NYC TEACHING PARAPROFESSIONALS
Class, Gender, and Race—and What It Means to "Work in Education"

Elizabeth Weaver

Writers and educators do many things to earn money over the course of a lifetime, and I am no exception. I've worked as a contingent faculty member, and I've also done temp work in offices to support what one might call my *teaching habit*. Considering how many teachers I know who've worked in restaurants just to be able to pay the bills, I am extremely privileged. Currently, I freelance and work as an adjunct writing coach for SUNY Empire State College, among other things. More specifically, I work for the college's Harry Van Arsdale Jr. Center for Labor Studies (HVACLS); it goes without saying that the questions of what higher education is for—and how we define *work*—are never far from my mind.

Political leaders continue to push for better standards of living and working conditions for many of the United States' most vulnerable. Their proposals include raising the minimum wage and making community college tuition free, a move that could presumably raise many citizens out of poverty.

Meanwhile, the so-called right-to-work movement threatens to further erode gains made by labor unions—unions much like the ones to which students in the HVACLS belong. Rhetoric about so-called *cushy* jobs—positions held by union members—tends to pit working Americans against each other. Members of the right-to-work movement argue that union members have things too good considering that regular working people do not enjoy the protections unionists do. The problem is that such antiunion rhetoric does nothing to better working-class lives, instead endorsing equally terrible working conditions for all.

Further, as well intentioned as simply raising the minimum wage and other initiatives may be, they serve as only small repairs to an

DOI: 10.7330/9781607327837.c014

increasingly broken system. After all, it is problematic that a college degree is largely considered a prerequisite today for even low-wage, salaried employment that did not even require a high-school diploma in the past. Stranger still, the privilege of earning less than $20,000 a year and no benefits—teaching a full course load for the academic year as an adjunct—today requires at least a master's degree, although candidates with PhDs are preferred. In 2013, the story of the death of Margaret Mary Vojtko, an adjunct who had been living in abject poverty, appeared in the *Chronicle of Higher Education* and elsewhere (Ellis 2013), thus bringing some public attention to the crisis before it faded back into the larger landscape of an exploited US workforce. There is no denying that holding a graduate degree and a faculty position—even an adjunct position like the one Vojtko held, much like the work I do—confers a higher level of social-class privilege. At the same time, the reality that so many faculty members qualify for food stamps and live and die as Vojtko did raises serious questions about the role of educational attainment in social mobility.

My current students—all of them union members—have chosen, one could easily argue, a much more sensible career path. Their official job title within New York City's school system is paraprofessional. During the school day, paraprofessionals assist students and NYC teachers in the classroom. During their weekends, however—and after work and during vacations—the students with whom I'm working are presumably free to spend time with their families rather than grading papers or planning lessons. The starting salary is as low as $27,000 (and in one of the most expensive cities in the country), but the workers are represented by a union and receive New York City employee benefits. Significantly, their union pays for this course work, which they're completing through SUNY Empire State College—and taking these courses allows them to qualify for salary raises.

This is some of what I know about my students. Most of them know much less, in turn, about me. I often wonder whether my students have any idea how little I actually earn.

In the course of introducing myself to my classes, I've told them a bit about my education and experience. I've told them I hold an MFA in writing and a graduate certificate in composition theory—and explained to them what that means. I've also told them that, many years ago, I took enough graduate-level education coursework to become a certified New York City high-school English teacher. I've explained that I went on to teach writing at several colleges and universities and currently do a number of things to earn a living, aside from serving as a part-time writing coach for their classes, and that this includes my work as a freelance writer. At some point, I may mention I'm the first person in my family to obtain a college degree. Sometimes the fact that I come from a very poor family comes up; I may or may not mention the welfare or food stamps that played a role in my life as a young person. The fact is, I do not come from a family in which we spoke about doing well in school and going to college, much less graduate school. As a result, there's a certain absurdity surrounding the fact that I would end up getting an MFA in poetry. However, I felt things could only improve for me financially if I continued with my schooling. That's the American dream, after all. I didn't have anyone to point me in a different direction, and my family did not have a high enough income to be expected to be responsible for even a small part of what my tuition would be. Therefore, they had no immediate reason to deter me from taking on my studies, so long as I could get enough scholarship money or other financial aid. The loans would all be in my name alone.

When someone says they're an adjunct or freelance writer, anyone who knows what those things actually are may jump to a number of conclusions:

First, there's a remote possibility the person in question has a lucrative writing career. Failing that, however, it is far more likely that the adjunct-freelancer either has *family money* or is partnered with someone who earns significantly more. Second, one might assume this is only temporary, part-time work; the adjunct-freelancer surely must still be in school (or must be *going back to school*), with many more years of pursuing the American dream ahead.

It certainly holds true that two of the instructors for whose classes I recently served as a writing coach are in graduate school. In fact, during our beginning-of-term orientation for writing coaches, the first question that went around the room was about who among us was "in school." It turned out that many of us were, but I am not. My contingent position does not feel like a temporary diversion on my road to a better life; this *is* my life.

There's another possibility. As a woman of a certain age who freelances or does adjunct work, I likely give strangers the impression that I've taken on this *flexible* work because I need to be at home with my children. The catch is—and this has come up in a few of the classes or in various one-to-one student meetings—I don't have any children; I have chosen not to have my own family.

Perhaps my students wonder whether my life simply got off track at some point, considering that I, at my age, have the level of educational attainment I do but currently hold only a handful of part-time jobs—and with not so much as even one child to show for my time on this planet.

Certainly, my students—most of them women and almost all of them parents—often cite work/life balance as a reason they chose to become paraprofessionals. In 2015, I served as a classroom-based writing coach in a women's studies course; in it, my students quickly steered the discussion to the fact that so many jobs traditionally held by women do not pay well, including the work of educators like them (and me). College-level composition faculty, as Eileen E. Schell's 1997 *Gypsy Academics and Mother-Teachers* points out, can rarely count on consistent employment or fair compensation. Some work—such as a mother's work—does not pay at all. In addition to working full-time—largely with young people who have special needs—and being in school in the evenings, several of my students are the primary caregivers, at home, of children who have challenges ranging from autism to chronic, debilitating asthma. One of my students recently shared with me her worries after being told she would not be permitted to drop her classes, which she'd hoped to do after losing all her course work when her laptop was stolen. That term, she had been balancing work with not only her routine family obligations but also the new responsibility of caring for an aging mother who had recently survived a stroke.

I, like my students, define work in many ways. Writing is work, and writers often are paid very little. Often they are paid nothing. Unlike me, my students don't necessarily consider themselves writers. This fact is one of many that highlight their lack of privilege compared to mine. There are experiences these students and I share, and there are experiences that set us clearly apart from each other.

One of the main experiences my students and I have in common is that we all might describe ourselves as *educators*. The classes I serve as a writing coach all take place at the teachers' union headquarters building in the Bronx; all the students are members of the United Federation of Teachers (UFT). Like me, my students work in classrooms, with students—but (also like me) they themselves are not currently serving as instructors (at least not technically).

As a former NYC teacher, I was also once a UFT member. Whereas a number of my current students made the transition from unpaid, stay-at-home parenting work to these unionized professions, I've moved in the opposite direction to some extent, leaving the stability and certainty of my UFT teaching position to venture into a less profitable life of an adjunct.

Having said that, as much as holding multiple positions of marginality (as I do) has a cumulative effect on one's disadvantage, *privilege* in one area also has a magnifying effect on one's privilege in other arenas (Nawyn and Gjokaj 2014, 85–106)—and I also undeniably hold many privileges. Most of my students and I have gender disadvantage in common, just as we share our backgrounds as members of poor or working-class families. Regardless of my current financial struggles, however, the cumulative effect of my many privileges is undeniable when compared to the lack of privilege held by most of the students I serve.

Most notably, I am a white woman with a graduate degree from Columbia University. As an adjunct, I also hold institutional power my students lack. By contrast, the majority of my students are many semesters away from even an associate's degree or salary increase, taking classes in the Bronx through a state university. The majority of my students these past semesters have been African American or Latinx. Unlike me, many are immigrants or come from families of recent immigrants. All of us lack privilege in multiple arenas.

Those enrolled in these UFT-sponsored courses, like me, work with students, not *with their hands.* In that sense, they are different from the majority of HVACLS students, who are in the local plumbers' and electricians' unions. Looking at the various types of work my students and I do, however, I circle back, over and over again, to the question of what labor is and how social class is constructed through not just the lenses of pay grade and educational prerequisites but also in relationship to where one works, with whom, what duties one performs, and what types of functions one serves. I'm interested in how our work experiences are similar and different. Above all, I wonder how much the cumulative effect of our similar social-class backgrounds and current incomes serves as materially relevant common ground in a country where pay has become increasingly exploitative.

As an adjunct who has often earned far less than $30,000 a year in New York City, I, like my current students, work with students, not with my hands. However, as a writer and teacher with sporadic earnings, who has also rented out rooms in my house to make ends meet, I *have* worked with my hands—a lot. And while the tax code dismissively calls rental income "passive," this labor has never felt passive to me when I've worked in my basement, for example, after someone has caused the sewer pipe to clog. It didn't feel passive, either, when, having neglected to wear gloves, my hands bled because I was installing wire mesh around the perimeter of the yard to keep rats away from the front door.

All the more reason, some might argue, to say I have little to nothing in common with my students—many of whom, as New Yorkers of modest incomes, may never be able to own their homes (and most of whom work with students so much younger than my own). After all, if we examine the various tiers of prestige in the field of education, a fellow adjunct told me, "the most important distinction is that educators who work with children and educators who work with students at the college level are two completely separate breeds."

I disagree that this is necessarily the case, and the underlying assumption strikes me as classist; it presumes that "work" is primarily a means of achieving personal fulfillment or intellectual or artistic prestige rather than financial survival—a view someone with my own financial struggles would have a difficult time holding.

As a writer involved in academia, I frequently get a glimpse into a universe in which the link between how people spend their time and how they pay their bills is tenuous. Last year, poet Tess Taylor's 2015 essay, "Report from the Field: But do You Have to Work?," argued that it is sexist to ask a woman writer who teaches for a living whether she does so because she actually "needs to work." While I didn't participate in this conversation and don't know the full context, if she says the question in this case was spurred by sexism, I believe her. After all, many low-paying jobs have historically been—and continue to be—held by women, thus discouraging many mothers from working outside the home. Taylor (2015) points to the fact that many women are constantly on the verge of earning wages so low those earnings all go—or almost all go—toward childcare. Adjunct, college-level composition instruction, a largely feminized position, presents exactly this dilemma for countless numbers of women.

The additional trouble with adjunct teaching positions and other types of work writers often do, as opposed to other low-paying jobs held largely by working-class women and other minorities, is that unlike manual labor or working with children, they are considered prestigious. Since the compensation level itself is not what makes these positions so sought after, the job market for adjunct work is flooded with highly qualified applicants (men and women alike) who are desperate enough for money to accept whatever these jobs pay, no matter how low the wages, right alongside the many others who can afford to these wages precisely because their source of *survival income* comes from elsewhere. The result is that adjuncts who wait tables to pay the rent are, on a regular basis, competing with peers living comfortably off family money. At the very least, they are competing with solidly middle-class men and women—many of whom are partnered with someone earning a salary that, no matter how relatively *modest*, affords them an amount of flexibility those with lower net incomes simply do not have. As a result, those of us from poor or working-class families struggle to feel we have any place in academic settings—as instructors or even as students.

Unfortunately, one of the most memorable moments during my time in the MFA program at Columbia came when one of the program's many privileged, white male faculty members bemoaned the fact that aspiring writers "didn't commit more of their time to traveling around the world." Apparently it did not occur to him that money could be an obstacle. It was certainly an obstacle for someone like me.

And I'm by no means alone. The inextricable link between race and disparities in wealth, for example, is an uncomfortable truth that undoubtedly affects the career choices of countless numbers of people, such as the students with whom I work. Despite the fact that I, a white woman, was raised in poverty, in a family with no property or wealth, there is no denying the extent to which the scales are unfairly tipped to far greater disadvantage for women of color. All these markers of identity play key roles in determining who can afford (or at least hope to be able to afford) to take advantage of unpaid and low-wage opportunities—whether in exchange for prestige or for an impressive line on a CV.

I acknowledge I am privileged to have a graduate degree from an Ivy League university—even if that means carrying a great deal of debt. And this privilege has afforded me choices. Giving up a teaching job for the New York City public-school system in exchange for a full course load as an adjunct was an enormous risk I did not take lightly and to which I could not (and did not) agree quickly. With no legacy or spousal safety net, I could not see myself trading in a stable job with excellent city and union benefits—even if it was a relatively low-wage position—for the unpredictable, poverty-level earnings I would be facing as a contingent faculty member. I wanted to work with older students at the college level, but financial survival has always had to come first.

Is it, then, simply the difference in race, class, or culture that made the students with whom I currently work choose to become New York City school paraprofessionals? Is there no chance they themselves would have wanted to become classroom teachers or adjunct professors or something else entirely?

Some may feel tempted to make blanket statements, neatly connecting the dots between the class or culture in which one is raised and one's intelligence, earning capacity, and professional interests and ambitions. It is true that most of my students have always wanted to work with children.

The majority of them probably have no interest in pursuing a master's degree or PhD, but the same can probably be said for most people.

However, the probable link between lack of wealth and lack of willingness to take on a risky, esoteric career path is undeniable. To deny that link is classist at best, if not sexist and racist. It is harmful, as well, to explain away how little many educators are paid by saying we're simply not in it for the money. Just because my students and I don't strive to earn what a CEO or lawyer (or even an accountant or a midlevel manager) might earn doesn't mean jobs that pay less than a living wage should exist. People who have creative, intellectual, or humanistic motivations in life also need to eat.

The fact that some adjunct job applicants are more financially privileged than others means we cannot afford to dismiss the question of whether everyone, financially speaking, "needs" to work—not so long as it means there will continue to be jobs that allow employed people to live in poverty. We cannot say education serves the purpose of bettering people's lives if institutions of learning don't set good examples in how they hire and pay their workers. Prestigious job titles do not pay the rent or the mortgage or medical bills.

When we ask ourselves what the purpose of higher education is, we must interrogate elitist assumptions. Those who view a college student's writing-skill level, for example, as a gatekeeping measure that's ultimately meant to determine how *worthy* a student is for one type of career—or level of pay—over another, must be kept in check. I, for one, certainly did not devote myself to becoming a better writer in order to financially prosper in corporate America or even academia; a person from my social class could have hardly comprehended what that would even mean. *Defending Access* reminds us there are many students who understandably (and perhaps rightfully) view courses such as basic writing as obstacles standing squarely between them and the pragmatic degrees they may otherwise be passionate about pursuing (Fox 1999, 48–51). (Author Tom Fox's former tutoring pupil, Monica, is certainly one of these students.) Most of my current students have very practical motivations; for the most part, they are trying to better provide for their families, not to impress anyone with an elite job title or degree. As an adjunct writing coach, I am privileged to continue to be able to do (for now, at least) something I love—something that feels like good, honest work—in an effort to financially survive. Just because some academics are committed to keeping the university as a place of refined poverty does not mean they have the right to impose that same struggle on others.

15

ACADEMIC CLASSISM AND WRITING CENTER WORKER IDENTITY

Liliana M. Naydan

I grew up the daughter of a first-generation college student who became a university professor, and watching the ways in which my father was able to advance through the ranks of academia led me to believe I could perhaps do the same, especially given that I had him as a mentor. But what I found as a graduate student earning an English PhD in the early part of the twenty-first century was quite different from anything my Ukrainian American father or other mentors in my doctoral program could prepare me for because academia had yet to see the likes of a problem like this one. What I found was the problem of *contingency*, and this problem is no stranger to contemporary news headlines and public controversies that have bubbled up at a slew of colleges and universities. If twenty-first-century academics look to the *Chronicle of Higher Education* or education-related pieces in major national newspapers, they are sure to see news of the ongoing labor crisis at colleges and universities as well as job actions surrounding that crisis. New faculty majority president Maria Maisto titles her May 14, 2015, *New York Times* piece "Unionization of Instructors Is Crucial for Colleges," and many members of the graduate-student, part-time adjunct, and full-time contingent postsecondary workforce would agree with her title's claim. Whether graduate-student teaching assistants are staging strikes as they did at the University of Oregon in December of 2014 or adjuncts are staging a nation-wide protest such as National Adjunct Walkout Day as they did in February of 2015, the underpaid and undervalued workers of the lower social classes of higher education institutions are suggesting that radical change in academic labor practices is necessary for colleges to best serve their students.

This essay theorizes contingency and worker identity as twenty-first-century news stories such as Maisto's make reference to it, and it in turn puts contingency into conversation with writing centers, spaces that self-identify as egalitarian, spaces that are themselves classed within

DOI: 10.7330/9781607327837.c015

their institutions, and spaces that have workers of different academic social classes working within them. In developing a discussion of worker identity in relation to academic social class—meaning social class within the context of university life—I reflect on my own range of lived experiences as a woman working in an array of postsecondary writing centers: my experience as an undergraduate peer tutor, a graduate-student tutor, a graduate-student assistant director, and a contingent full-time faculty director. In moving through these different positions at different institutions, I realized the ways in which academic social class paradoxically waxes and wanes as writing center workers, many of whom are women, move apparently up the ranks in the twenty-first-century university, which Marc Bousquet (2008), in *How the University Works*, says has "embraced the values and practices of corporate management" to produce "the return of the sort of dizzying inequalities formerly associated with the Gilded Age" (Bousquet 2008, 1). Ultimately, I argue that writing center practitioners must certainly investigate and confront issues of social class such as those Harry Denny (2010) discusses in his "Facing Class in the Writing Center" chapter in *Facing the Center*. But they must also consider the implications of manifestations of social class within the microcosm of academia and the ways in which class and gender intersect. And in turn, they must find ways in which to talk about and struggle against existing stratifications. Doing so will help them manifest more equitable working conditions for themselves and may result in an increased status for writing centers as academic entities.

PARADOXES OF CLASS IN ACADEMIC AND WRITING CENTER CONTEXTS

The *Oxford English Dictionary Online* (2016) defines *class* as "senses relating to groups, ranks, or categories," and theoretical conversations by thinkers such as Karl Marx, Max Weber, and Pierre Bourdieu have provided the foundation for many current considerations of class, including the one Bousquet (2008) engages in in *How the University Works*, an analysis of the state of labor in contemporary universities. As Bousquet suggests, contemporary colleges and universities rely heavily on disposable labor, and they underpay contingent faculty dramatically in comparison to what they pay tenure-line faculty. Perhaps as no surprise, writing centers, too, partake in and feel the detriments of the kind of labor exploitation in which colleges and universities engage. As Emily Isaacs and Melinda Knight report, "Writing centers are directed by people in non-tenure-track faculty positions predominantly (71%)," and many writing centers "[include] students in the mix of consultants" (Isaacs and Knight 2014, 48, 49). Likewise, women form a majority of the workforce in writing centers. As a result of all these factors, writing centers typically exist as marginalized. To quote Denny's 2011 essay "Queering the Writing Center," writing center professionals are akin to "queer people" in that they "continually confront [their] marginality" (Denny 2011, 264). They exist in a quasi-disenfranchised class within the stratified system of higher education that has tenured full professors as the institutional elite, and university administrators can dispose of writing centers and their practitioners on a whim, as evidenced by the proposed 2016 shut down of the University of British Columbia's Writing Centre (McCabe 2016).

My own experiences as a woman worker in writing centers speak to the problems and paradoxes of writing center labor, and those experiences began by way of my work as an undergraduate peer tutor at a public research university in the northeast. I pursued the work of tutoring in part because I struggled to succeed in my first-year writing course. As I readily tell my own first-year writing students, as well as the students I tutor in writing centers, I earned a C on my first freshman composition paper, and the grade hurt. I really had to buy into the idea that writing is a recursive process that requires writers—*me*—to revise *a lot.* For me, the work of tutoring writing was more fulfilling than working as a cashier at a local diner or babysitting, the jobs I had held before getting my tutoring job. It felt important because I was helping writers who were perhaps struggling as I had struggled. I was also helping bilingual Generation 1.5 writers like me. And I had attained a sort of status as an eighteen-year-old by way of this job that ringing out diner patrons failed to provide—even though restaurant work certainly isn't less valuable than any other and often easier work. This meaningful writing center work didn't pay much more than the diner paid, but I wanted to do it much more because it afforded me with a sense of making a difference and a line on my resume that had a bit more social or cultural capital, to use Bourdieu's (1986) terminology, than the diner line did. In other words, this tutoring job tapped my bilingual life experience and my struggle with writing in a unique and in turn productive way. I realized it might help me get accepted to grad school someday. And it likewise made me feel a bit more at home as a woman in academia since most of the peer tutors in my center were women.

Tutoring as a master's student and eventually as a PhD student, I felt the same kind of waxing in terms of class status even though, within the context of the universities I was attending, I was near the bottom of the barrel as an educator. I didn't realize it yet because I had been so fixated

on the valuable experience I was gaining and the great feeling a successful writing consultation gave me, but I was in many ways part and parcel
of the emerging problem of contingency in higher education. In "The
Rhetoric of 'Job Market' and the Reality of the Academic Labor System,"
Bousquet (2003) provides an explication of the problem as it pertains to
my field in particular, noting that

> under the actually existing system of academic work, the university clearly
> does not prefer the best or most experienced teachers, it prefers the
> cheapest teachers. Increasingly that means the creation of nontenurable
> full-time instructorships and other casual appointments, a casualization
> that has unfolded unevenly by discipline and is especially pronounced in
> English and writing instruction. (Bousquet 2003, 222)

I loved my work, and I probably more than once naïvely said to fellow
grad-student consultants that I would do this work for free—even though
I was at one point living in a pretty dilapidated basement apartment that
flooded regularly when it rained because it was all I could afford on my
below-the-poverty-line teaching assistant's pay. But I realize now that the
universities at which I was working didn't value me as much as the writers who visited the center did. To these institutions, I was merely cheap
labor. And these institutions were knowingly or unknowingly exploiting me because of my desire to ascend the ladder of academic status.
Indeed, this might be labor exploitation at its finest in that I felt wholly
satisfied with my work and these universities, as a result, felt wholly justified in paying me quite little in relation to other instructors.

Around the time I was working as a graduate-student assistant director of a writing center on a teaching assistant's line, I finally came to
acknowledge more readily the labor problem in which I was implicated:
I began to see the strange paradox of class in higher education. I remember my enthusiasm for the great administrative experience I was acquiring as a graduate student and also for this great new line on my CV. I
was masquerading as having what Michael Zweig's (2003) *The Working
Class Majority* calls a higher social class via power on the job—via some
semblance of "control over the pace or content of [my] work" (Zweig
2000, 3)—even though, in some ways, I held a working-class position.
But my work in my graduate employees' labor union made me aware
of systematic problems in labor practices at colleges and universities, as
did my position working for a verbally abusive writing program administrator (WPA) who belittled and undermined grad-student employees
in our program. I remember this WPA reading aloud and ridiculing a
classmate's paper in our practicum on teaching writing and, sadly, leaving this always quite conscientious, thoughtful, level, and kind classmate

humiliated and in tears. This was no way to treat a graduate student or, for that matter, any worker. I was learning the hard lesson that opportunities to obtain experience exist, but there is no certainty of ethical or humane mentoring of graduate-student employees, and grad students often lack power to combat unethical treatment. The best we could do in my own program was organize ourselves to articulate, in teaching evaluations we wrote, the abuse we collectively experienced, and we were fortunate that faculty in positions of power who read those evaluations responded to our concerns—because in many cases graduate students' concerns are overlooked if their concerns don't speak to administrative goals for graduate programs. I am recalling here the graduate students at my alma mater protesting at the office of the graduate school's dean because we didn't agree with his decision to give a $2,000 per year raise to incoming students but not to the current student employees who had more teaching experience. He felt some pressure as a result of the protest, but he had little sympathy for our concern and, in the end, gave us no raise. Recruitment won out over retention in his thinking, and seasoned graduate-student labor remained disgustingly cheap.

In addition to outright abusive treatment of graduate students as well as actions such as those described of this dean, who exhibited little value for graduate-student instructors, there exists a void in effective mentoring of graduate students because even many of the best mentors lack knowledge of contemporary labor problems that pervade higher education. Too many of my mentors seemed surprised by how few publicized jobs seemed suited to my skill set—faculty jobs, especially tenure-line faculty jobs, were few and far between and the job market was something of a myth, as Bousquet (2003) documents. Too many of these highly educated, dedicated, and knowledgeable mentors had to accept the reality that apparently moving up the ladder in academic social class by working toward a PhD didn't necessarily result in a job with the kind of status available in *old* academia. I came to accept something I had been suspecting: that while a PhD promised a piece of paper and a mind enlightened from years of reading and writing, it did not necessarily mean anything more. I knew well that I might not find an academic job at all, let alone a tenure-line one. I also saw evidence of the paradox of class in higher education in the reality my supervisor, the writing center's director, faced. He was working on a contingent faculty lecturer line even though a previous director had directed the center on a tenure line, and this contingent-faculty director had virtually no hope of seeing a promotion of the sort a tenure-line job affords, at least if he opted to stay at our institution (which he did). He likewise appeared to struggle with improving circumstances for his center more than the previous tenure-line director did: he appeared in ways not as poised within the institution (because of his contingent position) to develop the center into something more than it had been historically, and to me as someone who hoped to one day run and develop a center, this reality seemed unnerving to say the least.

My former director's reality resembled my own in my first full-time job following graduate school—a job that further exemplified the paradox of academic labor in the age of the corporate university. In terms of the education I had acquired, I had climbed quite a ways beyond the knowledge I had as an undergraduate peer tutor. But my status plummeted via the full-time contingent-faculty lecturer position I accepted. The position had me directing an undergraduate writing center and teaching as a lecturer on a faculty of predominantly women. Some of these women scoffed at the notion that they were workers rather than academics because identifying as a worker somehow impedes one's status, and some of them regularly attempted to convince me of the benefits the contingency of the position had. Contingency would help me have a family, they'd say. Contingency affords flexibility the tenure track doesn't, they'd say. I never bought into these ideas even though I heard them regularly, but hearing them was helping me conceptualize how we'd gotten to this state as a field.

To whatever degree authority exists in writing centers—spaces practitioners idealize and perhaps manage to realize as egalitarian—there existed in me a sense of merely masquerading as an authority for writing consultants who saw me as being in charge of the center. I wasn't listed as the center's director online, and I was too apprehensive to draw this fact to anyone's attention. More notably, I had no control over the budget, and, to put it bluntly, I had never even *seen* the budget; every expenditure had to be approved by someone else—someone who was privy to information I would never come to know. I remember vividly the detriment of my lack of control of the budget coming to a head for me on a train ride back from the 2012 National Conference on Peer Tutoring in Writing in Chicago, a conference at which the wonderful tutors I had brought with me were introduced to numerous exciting ideas for developing our center. I sat in my seat on the train with the consultants crowding around me, enthusiastically enumerating all the developments we should pursue—developments that would cost money I wasn't sure we had. I had never seen these consultants so excited, and their enthusiasm certainly made me feel as if I was doing something right. I was also sure these undergraduate peer writing consultants' voices were far more valued than my own by my supervisors. Hence, in the face of these consultants' wide eyes and creative thinking about possibilities for writing centers, I sat there feeling quite small and utterly unable to commit to a single brilliant and exciting change they were proposing. I felt frustrated that no one saw the dirty secret of my employment situation. And I had no clue—at least at that point in my career—as to how to begin the process of explaining to them, or to anyone, the reality of contingency, that liminal identity that had designated me and my colleagues as professors but not *really* professors, as worthy to teach and mentor undergraduates but not worthy of institutional respect or investment. This wasn't flexibility for women workers. These were oppressive working conditions for mostly women workers.

Having cultivated a sense of empowerment among these particular consultants—a sense that they could affect institutional change, as evidenced by their enthusiasm on the train—I soon came to reflect on my own days as an undergraduate peer tutor, and I gained a new sense of understanding of the power dynamics in and around writing center work—power dynamics that far transcend those between tutor and writer as, for instance, Peter Carino (2011) explores them in "Power and Authority in Peer Tutoring" and as many writing center practitioners circumscribe them in scholarly and everyday conversations. I was living the reality of climbing the apparent ranks of academia, all the while, paradoxically, losing status. I was living the reality of becoming part of the easily replaceable glut of English PhDs. And I was realizing the apparent inevitability of existing in a stratified, counteregalitarian system as long as the university sustains corporate interests—a system that masquerades as equitable and that I so hoped would function as an enclave away from the corporate world, but a system run by CEOs who are in many ways at the forefront of creative and oppressive corporate thinking.

TOWARD A REVISED WRITING CENTER WORKER IDENTITY: TALKING ABOUT LABOR EQUITY IN WRITING CENTERS

Despite the challenges I was facing in negotiating my own worker identity, I realized it's true that tenure-track status doesn't wholly define workers' feelings about their jobs—that job status is far from everything and that academic workers can define their identities in ways that transcend questions of status, as Anne Ellen Geller and Harry Denny (2013) keenly point out in "Of Ladybugs, Low Status, and Loving the Job: Writing Center Professionals Navigating Their Careers." As Geller and Denny describe, "Both staff and faculty WCPs" they interviewed for their study told them "about their desire for writing center positions that would provide them with more satisfying professional experiences. But the more satisfying professional experiences they sought were not necessarily aligned with position classification" (Geller and Denny 2013, 112). And certainly, there is value in the "deeper conversation that transcends" the tenure/nontenure line binary they critique (Geller and Denny 2013, 111). I wonder, though, how we can acknowledge the complex reality of twenty-first-century universities' labor practices and the complex reality of contemporary academic-worker identity—especially as they pertain to women—while working to counter a system that increasingly places a majority of workers at risk of losing jobs and that is in many cases failing to pay workers a living wage.

Much like the field of writing center studies has revealed complexity in power dynamics in centers and problematized the notion of *peership* in peer tutoring as a practice, writing center practitioners interested in organizing against corporate dynamics in the university must realize that notions of egalitarianism and equity in contemporary colleges and universities exist as a fiction. They must come to accept the uncomfortable reality of feeling pride in and love of writing center work while recognizing what is often implicit or explicit academic classism and labor exploitation—of undergraduate peer tutors providing a crucial service for relatively little pay, of graduate-student tutors and administrators seeking CV-building experiences, and of contingent directors who are often women and who often lack institutional positioning to transcend the status quo in and through their centers. In other words, I am recommending that by embracing a more complex worker identity that acknowledges the complexity of waxing and waning academic class status, writing center practitioners might better position themselves to position their centers as more influential forces from the margins, from the center, or from wherever they may reside in the stratified and increasingly classed system of higher education.

Although I felt least empowered and least respected in my position as a writing center director because of my contingent status, I realized somewhat late in the game that whatever influence I had, I had acquired through undergraduate tutors who respected me and my work—even if the institution did not. I realized that revealing my own disempowerment to tutors would help tutors who paradoxically had more power than I had to organize on my behalf and on their own and to advocate for the kind of center all of us wanted. It was through the help of tutors that changes such as an investment in scheduling software became a reality in my former center. Likewise, it was through the help of tutors that longer appointment times eventually became a reality. Foregrounding undergraduate student tutors' needs in conversations with my own supervisors helped me to effect change, and if I had to direct a center from a contingent line again, I would encourage undergraduate tutors to speak in more direct ways to my supervisors. If we as writing center administrators recognize that undergraduate tutors may well have more influence than we do, we can work via grassroots organizing drives of a sort to build the centers we desire and ones students in the twenty-first century truly need to succeed.

Sadly, though, very few undergraduate tutors realize the complexity of the power dynamics at play around them—something I only realized after I left my contingent directorship. I remember one tutor in particular coming to my office in tears to ask me why I was leaving. She had no concept of how unhappy and powerless I felt in my precarious position, nor did she understand what contingency means within the context of twenty-first-century academic life. She in many ways saw the situation in our center as idyllic—and perhaps it was, at least from an undergraduate's perspective, and especially an undergraduate woman's perspective. I likewise remember overhearing two other tutors chatting and wondering aloud why I had opted to leave for a lower-profile institution than the one at which I was working. They had no concept of the great degree of respect I felt in my soon-to-be position as opposed to the overall disrespect I inevitably felt in this contingent directorship, and, to my disappointment, the elitism that stratifies postsecondary institutions and the educators within them was pervading the students' own thinking, based on their conversation. *Boy, it starts so early*, I thought to myself. Finally, over a year after leaving my job, I received an e-mail from a former tutor complaining about how corporate her university and writing center had become. She actually used that word: *corporate.* I responded with empathy and sympathy, with kindness and respect, but I couldn't help but think to myself that the institution and center had been that way when I was there. This tutor—and certainly other tutors—just didn't realize it. And how could she or tutors like her realize it if contingent faculty don't take the chance, or risk, of revealing the behind-the-scenes workings of things? How could she or tutors like her realize it if faculty don't share stories about the problems with their positions and motivate undergraduate tutors to think about the possible detriments of their own contingency, too—about the possible exploitation involved in relying on undergraduates who can serve as cheap labor because they seek work experience or a resume line?

Ultimately, I propose that conversations about contingency—*told* stories about the detriments of what it means to be a contingent worker—must emerge as staples of writing center professional development at staff meetings if writing centers want to cut through the systematized stratification that keeps academic workers working within them (many of whom are women) on the lower rungs of the academic social order. I wish I had told my own stories sooner and spoken more openly, and without fear of possible consequences, about the developments I saw evolve in my own woman-worker identity at different institutions and about what it means to do our crucial work without, in some cases, the respect, pay, or job security we deserve. I wish I'd had back then what I have more of now: the confidence to talk about the problems emerging in writing center labor and writing center worker identity.

16

OTHER PEOPLE'S HOUSES
Identity and Service in Writing Center Work

Beth A. Towle

For several years during my childhood, my mom cleaned other people's houses. She took my younger brother and me with her, and so we spent our Saturday mornings watching other people's cable television and playing with toys left over from children who had moved out of those houses years before. These were people from the small Indiana town where we lived, the same town where my mom had grown up, and her mom, and her mom, reaching back over a century. So everyone knew who we were and helped us out, even if it caused some shame and dismay on the part of my parents. I never ran out of hand-me-downs. As I got older, I realized we were not as destitute as some in our town, but we were also just always on the wrong side of doing okay. The safety net had too many holes to do much good. We had our own house, but that didn't keep my mom from having to take care of other people's.

Other people's houses.

Other people's houses were what continued to sustain me as I got older and went to college, too. I had always wanted to be a writer, and when I got to college, I found myself easily swayed to change from writing primarily fiction to primarily poetry. Charming and kind professors persuaded me to do an MFA in creative writing, which I eventually did. And then, while unhappy in my MFA program, I was persuaded by the director of the university writing center where I worked to pursue rhetoric and composition. I continually changed fields and paths in order to please others and to do the work they asked of me. I came into their houses and I did not leave because, to be honest, I needed the charity. As a first-generation, working-class student, my path through education and toward a career was entirely unpaved, so I relied constantly on other people as a way to help me understand what came next, over and over again, until I ended up just following through doors that weren't really mine.

DOI: 10.7330/9781607327837.c016

As a child, and then eventually as a teenager and college student, my number-one goal was to never be put in the position of my mother. I did not want to clean or to take care of other people as a service. And yet, my eventual path through life led me to choose the path of writing program administration (WPA) and writing center studies, and I am fully aware of the ways in which I will be essentially committing myself to a position of service. The material and emotional labor of writing center professionals is profoundly different from the labor my mother did when cleaning houses or my father did when he restocked grocery-store shelves. The work I grew up with and the work I am being trained to someday do are profoundly different in terms of both the material and the social privilege they afford. And yet, as scholars such as Donna LeCourt (2004), in *Identity Matters*, and others have pointed out, you can never truly leave your class identity behind, even as you move on to the next thing. Worse, every move you make forward forces you to reckon with what you are leaving behind and sometimes to mourn it. LeCourt (2004) argues that the very nature of class in the United States asks working-class and first-generation students to disavow the worlds they grew up in.

> If identities are only valued when categorized and named, it should come as no great surprise that maintaining a working-class identity is something few of our students are likely to do: After all, if they recognize the influence of class at all, they assume their goal in attending college is to leave behind such a legacy rather than laying claim to it. The very fact that students have entered college suggests to them that their goal should be to erase class markers in their pursuit of economic or cultural advancement. America's very national consciousness typically excludes class as a category of difference that might be recognized as a source of power. (LeCourt 2004, 160)

LeCourt argues that the most devastating aspect of being a working-class student in higher education is the way in which erasure is not only engendered but encouraged by the system. The assumption made by academics and public alike is that to be working class is to want always to not be working class, that a person should be embarrassed by their low socioeconomic status in order to be motivated to move to a higher class. This message leaves working-class students with an in-betweenness, a sense of not belonging to any one place.

While I have come to be very proud of my status as someone from the working class, I also realize that pride arises out of the very problem LeCourt (2004) describes. I have the pride because I succeeded in *beating the system* and overcoming class in order to do well in higher education, a rhetoric we are asked over and over again to buy into, no matter which side of the economic divide we may live on. Therefore, I repeatedly feel as though I must disavow the hard work I grew up with, and my disavowal is largely supported by the bootstraps narrative that, as LeCourt (2004) also points out, is part of the very identity of working-class people in the United States (162). I am proud of where I have been and where I'm going as a doctoral candidate, but I also am continually exhausted by the high-wire act of trying to hold onto all my identities at once—academic, creative writer, member of the working class, and so forth—without losing the momentum of trying to move forward. But forward to what?

Again, I return to the idea of working-class identity being connected to homes, houses, and residences. In this case, the metaphor of taking care of someone else's space is fitting to describe the ways in which academia in general and writing centers in particular are complicit in forcing already marginalized identities to conform to a kind of monolithic *academic* identity, or at the very least a near-monolithic disciplinary identity. Students whose identities do not fit the typical academic profile of white, Judeo-Christian, middle-to-upper-class men who speak and write in standard academic English are asked over and over again to give up their homes in order to go into someone else's and do the work the homeowner cannot or will not. In this case, the labor of conformity is entirely on the one who is already disadvantaged by being seen as *Other*.

For me, the home I was asked to give up was working-class identity. I realize I have faced less hardship in my entrance to academia than many: I am white, and cisgender, and heterosexual. Despite some issues with chronic pain, I am not considered disabled, and I rarely identify as such. The privilege of being white, working class, straight, able-bodied, and so forth has allowed me to mostly address my identities on my own terms. Intersectionality adds an extra dimension to what I discuss here, and the ideas of home and of houses we have had to leave behind become even more fraught when we consider how race or ethnicity, sexuality, disability, and language intersect with working-class or first-generation identities. In addition, I must consider how the metaphors of home and of house have been used by working-class people to close off their communities and make drastic political decisions.

For me, the idea of constantly entering and exiting other people's houses, even while you have your own somewhere else, is the best way I can make sense of the ways in which I move through the various communities I belong to, from my hometown to my poetry workshops to the academic communities in which I participate. Nothing ever feels wholly my own, and I am constantly yearning for a place somewhere else that is *mine*, even if that place is no longer accessible to me the older I get and the more complex my life becomes.

The metaphor of housekeeping applies to writing center work as well. As hard as we try to avoid the status of service work, both as tutors and as administrators, it is constantly dumped upon us. And it really *is* service work; we provide a service for students who otherwise would be left in the dust. I have no illusions that a large number of the students I see in the writing center are fellow first-generation students who are in need of the services the writing center provides. And yet, because it is so hard to claim a socioeconomic identity in any academic context, the service aspect often may feel like a burden to both the student and the tutor.

Recently in the university writing center where I work as a graduate teaching assistant, a first-year student who was working on a scholarship application met with me to discuss her personal statement. She just wanted to be able to study abroad, she told me. "I have financial issues and work a lot, so . . . ." I asked her if she was a first-generation student, and she said yes. Because I am constantly looking for mirrors, particularly when I am on campus, I excitedly told her I was first-gen as well. She gave me the response I often get from first-generation undergraduate students I *come out* to: a vague look of disappointment. It took me an embarrassing amount of time to realize why it was that other first-generation students did not seem excited about meeting an older first-generation student—and a doctoral student, no less!—in an academic context. Here's another person who doesn't know what's going on, they must think.

And I can't blame her. I often have wanted only the advice of expert insiders, and it took me a long time to discover I actually get the best advice from the people who have been fighting the same fight for a long time: other first-generation scholars, other working-class graduate students, and even my own parents, who have luckily seen my academic work as genuine labor and therefore have been able to offer their own advice on how to separate myself from the labor I do. In some ways that has been the most difficult aspect for me of becoming an academic. For many academics, their jobs are a very large part of their identity. And I did not grow up in a family in which that was true. My parents had jobs that consumed their lives, but they would never consider their jobs an essential part of who they are. As a result, I have often found myself as a graduate student trying to thrust a cleaver between who I am when I'm on campus, or even when I'm researching and writing at home, and who I see myself as in my daily interactions or inner life. I still do not see the Beth Towle who teaches tutor-education classes and works on her dissertation as the same Beth Towle who later that night works on her art journal or writes poetry or even watches television.

So the undergraduate student who came to the writing lab and didn't actually want to hear a graduate student talk about identity is not as misguided as I may have originally believed in our session. Rather, who she is as a student may be separate from who she is as a person going to college for the first time. That cleaving of identities is, in some ways, part of what it might even mean to claim a working-class identity. It is not an easy fix, nor should it be.

Of course, it goes both ways. I have students in the writing center who really do want to hear about my own experiences as a first-generation student. They so rarely meet people with similar experiences that they hunger for it. So, yes, writing centers provide a service, even if it is not always the service we expect, just by being a collaborative contact zone.

And yet, despite this, I still bristle a bit at the idea that I have given myself to a career I know will largely be considered a service and not an intellectual activity. Writing center studies has struggled to be seen as a legitimate intellectual pursuit, and writing center administration is still largely made up of people who are inexperienced in writing studies as a whole, and writing center scholarship specifically (Geller and Denny 2013; Purdue OWL Research 2016). Unlike WPA studies and the Council for Writing Program Administrators (CWPA), which has emerged with a clear agenda of promoting WPA labor as intellectual work, writing centers have yet to make the same strides within institutions or within writing studies. A long history of being tied to remedial training of underachieving students (you know, those working-class kids who already are disadvantaged and have asked to lift themselves up to the academic discourse prized by higher education) has allowed institutions to view their writing centers as places of only service rather than intellectual pursuit.

So, despite a lifetime goal of wanting to avoid taking care of other people's property, I find myself pursuing a career deeply tied to service. As explained before, I do think writing centers perform an important service, and as I have become more involved in volunteer work in my own community, I no longer see service as a negative concept. However, I do struggle sometimes with committing myself to five years of PhD work for this profession. Because even if I do get a tenure-track job as a faculty director of a writing center, I will likely never have as much time for research and scholarship as my PhD cohort mates. Part of me feels that this is a blessing, that a life dedicated to helping others and doing invisible but important work is certainly one worth pursuing.

But another part of me feels as if I am retreating into what I already know and can only know: a life of laboring on the behalf of an institution I have never felt I was welcomed in or wanted by, at least not without changing some fundamental piece of my class identity. A lifetime of working in other people's houses.

17
CLASS DIVISION, CLASS AFFECT, AND THE ROLE OF THE WRITING CENTER IN LITERACY PRACTICES

Anna Rita Napoleone

One of the first midterm conferences I held as a first-year PhD graduate student teaching a composition class at UMass Amherst revealed how difficult it is to talk about social class. Because I had been a tutor, one-on-one conferences were familiar and enjoyable, and I was looking forward to them; however, positioning myself as teacher shifted how I talked about class politics in the university. In "On the Subjects of Class and Gender in 'The Literacy Letters,'" Linda Brodkey (1989) notes how "attempts to transform classroom discussion into conversations between peers are thwarted to the extent that teachers fail to realize that their interpersonal relationships with students, as well as their institutional ones, are constituted by educational discourse" (Brodkey 1989, 130). Therefore, teachers, even when they think they are helpful, critical, and reflective, fall in line with middle-class norms. I recognized this through my own experiences with taking on a teacher role.

During midterm conferences, John (pseudonym) told me he did not want to be in school. He explained that he did not like school, but he attended because school was what his parents wanted for him. He would have preferred to work as a laborer. He spoke of the disconnect he felt but could not fully explain why. He said school wanted to change him, but he couldn't articulate the change. I listened and attempted to discuss the difficult transition to college many first-generation, working-class students experience. However, I fell short of fully articulating what it means to feel as if you don't belong. Unfortunately, at the end of the semester, during another conference, John said he was not coming back to school and that he had already shared his decision with his parents. I did not know what to do. Part of me was thinking, "If you find something better go for it because school ain't all it is cracked up to be." Another part of me was thinking, "No! Don't go, not yet. Give it a chance!" I

DOI: 10.7330/9781607327837.c017

wasn't sure whether that is what I was feeling or what I thought was the correct response. I couldn't help but get teary eyed and explain to him that college could sometimes be difficult. Like John, I felt academia was a contentious space that did not allow him or me to be. This form of academic literacy is one that I, and perhaps John also, hold as suspect.

I told John I understood his decision and that he should never close the door on his education because of things that seemed inexplicable. I told him that perhaps he should question why he felt the way he did, and if he felt that way, might there be others who also feel the same. He said he knew and that he really would prefer to work right now. As a graduate-student teaching associate (TA), what should I should do in terms of the institution and teacher etiquette were different than what I was thinking and feeling, as I too was feeling that sense of not belonging. In this interaction, I did not fully discuss with him understandings of class. In that moment, due to my own complicated feelings about my own position in academia as a first-generation college student, I attempted to depoliticize my body.

Like John, I was having a hard time at UMass. Often, during my first semester, I went to campus, parked my car, and walked for ten minutes to Bartlett Hall, where I taught. Most days, I teared up or cried as I felt the strain of being in this space. A close friend of mine said it was because I had often been in immigrant working-class spaces. She was right. I felt my class in ways I hadn't before because I was always in schools where the majority of folks weren't middle-class white folks. I recognized my own emotional labor while in a position in which I was to be an emotional manager. As Julie Lindquist (2004) points out,

> literacy learning generates its own complex dramas of motive, desire, and affect—dramas scripted and staged by experiences of class difference; and only by giving more explicit attention to the performative and relational dimension of affect in classrooms where literacy instruction happens will it be possible to disrupt the usual arrangements of students-as-emotional laborer, teacher-as-manager that are especially pernicious when teaching working-class students. (Lindquist 2004, 189)

My affective relationship with schooling and school practices is what I was negotiating when I was talking to John. That negotiation had much to do with class and the ways class is not seen as a way of being but rather as an economic and mutable space that one wants to exceed/surpass. For me, and perhaps for John, as I cannot speak for him, this sense of being is strong and throws into question academia and our place in it. The affective investments that connote working-class ways of being make it difficult to want to be in that space. Lines are drawn. In a predominately middle-class space, I often feel misaligned with the space, and I believe John did too. John noted boundaries/divisions between him and academic space, as did I. Academic spaces and the bodies in those spaces can determine where one ends up. For John, he ended up out of the university.

(DIS)ALIGNED FEELINGS

Writing centers as part of the social space of academia allow for an affective reorienting of academic space. Writing centers present moments in which boundaries are pushed and literacies are made available and legitimate in the academic space; however, more space must be made for undergrads and graduate students alike. My experience in a writing center at a diverse university in Brooklyn cultivated an awareness of multiple literacies tutors, tutees, and faculty engaged in. It was in a sanctioned space in the university where identity and language were understood as inextricably linked to the material, and the space allowed for the politics of language to *be* not just in texts being read but also in the very bodies in the space. There were many moments in which divisions/borders were present because of class, but more as I continued on to my PhD, in part because of the space I occupied as teacher.

In "Performing Working-Class Identity in Composition: Toward a Pedagogy of Textual Practice," Donna LeCourt (2006) notes, "In reality, universities don't just reflect class identities. They actively produce class divisions" (34). Literacy practices of working-class students manifest discursive reverberations of working-class social practices grounded in material conditions. However, these literacy practices are defined and interpreted in academia as anathema to academic discourse, thereby producing and perpetuating class divisions.

Literacy practices are ideological (Street 2001, 434); James Paul Gee (2001) notes that "any socially useful definition of 'literacy' must be couched in terms of the notion of Discourse" (529); therefore, literacy and discourse "crucially involve a set of values and viewpoints in terms of which one must *speak* and *act* at least while being in the discourse; otherwise one doesn't count as being in it" (Gee 2001, 538; emphasis mine). In "Language with an Attitude: White Girls Performing Class," Stephanie Jones (2006) notes the importance of a sociocultural approach to discourse and how it can illuminate how class functions in relation to performance, affect, and body (116). Jones discusses the construction of primary discourse. She notes, "These ways of being in our body and with other bodies come together to form our primary discourse, acquired socially and culturally and developed across time within families where love, loyalty, anger, fear, and other complex emotions are initially felt" (Jones 2006, 119). Therefore, emotions are not individualistic but are reverberations of larger ideological power relations in the social space of academia. As Sara Ahmed's (2004b) *The Cultural Politics of Emotion* notes, "Emotions create the very effect of the surfaces and boundaries that allow us to distinguish an inside and an outside in the first place" (10). Transitioning into academic space may be easier for some, which in part has to do with one's social class. *Fitting into* an academic space can be a complicated process because that may mean, for some, affective investments in or divestments of ways of being.

AFFECTIVE DIVESTMENTS AND INVESTMENTS

Affectively I note how certain ways of being create surfaces and boundaries that are a result of my working-class identity. Although working class, my whiteness grants me privileges people of color are not granted in academia. My whiteness grants me the opportunity to depoliticize my identity in the space. In a sense, I could/should disappear in the space. My educational experiences leave me wondering, how do middle-class practices in academia work on working-class ways of being and continue to create borders that are felt because of institutional and social structures? This is not to essentialize classed ways of being but rather to point to affective investments in ways of being that are part of material realities.

In an article Donna LeCourt and I (2011) wrote, we discuss the embodied and affective nature of class by highlighting how our investments in school were different and how we reacted to similar academic practices differently even though we are both working class (LeCourt and Napoleone 2011, 81–108). For example, LeCourt worked to lose her accent when in college, but I didn't. LeCourt explains her reaction to the "difference" of her accent when in college and her attempts to alter it. Although the quote is lengthy, I believe it is important.

> This mark of difference was one I did not know how to attend to. I learned to alter my clothing and makeup, but how does one learn to speak differently? My way of speaking had become "naturalized"; my accent and pacing . . . were an invisible aspect of self, a connection between body and mind where the vocalization of sounds seemed to emit from an enfleshed self. When I began trying to change my accent—I practiced throughout my time in Washington in front of a mirror—it felt as if someone else were speaking. I was so focused on how I wanted to signify to others—as intelligent, as an academic—that my language no longer seemed my own. I was not performing in any way transgressively; I was literally acting in response

to the social gaze in a way that disconnected my body and mind. After all these years, that performance now feels as authentic as the more accented language I still use at home, a part of the multiple identities I recognize as "normal." When trying to alter the accent, however, my mind and body felt separated, as if one were warring with the other; I lost many battles as my accent or ways of speaking would "pop up" when least expected, marking me as different in a context where I wanted sameness. Not incidentally, this still occurs when I am angry or frustrated, reminding me that such an accent lives deep in my affective core, seemingly more closely tied to body than my other identities. (LeCourt and Napoleone 2011, 90)

In higher education, university academic discourse is equated with middle-class discourse, as many scholars in composition studies have noted (LeCourt 2006; LeCourt and Napoleone 2011; Lindquist 1999; Villanueva 2003). In order to "signify" as professional, LeCourt has actively worked to depoliticize her body. She works to alter her looks and her speech in order to disappear in the space. She does so by actively working to perform sameness yet finds moments in which her working-class accent is "closely tied to [her] body" and therefore presents difference, and as she notes, that difference is something that continues to occur even today and "when least expected" (LeCourt and Napoleone 2011, 90). LeCourt notes that she is responding to the social gaze of institutional expectations of what is professional. Such expectations are tied to classed identities and, therefore, reveal the lines drawn. However, as LeCourt and Napoleone note, the affective investments and attachments to a classed identity and discourse do not easily disappear (LeCourt and Napoleone 2011, 84–85).

CLASSED LANGUAGE AND CLASSED AFFECT

I recall a time during undergrad when I took an Italian conversation class with many other Italians and Italian Americans, mainly women, and the professor remarked about the kind of Italian we spoke. Most of the students were southern Italians, and most were from the working class. When we were speaking Italian, we often used the word *mo*. The Italian professor looked at us and said there was no such word. We all looked around at one another and told him that there was and we all used it. *Mo* means "now." You could see exasperation on his face. We were exasperated, too. He was not going to have it. He said *mo* was not a word. We had to make a case for the various differences in languages in the south and the importance of them. One of the Neapolitan American women discussed the ways Neapolitan is a language her family speaks; she asked how he could speak about these dialects (languages) in this way, considering most of us were from southern Italy. He could not see that. What he also did not see was how our identities were inextricably tied to our language, and we were not going to accept the kind of linguistic terrorism (Anzaldúa 2007, 81) academia, in this case standard Italian, was placing on us. Furthermore, our dialects (languages) in Italian intimated a classed understanding of who we were. We were not aligned with the professor and what he saw as valuable and legitimate.

What we can note is that the divisions are as affective, as our dialects (languages) are part of our primary discourse that is embodied. Again we note, as LeCourt (2006) states, the ways in which academic discourse actively works to "produce class divisions" (34). Divisions are perpetuated by understandings of classed literacies, thereby creating us and them. Jones (2006) argues that "white children of the poor and working classes are struggling to construct hybrid language practices that will work in their favor in academic settings where their own dialect is often criticized as poor language use" (117). What Jones (2006) notes is that these students are viewed, by some of the students themselves as well as some of the educators in the school, as having an attitude because of their language practices and behaviors. Jones notes that such students are seen this way because they are not performing/acting/reacting in ways deemed appropriate in school. I believe Jones's (2006) use of sociocultural theory on language can apply to language practices regardless of age. Her thoughts on sociocultural theory and discourse, and how she sees the attachments to a way of being these second graders have in contrast to the ways in which the educators and administrators understand them, stirred in me one of those *ding-ding* moments in which class can be seen affectively by the way the children felt and acted. Jones (2006) looks to inform us that hybridity is possible. She uses "hybridity and hybrid language practices to describe the use, or performance, of more than one Discourse to communicate and make meaning in different settings" (Jones 2006, 116). Yet her discussion around hybridity is not discussing diverse discourses but rather that the kids need to learn the rules because they are the ones crossing the borders and entering the social space that requires them to learn middle-class practices. Jones's (2006) understanding that we perform and work with more than one discourse is important. However, I do think, when studying working-class discourse, that we need to be wary of her understanding and use of hybridity. The reality is that students are aware that there are expectations of performing certain literacy practices. What those expectations are and how/if they conform to standards (this may be perception or what they have learned via their own schooling) of the dominant culture in order for their performances to be considered acceptable might reveal classed expectations and practices. Such revelations of classed expectations speak to the divisions produced in academia.

POLITICS OF LANGUAGE FRONT AND
CENTER AT THE WRITING CENTER

In my earlier years as a recent graduate student in a master's program, the writing center seemed to cultivate tutors' experiences as much as cultivating tutees' writing experiences. Tutors from different backgrounds and literacies were present. The kinds of Englishes I brought with me to the writing center (working-class English, English as a second language (ESL), Generation 1.5), although dismissed in the classroom space, for the most part were validated in the writing center. I soon came to note that it wasn't just language that marked differences but also the ways in which *engagement* with literacy happened.

Often there were discussions among the tutors about how we aligned or did not align with the politics of the classroom, as many of us were practicing literacies not often sanctioned in academic spaces. There were also, as in my Italian class, many of us who knew our literacies were legitimate regardless of professors' lack of facility with different literacy practices. The writing center of my earlier days seemed to fit with a sense of difference that was often embraced and that really put front and center the politics of language and identity. I felt I could *be* in the writing center, in our daily interactions as well as in larger interactions within an academic space. There was a sense of constant negotiation with Standard American Edited English (SAEE) that made the politics of language evident and suspect and that was crucial to our continuing work on how our identities *fit*. This sense not only makes us critical but also reorients us affectively. "One fits, and by fitting, the surfaces of bodies disappear from view. The disappearance of the surface is instructive: in feelings of comfort, bodies extend into spaces, and spaces extend into bodies. The sinking feeling involves a seamless space, or a space where you can't see the 'stitches' between bodies" (Ahmed 2004b, 148). Fitting in, in this sense, does not mean sameness but rather making it possible to have space for other bodies. In the writing center, our bodies could extend in the space. In other institutional spaces, the lines were deep.

In terms of class, where ways of being and those attachments to ways of being are seen as mutable, I can't help but think of white working-class folks who often feel misaligned with the space, yet whose white bodies are depoliticized in the space of academia, making it seemingly easy to pass in the space. Class markers (specifically accent, gestures, ways of speaking, etc.) are seen as mutable. I am an ethnic white immigrant and working class and thus seen as mutable. Therefore, I should/could pass if I cover those seemingly mutable aspects. I recognize it is due to my whiteness that class can be placed front and center. This kind of passing and/or covering can definitely feel coercive (Yoshino 2006, 93), and institutional structures are implicated in this coercion. Attempts to depoliticize the body in order to pass/cover and sink into an academic space can be a complicated process because that may mean, for some, affective investments in or divestments of ways of being. Discussing affective investments/divestments may sound like a move into an essentializing space, a call for authenticity. That is not the case. Rather, what should be noted are the ways in which we have affective attachments to ways of being.

Although theoretically we may understand that an attachment to a way of being is a construction, the feelings and attachments we have to an identity, in practice, seem for many disconnected from theory. For example, LeCourt (2004), in her chapter in *Identity Matters*, discusses identity, materiality and power. She says,

> Identity is never prefigured deterministically, but is a continual process of occupying new subject positions and discarding others. . . . While identity might best be defined as "points of temporary attachment to the subject positions which discursive practices construct for us," introducing power into the formulation forces us to consider whether attachments with discourse are felt and enacted as if they were temporary, or whether certain attachments come to be seen as inextricable while others are open to reformulation, distancing, or even detachment from our sense of "primary" identity (Hall, "Who" 6). (LeCourt 2004, 143)

Feelings of misalignment in a space that often wishes to erase class and other identity markers seem to point to the importance of recognizing how affect works on our identities. Also, recognizing how affect moves/circulates in academic social space brings to the fore how bodies are marked in the space.

The importance of affect as a point of entry into critical inquiry is crucial to understanding the ways in which boundaries as a result of class work in academic spaces. Class happens in moments of contact; difference is noted in moments of contact, and understanding hierarchy due to power relations/structures one encounters is a process that becomes embodied and felt. As Ahmed (2004a) notes, "Rather than seeing emotions as psychic dispositions, we need to consider how they work, in concrete and particular ways" (119). My academic experiences have made me realize that class must be seen as more than a discursive position; we must see it as an affective process. Writing centers are spaces that can assist in affectively reorienting the politics of language and identity one encounters in academia by making visible the classed discourses that often go unseen or are misunderstood.

PART V: CLASS
Review

As Julie Lindquist (2002), in *A Place to Stand*, writes, "The experience of class in America is impossible to explain, difficult to render, and dangerous to address" (vi). Class is at once everywhere and nowhere. Unlike other cultural markers, it lacks galvanizing identifiers and is easily disguised by an ornamental culture—the clothes we wear, phones we carry, and cars we drive. Although the 2016 election made clear several pressing social concerns, perhaps no contemporary issue was cited more than economic class. Whether overtly stated calls to support the middle or working class, chants to dethrone the elite upper class, rallies to bring back US labor, or more nuanced, implicit offerings to engage *hardworking Americans* or *struggling citizens*, such discourse reminds us all of the uncertainty and fear that grips much of the public, that perhaps meritocratic ideals and egalitarian opportunity are more fiction than actual fact. Many are left to understand financial standing in simple terms: the haves and have nots, a zero-sum paradigm in which a loser must exist so someone may win.

Despite the ambiguities associated with class, the power and lore of the middle class prevails. However, what exactly constitutes middle-class standing is far more obfuscated, if not outright contentious. A basic Google search of the term identifies a litany of definitions without any sense of consistency, and "The Census Bureau does not have an official definition of 'middle class'" (US Census Bureau 2017). What is left is a vague outline of possibilities: *you'll know it when you see it, a comfortable life, a college degree.* Without clear demarcations, the middle class consists seemingly of us all, or so we may tell ourselves. Often, the working class tends to identify accordingly to escape the stigma attached to such lives, while the wealthy, blushing, work to hide their opulence in the middle just the same. Perhaps, for some, the middle class signifies homeownership, savings for retirement, and minimal debt.

What is concrete, however, is that the technology-based, service economy of the present drives students to the academy in order to stabilize or raise their class standing. No longer a privilege, a college degree stands

DOI: 10.7330/9781607327837.p005

as a necessity. David Leonhardt of the *New York Times* (January18, 2017) recently published "America's Great Working-Class Colleges," an article that praises particular schools for their ability to increase students' earning abilities and provide access to the middle class. Days after its publication, the marketing wheels of the noted institutions were immediately spinning, selling prospective students on upward mobility. Lost in the data and subsequent peddling are the finer truths, that students who enter college from a lower socioeconomic standing will with great consistency achieve higher salaries than their parents who did not and that specific programs or degrees will widen that margin even further. Not surprisingly, these students value majors and careers that increase opportunities for economic mobility. Attending college is understood as a financial pact based on economic necessity rather than on the luxury of interest alone. However, the 34 percent of first-generation incoming undergraduates who are the first in their families to attend college (US Department of Education 2014) often encounter a space far less inviting than publicized.

Higher education functions as a mechanism to accentuate issues of class: "In reality, universities don't just reflect class identities. They actually *produce* class divisions" (LeCourt 2006, 34; emphasis in original). With great frequency, we in the writing center are prodded by the institution to overtly clean up students' prose and covertly wash away any affect associated with the working class, to make these students sound, look, and perform like they *belong*. Most notably, Lynn Z. Bloom (1996) has shown the clear line of classed demarcation that exists in writing studies, noting what she considers to be middle-class values, such as self-reliance, responsibility, propriety, moderation, thrift, efficiency, order, cleanliness, punctuality, and delayed gratification, that are instilled by way of instruction. Although one would have trouble contesting that the academy actively works to acculturate students to the middle class, we, like others, are wary of assigning such values to a single cultural faction. Nancy Grimm's (1999) response reminds us all that these values cross class boundaries, stating that "Bloom appears to be claiming for her class many of the same values that were practiced in my working-class family" (60), and Donna LeCourt and Anna Rita Napoleone (2011) go forward to question what constitutes a normative academic body.

In fact, Bloom's attempt to provide an answer is what poses a problem for us: the implication that the working class is somehow *not* self-reliant, responsible, and so forth. Instead, in a relational theory of class, we recognize working-class subjectivities in academic contexts primarily by their transgressions (LeCourt and Napoleone 2011, 86).

In essence, the virtues assigned to the middle class are also evident in the experience of the working class; however, how these moral codes are performed and subsequently signify are determined proximally to the middle-class norm—adeptness with academic language, ability to present a calm and cool demeanor, both in prose and in rhetorical/affectual performance, and so forth. Much to the dismay of LeCourt (2006), any deviation from these norms may leave students feeling that they are on the outside looking in, that they must "live with alienation or pack up their culture with their clothing and return home" (32). Such digressions can lead students to experience dual estrangement from both home and the institution, leaving them to feel as though they do not have a place in either setting.

And for those who decide to move forward with their studies, mediating the expectations of home and school, their public and private selves, presents its own set of difficult circumstances. In "Inventing the University," David Bartholomae (1986) argues that students are asked to write in the language of the academy before having the ability to do so (4–23). If such thinking applies to all students, the working-class or first-generation population works from a greater disadvantage, as they are simultaneously learning one form of discourse, many times artificially mimicking what they believe to be right and proper, while discarding another, often out of shame, quickly learning that their vocabulary, register, and/or approach to writing is far from what is held in academic high regard. When students elect not to cover or are unaware of how to do so, they, as Irvin Peckham (2010) writes in his *Going North, Thinking West*, are said to be either resistant or incapable of being educated (48). Working-class language and academic discourse become falsely compartmentalized. According to Lindquist (1999), the two function as mutually exclusive of one another rather than using the benefits of their overlay and the rhetorical pragmatics that exist across class lines.

Upon initial review, class seems nebulous. Thankfully, the rich history of working-class writing does provide opportunities to reflect on these lives and challenge the misperception that the academy sees no class. Richard Rodriguez's (1981) *Hunger of Memory*, David Borkowski's (2004) "'Not Too Late to Take the Sanitation Test': Notes of a Non-Gifted Academic from the Working Class," and Mike Rose's (2005) *Lives on the Boundary*, among others works, have sought to provide a language for working-class identities in the academy. These voices penetrate and disrupt longstanding assumptions that language is fixed, that experience is isolated, and that the academy is sedentary. In an effort to render class less voluminous, the authors of this collection follow suit and, as Gary

Tate, John McMillan, and Elizabeth Woodward's (1997) essay suggests, "try to understand and come to terms with our own individual class histories, complex as they may be" (Tate, McMillan, Woodward 1997, 14). As we have discussed elsewhere in the text, such complexity stems from, among many factors, the simple truth that we are never simply *class* alone—that our identities are not monolithic and therefore never easily managed, never presenting as stable or being read with utter consistency. Rather, as Nancy Grimm (1999) posits, identity is multifaceted and multivalenced. To her point, "It is hard to imagine class cleaved from other aspects of who we are since they are so intertwined with one another" (Denny 2010, 62–63). Class, however, operates surreptitiously, a less visible marker given our propensity to enact middle-class culture. Yet, it remains ubiquitous, at times undergirding existing privilege or functioning to undermine socially valued aspects of who we are. Class, therefore, is raced; it is gendered and sexed; and, of course, class functions as part of national and ethnic identities.

Through the specific lenses of place, space, labor, and culture, the contributors of part 5 address the overarching nature of class through their distinctive voices and do so with an eye fixed on the intersectional nature of their identities. Beth (chapter 16) considers the tensions associated with place by complicating the *cozy-home* metaphor often associated with writing centers. In fact, to her, they are neither cozy nor reminiscent of home. Instead, they are spaces in which little of her own identity resides, places she does not own. She sees herself as a housekeeper, a term loaded with classed and gendered implications, disinfecting sullied writers, possibly even herself. Elizabeth's (chapter 14) piece pairs nicely with Beth's (chapter 16) work, bringing to the forefront a critical discussion on the issues of contingent workers and the intersections of race, gender, and class. If Beth is clearly not the homeowner, per her own admission, Elizabeth, white and educated, may look the part but as a contingent worker lacks any status to claim such an identity. Like Elizabeth, Anna Rita (chapter 17) speaks into the intersection of class and race, moments in which her whiteness, which carries with it assumed privilege, is checked when the politics of class are read in her performativity. Liliana (chapter 15) in essence speaks on behalf of her fellow contributors, explicitly addressing the marginalization of contingent labor within the writing center brought about by the corporatization of higher education.

Given the complications associated with unpacking class identities on a national level, writing centers would do well to pay closer attention to the local communities of which they are a part and that they

subsequently service. Since the experience of class differs given geographic locale, writing centers "must address the specificities of the
experiences, problems, languages, and histories that students and communities rely upon to construct a narrative of collective identity and
possible transformation" (Giroux 1993, 24). Stephen Parks (2000) con-
cludes *Class Politics* by calling on the composition community to engage
in community-based critical pedagogy.

Through such means, staff is compelled to consider the politics of
the specific places they inhabit, well beyond the center. Time and time
again, we claim to meet students where they stand, but instead we often
ask them to meet us where we are found. To effectively address issues
of class, we must understand how it circulates in and out of our centers,
how it embodies lived experience, and how it provides meaning in various contexts. In order to do so, we might ask ourselves the following
questions: How can we discuss tensions between academic and home
discourses while still providing students their own agency? How can we
help students utilize their lived experience to their benefit as writers?
How can we help students to code mesh rather than code switch? In
what ways can we be self-reflective in the work we do? How introspective
are we with regard to our own selves as classed beings? How willing are
we to openly discuss our classed identities? How can we help faculty/
staff become more cognizant of issues related to class in the center?
In what ways can we challenge the academy's perception of what constitutes academic writing? What measures have been taken to provide
mentorship to working-class students?

What we have noted above is pretty rich in terms of guiding staff
to engage with issues of class. Whether one, several, or all proposed
questions are employed will certainly vary according to the centers in
which we work and the needs of both staff members and students alike.
What is a necessity, regardless, is addressing the complexity of class,
particularly in the confines of the academy. Dialogue, therefore, must
pay close attention to what higher education purports to be its truth:
that all are welcome and all can succeed. The caveat often left out is
that such success is largely predicated on the ability of the student to
accept *challenge*—to be *gritty* and *resilient*, two strikingly classed terms
if we consider Victor Villanueva's (1993) bootstrap metaphor. Perhaps
a hard truth may serve as the greatest reminder as to what is at stake:
the academy is not class neutral. Students will enter our centers scarred
from this realization, moments when they are told they should never
dare "write like they speak," times in which they are said to be "too emotional," and occasions in which they feel compelled by others to choose

between home and school. We are not obligated to provide cover in our centers or work to remediate what/who has been thought to be *broken*. Instead, we must be conscious of what institutionally transpires in the day to day, helping students understand the schism between home and academy, identify the markers of cultural dominance, and learn that language and writing are not class-specific tools designed for a select few to accomplish a favored outcome.

PART VI

(Dis)ability

18

EMBRACING LEARNING DIFFERENCES
Spreading the Word to Writing Centers and Beyond

Tim Zmudka

I feel like a complete *moron*! I'm such an *idiot*! Wow, that was *retarded*! Have you ever heard such outcries spewing from the mouths of agitated students, tutors, or faculty during a tutoring session? While I have not witnessed them myself within the confines of the writing center, I have overheard several students express these exact utterances after receiving a recently graded exam or paper and noticing they made an embarrassing mistake—the type of mistake they wish could be fixed. I have made such self-ridiculing statements in class, but let me ask you this: how do you feel when you read the words *moron, idiot,* and *retard*? I'm willing to bet the majority of you who gaze upon this page would recognize *retard* as the most slanderous of the three terms.

The US Congress (2010), former President Barack Obama, and the federal government recognized the derogatoriness accompanying the term when they signed Rosa's Law, which required all federal legislation to replace *mental retardation* with *intellectual disability*. Even though *moron* and *idiot* are socially acceptable terms, most don't realize they were once equally as derogatory as *retard*. Just as *intellectual disability* replaced *mental retardation*, it wasn't long ago that mental *retardation* replaced *moron* and *idiot*. All three terms now stand together on the euphemism treadmill of words that once described individuals with intellectual disabilities. Coined by psycholinguist Steven Pinker, "euphemism treadmill" refers to the linguistic process by which pejorative terminology is replaced by a more acceptable euphemism. Gradually, the process continuously repeats itself whereby the replacement term acquires similarly negative connotations and is replaced itself by another euphemism (*New York Times*, April 3, 1994).

Although Rosa's Law rightfully expunged the now maligning use of the word *retard*, how long will it take until *disability* joins its predecessor by stepping onto the same wearisome euphemism treadmill? Originating

DOI: 10.7330/9781607327837.c018

with the Special Olympics Global Youth Activation Summit in 2009, the R-Word: Spread the Word to End the Word campaign is attempting to stop this euphemism treadmill in its tracks by educating society on the belittling effects of the word *retard*. Instead of simply challenging the rhetorical use of the word, the campaign also aims to promote the positive attributes and unwavering potential of individuals with intellectual disabilities (R-Word 2009). While the campaign's efforts are succeeding in helping individuals with intellectual disabilities gain their footing in society, their endeavors foreshadow similar challenges facing another faction of intellectual differences—college students with learning disabilities.

Despite the resources available to students with learning disabilities through disability services, many individuals are still hampered by outdated pedagogical practices and inaccurate preconceptions regarding the abilities of students with learning differences. As a result of such misinformed ideologies, the euphemism treadmill of disabilities continues propelling itself onward. Institutions of higher education and writing centers face a significant dilemma with instrumental outcomes for these students. In *Enabling University Impairment, (Dis)ability, and Social Justice in Higher Education,* Tara Brabazon (2015) writes, "One of the most damaging cultural forces imposed on men and women with impairments [or disabilities] are the labels that restrict, limit and deny their potential, ability and independent decision making. A diagnosis becomes a label and transforms into a narrative that caps and culls expectations, hopes and aspirations" (Brabazon 2015, 67–68). As a student who faced speech and language impairments, reading remediation services, and attention deficit/hyperactivity disorder (ADHD), I have personally experienced the constraining effects of such labels. Fortunately, I overcame self-limiting beliefs and feelings of inferiority largely due to my time as a writing center tutor.

I have come to realize that learning disabilities are nothing more than learning differences. Even though it is expected that students with learning differences will find traditional pedagogical practices challenging, the most disabling aspects facing them are the misconceptions surrounding their unique learning styles. As a progressive entity on college campuses, writing centers must lead academia by not only replacing *learning disability* with *learning difference* (LD) but also by transforming the stigmatizing narrative that is restricting these students from fulfilling their true potential.

MY NARRATIVE OF LEARNING DIFFERENCES

The Special Olympics' (2009) R-Word: Spread the Word to End the Word campaign's battle cry was founded upon the efforts to censor the barrage of degrading language aimed at individuals with intellectual disabilities; however, the origin of my verbal-linguistic bouts was much more pronounced—literally. While I have faced a variety of learning and developmental challenges pertaining to language and rhetoric, my story began when I was a young child with a speech impediment. My speech was characterized by inaccurate sound productions and consistent stuttering. I scurried around my house as a child unintelligibly uttering, "W-w-w-Windsay, wahh ah mah W-w-w-wegos?" This is a question I often asked my sister, Lindsay. If you're having trouble deciphering it, I'm asking, "Lindsay, where are my Legos?" My stuttering tendencies were sporadic, but my mispronunciations were constant. Yet both had significant implications for my abilities beyond speaking.

Like many children with similar speech and language challenges, my difficulties led to phonological awareness delays. Phonological awareness skills are a critical component of spoken language. These skills allow us to discriminate, comprehend, and manipulate sound patterns within words. While phonological awareness is rooted in oral language, it is also an essential aspect of reading. Unfortunately, children with similar language impairments to mine throughout elementary school are significantly more likely to struggle with reading throughout their lives (Justice 2006). My story is no different. Learning to read begins with learning to speak, and I found both tasks to be extremely arduous throughout elementary school.

My reading scores were near the bottom of my class and the State of Michigan's standardized testing percentile rankings for my grade level. I struggled immensely in the classroom because of the challenges I faced with my speech and reading skills. However, my poor test scores were the least of my worries as an elementary-school student. I was much more impacted by the social ramifications that accompanied my challenges. I agonized over the task of simultaneously speaking and reading in front of my classmates, which led me to avoid reading aloud at all costs. As my teachers announced reading activities, I began my daily mission of isolating myself from the class. I asked my teacher if I could use the bathroom. I hid under my desk pretending to tie my shoes. I left my desk to blow my nose or get a drink of water; and as a last resort I looked down at the reading material praying my teachers wouldn't call on me. I became an expert at eluding group reading activities. I became an expert at eluding reading activities (or so I thought).

To my disappointment, my covert antireading operations weren't as clever as my seven-year-old mind had thought. My teachers and parents noticed I needed help. I was enrolled in four years of extensive speech therapy and two years of reading tutoring. I don't remember very much about these sessions, but I do remember how much I dreaded them. Like most kids, I hated sitting at a desk and practicing tasks I wasn't good at. What child would enjoy this? I would have rather been playing football with my friends, watching Power Rangers, or trading Pokémon cards instead. Even though I disliked my therapy and tutoring sessions, they came at the perfect time. I now realize how essential these sessions were for changing my educational and social trajectories through my adolescent life.

I graduated from therapy at the end of fifth grade and entered middle school with a fresh start. Other than minor bouts of stuttering, my speech and reading abilities were on par with my peers'. Nevertheless, I face linguistic challenges that still persist to this day largely because of my ADHD. My challenges as a student that stemmed from adversities with verbal language evolved into reading difficulties and culminated in challenges with literary composition. Yes, as a former writing center tutor, I frequently find the writing process extremely burdensome. Yet I can also say I truly enjoy writing. I know you are probably thinking, how can a former writing center tutor renounce writing yet enjoy being a writing tutor? Before I lose credibility, please know I'm completely aware of my contradictory remarks. I can assure you my feelings make complete sense in my ADHD mind. In fact, I have learned over the course of time that my ADHD is the culprit behind both my strenuous writing process and my affinity toward being a writing tutor.

I'm not alone when it comes to the challenges my ADHD mind faces when participating in the writing process either. ADHD students are five times more likely to have writing difficulties compared to their non-ADHD peers (Yoshimasu et al. 2011). While I have never been diagnosed with a writing difference, many of the common traits of ADHD extend into the writing process. Such traits are embedded in the ADHD brain's physiological difference when releasing and replenishing dopamine and other neurotransmitters within the frontal lobe of the brain (Wu et al. 2012). The frontal lobe is responsible for a variety of higher-level cognitive functions such as movement, learning, personality, and decision making. Another primary function of the frontal lobe involves our executive function skills, which include skills such as attentiveness, planning, problem solving, impulse control, organization, time management, and information processing. Executive-function skills encompass the challenges experienced by individuals with ADHD while writing.

A writer relies on many of their executive function skills simultaneously when engaging in the writing process. A writer must manage their time wisely while collecting evidence and formulating ideas. They must coherently organize their ideas so they do not confuse their readers. They must process information efficiently while planning and composing their work in black and white. They must pay attention to the task at hand. Considering all the components of the mind's executive-function system, it is not surprising that writing can be a mentally fatiguing process for students with ADHD.

With *attention deficit* making the first half of the ADHD acronym, it's no secret that my identity as a student with ADHD begins with attention. Throughout the day, my mind constantly drifts during class, work, and even in the middle of conversations. When it comes to writing, my inattentiveness can be even more prevalent. In fact, I've looked away from my computer screen at least five times for just the past two sentences. Other than giving objective measures like how many times I look up from my computer screen, it is difficult for me to explain how my inattentiveness works when I write.

I don't smoke cigarettes, but I imagine my inattentive urges throughout the writing process are comparable to a smoker's craving to light up. The feeling starts as an itch to divert my attention to something else near me and quickly grows into an incessant urge that stampedes through my nervous system. Many smokers say their urge to smoke is influenced by those around them—if someone else is smoking, they're more likely to smoke more often. Their smoking is a product of their environment, which is exactly the case when it comes to my inattentiveness. As the number of environmental stimuli increases, so does my ADHD mind's inattentiveness. It doesn't take long to realize how much this urge increases when I'm writing at home with a playground of distractions.

Based on this recurring storyline, the first step I take when I'm writing is to leave my house and go to the library. I need an area where I can avoid all the distracting stimuli in my room. This strategy isn't always successful though. The otherwise typical sounds at libraries can also scream for my attention. This leads to my next tactical strategy. I wear ear-bud headphones whenever I'm studying or writing. I don't wear them to listen to music like most people do. I find music lyrics equally distracting when I'm trying to focus. Instead, I wear them as if they were earplugs and listen to ambient noise. This strategy doesn't always block out distracting noises, but it still helps with reducing distractions and keeping my attention on my writing for longer periods of time.

While the tangible act of changing my writing environment is instrumental when it comes to avoiding distracting stimuli, my ADHD mind still finds other aspects of writing challenging. The most challenging aspect for me involves planning and organizing my ideas throughout the writing process. My brain works like a pinball machine in an arcade room. Each pinball bumper represents an idea, topic, or distraction my neural network wants to attend to, whereas the metallic pinball is my attention span randomly firing in all directions. No matter how many or little relevant ideas my pinball-like attention span bumps into, it doesn't have the ability to stop and fully process each idea before randomly flinging itself toward another idea. When it comes to writing, my work resembles that of an inexperienced pinball player who frantically mashes the buttons on a pinball machine to keep the pinball in play. Ideas fling themselves at me in all directions, and my attention span bounces around too fast for my fingers to keep up with typing each idea. Even if I could type as fast as a legal transcriptionist, the unpredictability of my ideas creates its own set of challenges during the writing process.

I'll start writing about an idea or topic, and then another unrelated topic rushes to my head and I have the urge to start writing about that one before I forget it. The only problem is that I forget to return to the previous topic the majority of the time, thus leading to a jumbled outline of ideas I have difficulty puzzling back together. If I'm not extremely careful, the unorganized ideas can throw my work completely off track for long and unproductive periods of time. Some of these bouts last only ten minutes while others last for hours at time until I finally throw in the towel for the night. Such agonizing nights are mentally grueling. During these strenuous stretches, I only produce one or two paragraphs over the course of hours. I spend the rest of the time producing irrelevant tangents or having my mind veer completely off track.

For this piece alone, I have written over ten single-spaced pages of irrelevant information. A lot of this unused material is in paragraph form, while the rest is a collection of thoughts made up of one to two sentences. I also forgot to mention I have saved seven separate yet largely overlapping drafts. To tell you the truth, I can't even explain, or fully comprehend, how I ended up with that many separate drafts for one piece of work. I am confident in saying that this haphazard practice of mine is largely due to my less-than-ideal organization strategies.

It is important to point out that my ADHD doesn't wait for me at the writing center door to finish tutoring sessions. In fact, my tutoring sessions often feel as if I'm back in an arcade, as my ADHD mind pinballs during conversations as well. This happens so suddenly I don't even realize it. At any second my ADHD can cause me to miss pertinent information within the conversation. It only takes a single word or distraction for this to occur. This happened just last week during my first day working in a new supervisory role. I was speaking with my new supervisor for one of the first times. The conversation was running smoothly until a single word caused my mind to bounce in an entirely different direction. I only missed a few moments of what she said before noticing that my attention wandered, but that was enough to change the entire meaning. I took her comments as sarcasm and responded in the same manner. It turns out she was far from being sarcastic, causing me to stammer through explaining my awkward comment.

Similar situations are likely to occur during tutoring sessions if I'm not careful. While reading someone's work, I'll come across a random word or phrase that flings my mind in another direction. These errant thoughts aren't reserved for points I feel I need to address with the student during the session. Instead, it is more likely that the word or phrase that catches my interest reminds me of an unrelated topic. My mind grabs hold of these thoughts and takes off. It doesn't matter whether I'm reading or the student is reading their work; I stop paying attention to the words on the page and lose track of what's being read. During my early days as a writing tutor, I would make the mistake of haphazardly trying to fill in the gaps of what I missed by formulating assumptions. Most of the time I would be completely wrong, resulting in a problematic tutoring session. This reckless approach not only hindered my reading comprehension but also was a disservice to the students with whom I worked.

I knew I needed to find a solution for this recurring tutoring faux pas in order to truly support students in the writing center. I resolved my predicament by consciously violating a tutoring method that was engrained in my mind in my training at my writing center. I do not ask the student to read their work aloud. Instead, I prefer that both of us read silently together. I completely understand that having students read their work aloud is a terrific strategy that enables students to develop independent revision skills. I also understand that reading aloud further encourages a collaborative environment by allowing the student to become an active participant in the tutoring session. It allows them to develop confidence and a sense of ownership in their writing.

Even though it may seem like a rational choice to have students read their work aloud, I have learned this is just not the best approach for me. My best tutoring sessions occur when both my peer and I read their piece silently together. This gives me the chance to read at a slower pace and reread areas where my mind may have gone astray. I understand I could accomplish the same outcome while a student reads aloud by simply asking them to repeat themselves. This practice would also accomplish the aforementioned benefits we see when students read their work aloud.

Unfortunately, this is not always the case. I have found that I need to frequently reread sentences and even paragraphs throughout any given composition, which may negatively impact a student's self-confidence. Students take my asking them to reread the wrong way by believing there is something wrong with their work. If I implement this strategy multiple times in a session, it can lead students to mistakenly lose the confidence they hold in their writing abilities. They could easily presume that I reread portions of their work because I find their writing is subpar, but in reality that is most likely not the case. The majority of the time I reread aspects of a student's writing to ensure I'm able to tutor effectively—it has nothing to do with the quality of their work. If a student misinterprets my motive for rereading their work, it can greatly hinder the outcome of the session and also be extremely disempowering to the student.

This doesn't mean I don't make my own compromises when students need them, especially when considering my collaborative efforts with students with LD such as dyslexia. Due to the nature of their difference, many students with dyslexia find it even more challenging to comprehend text when reading silently compared to aloud. This is where I reach my dilemma: do I still use my silent-reading strategy even though it creates an almost exclusively directive pedagogical approach? In my opinion, this would be a selfish solution on my part by completely constraining the conversation in order to cater to my learning style alone. Not only is this strategy egocentric on my part, but it also disengages the student from the session and greatly limits the conversation. My peer would be required to recall their work from memory alone. As a result, it disempowers the student by building a conversational barrier between both of us and creating an unbalanced tutoring session.

Instead of generating a purely directive tutoring environment by reading in complete silence, I compromise ideal tutoring conditions for me so my peer can also benefit from the session. I suggest that I read the work aloud, which allows the student the opportunity to comprehend the text audibly. This negotiated strategy also gives me the opportunity to pause and to reread portions of the work if needed. Although this approach doesn't fit the most conducive conditions for my ADHD, it shifts the otherwise exclusively directive approach toward a balanced medium. Even though I know this isn't the most optimal approach for me, I remain open-minded and realize I must be willing to make this sacrifice when needed.

THE DEBILITATING MISCONCEPTIONS OF ADHD

You may be asking, why didn't you just reveal your ADHD to others? That would make sense given that I'm striving to empower LD students within writing centers and academia. The truth is that I felt a sense of disempowerment because of my ADHD throughout my entire undergraduate career. I did everything in my power to keep it a secret during my time at the University of Michigan. I never revealed my diagnosis to academic advisors, professors, classmates, or even my friends and roommates. In fact, I never even revealed my actual diagnosis to my writing center director until she asked me whether I wanted to contribute to this book. She only knew of my interest in learning differences based on the capstone project I completed during my senior year as a writing tutor. My capstone project focused on learning differences within the writing center, but I never openly acknowledged my ADHD diagnosis.

Unlike my earlier efforts of hiding my reading difficulties, it was much easier for me to conceal my ADHD from my professors given that my diagnosis was categorized as the inattentive type of ADHD, which has minimal hyperactive/impulsive tendencies (ADHD is diagnosed according to three categories: inattentive type, hyperactive/impulsive type, and combined type). Since I didn't display the hyperactive traits, my ADHD went largely unnoticed in classrooms and lecture halls that were filled with over two hundred students.

However, my desire to keep my ADHD diagnosis a secret didn't come without sacrifices. By hiding my ADHD, I forfeited helpful accommodations offered to students with LD. Specifically, I missed out on the typical ADHD accommodations, such as additional time for exams, testing in quieter/smaller rooms, and academic coaching. I thought that surrendering potential accommodations was a price worth paying in order to keep my ADHD hidden. I believed I could compensate if I just studied harder and lived on caffeine. I remember thinking to myself, "How hard could it be?"

Well it was extremely hard. I agonized through my coursework, no matter how much time and energy I put into sitting at my desk studying. No matter the amount of effort I put forth, I didn't believe I was capable of succeeding because of my ADHD. My grades plummeted from the first day I was in college and at the beginning of each term, and I found myself dropping courses in an attempt to stay afloat academically. I ensured that I kept my status as a full-time student, but I only did so in order to meet the requirements of my scholarships and financial aid. Even after limiting my course load during the fall semester of my sophomore year, my fate as a college student hinged on my final exam in cellular biology. I can't recall the exact grade I needed on that biology final, but I do remember anxiously knowing that my time as a University of Michigan student could very well end if that final exam didn't go well. So how hard was it really? I barely made it past my sophomore year.

I put all my energy into overcoming the hurdles of my ADHD and ignored the fact that my decision to not seek help dug me into an academic hole. I overlooked how difficult it was for me to control my ADHD mind's inattentiveness when I couldn't control my environment (especially in lecture halls with hundreds of my peers). I couldn't ignore distracting stimuli, such as students sniffling through sicknesses in the dead of winter, the sound of shuffling feet in rows of seats behind me, or pencil erasers rubbing against paper during exams. I needed additional support to learn study skills, such as managing my time and prioritizing my college course load. I needed additional time and a controlled environment in order to remain focused while answering essay questions. I needed guidance.

Why did I falsely believe I could flourish academically as a college student when I knowingly hindered myself? Why did I choose to go through my first two years of college in anguish rather than revealing my ADHD? It's not like the accommodation process was laborious for me. I didn't need to be interrogated by the university or to perform any additional diagnostic testing. The only requirements were to submit paperwork from my doctor, meet with an advisor from the Office of Services for Students with Disabilities, and coordinate accommodations with my instructors. Despite such a simple process, I still didn't seek accommodations. And I'm not alone. While 87 percent of high-school students with LD receive accommodations because of their LD, only 19 percent of these same students with LD receive accommodations at the postsecondary level (Newman et al. 2011, 32). Why is there such a sharp decline in accommodations from high school to college? As one of the many students who didn't apply for accommodations in college, I can tell you many students avoid accommodations due to motives similar to mine.

I think that, unfortunately, many students try hiding their diagnosis because of the climate surrounding LDs on college campuses. I didn't fully comprehend my irrational thinking at the time, but my apprehensions toward revealing my diagnosis largely stemmed from the negative perceptions surrounding ADHD on college campuses. As I entered my freshman year, media coverage was in the midst of heavily discussing ADHD medication abuse among college students. Unfortunately, many college students view ADHD medications as miracle pills to pull all-nighters for writing papers and cramming for exams. I'm not denying that the abuse of ADHD stimulant medications is a disturbing concern. Just a couple months ago, I overheard students at my current university's library openly talk about their use of Adderall as if it was a steroid for studying. They were telling their friends how much more they were able to accomplish when they took the medication. These students were sitting more than thirty feet away from me, yet I could heard them as clear as day. Obviously, college-student stimulant abuse is a serious issue and something that shouldn't be taken lightly.

Nonetheless, students with ADHD are unequivocally caught in the crosshairs of storylines surrounding both peer stimulant abuse and the potential overdiagnosis of ADHD. Some completely disagree with the overdiagnosis of ADHD, while others blame the influential pharmaceutical industry. It's also common to hear blame being placed on lazy parents who resort to medicating their child. I have my own beliefs regarding these issues, but my ADHD mind resists the urge to venture into those topics. The point is that no matter your stance on these issues, one outcome is obvious: these intricately tangled debates sensationalize ADHD for college students. As a result of this controversial debate, opposing parties demonize the diagnosis and mislabel students with ADHD as unintelligent, lazy, and undeserving of accommodations at the postsecondary level.

That is exactly how I felt as an undergraduate student. My studies revolved around the fear that my peers and professors would believe I was a stimulant-seeking fiend making excuses and trying to cheat my way through college. I ignored the reassuring evidence backed by my unique learning style, my documented diagnosis, and the challenges I faced with traditional teaching styles. Despite my unwavering perseverance to accomplish my lifetime goal of attending the University of Michigan (albeit my childhood motive was because of the football team), my mind continually repeated, "How could you have ADHD if you're attending this prestigious university?" I overlooked everything I had done prior to that point in order to achieve my dream. I overlooked the countless hours I spent in high school working laboriously through homework while my friends tried to persuade me to hang out with them. I overlooked the additional ACT/SAT preparatory courses I took on the weekends. I overlooked the fact that all my accomplishments were a direct result of my relentless effort. My achievements had nothing to do with having access to stimulant medication.

Unfortunately, many students with LD face similar adversities due to social intolerances. Alison L. May and C. Addison Stone (2010) found that many typical-learning peers and faculty believe students with LD are intellectually inferior and possess lower academic abilities compared to typical-learning students (May and Stone 2010). Such stereotypical views are far from the reality, as supporting research suggests students with LD are no different from their typical-learning peers when it comes to intelligence (Sparks and Lovett 2009). Despite no difference in intellectual abilities, students with LD are still wrongfully targeted. Their character is continually questioned through false accusations alleging that they are working the system in an attempt to gain academic advantages (Marshak et al. 2010). Similar reservations have even been found in faculty who blatantly voice their aversion toward providing accommodations for students with LD by telling them, ""Well, I don't know if you need to be taking this class if you have a learning disability"" (Denhardt 2008).

Fortunately, it appears that some scholars have found that faculty perceptions of learning differences are improving (Murray, Wren, and Keys 2008). My hopes are that your institution and writing center have implemented progressive approaches over the past decade to improve the chilly climate facing students with LD. In my relatively small sample base of Michigan colleges and universities, I have witnessed improvements in faculty and staff education as well as improved instructional practices. Nevertheless, more must be done in order to reach the point at which the stigma surrounding learning differences is eradicated in the eyes of everyone, including students with LD. Until we reach that point, students with LD will continue hiding in the shadows and be afraid to embrace their unconventional learning styles.

Academia and writing centers must recognize this and be willing to advocate for students with LD to ensure they receive the support they need when participating in traditional modes of instruction they find challenging. In order to do so, faculty and staff must be further educated on the self-limiting beliefs many students with LD face. Such limitations hinder their ability to actively seek out support. I've indirectly experienced a faculty member's neglectful practice that overlooked the apprehensions of many students with LD. Although I was never enrolled in the class, a professor teaching a course with well over two hundred students gave pop quizzes as the primary grading assessment. The professor made every effort to offer accommodations by reserving separate classrooms for individuals who needed extra time or a quieter environment. At first glance, there is nothing out of the ordinary for this type of accommodation. It's a standard practice for almost every college exam. Yet even though this professor offered accommodations, they overlooked how the nature of the pop quizzes impacted students with LD.

Unlike typical testing accommodations for which students know their alternative location in advance, these students were required to stand up in front of the entire lecture hall and proceed to the new room. This procession may not have mattered for some students who were comfortable disclosing their learning difference to others, but it could have been a polarizing experience for students on the other end of the spectrum. It's highly likely that many students in this class avoided the demoralizing walk out of the lecture hall by forfeiting their right to accommodation. Although this professor had good intentions of offering accommodations for his pop quizzes, he overlooked the potential ramifications of his actions in implementation.

The practices of this faculty member exemplify the current debilitating state of higher education toward students with LD. In a study of the top four higher education research journals (based on number of citations and articles published from 1990 to 2010), Edlyn Vallejo Peña (2014) found that only 1 percent of the articles examined learning differences. I'm not suggesting that learning differences are completely ignored by research. Many journals publish relevant empirical research providing great insight into the difficulties students with LD face with current educational practices. Such research is imperative for developing the best instructional strategies for all students. Writing centers have also increased discussions and implemented a variety of improvements regarding strategies to further support students with LD.

Even though the efforts currently being put forth are well intended, conversations narrowly focus on the medicalization of students with LD. Research is trying to find *cures* for learning differences by emphasizing atypical learning traits. By almost exclusively focusing on the challenges these students face, the misconceptions surrounding learning differences are only reinforced. As a result, these conversations, due to their focus on cures and challenges, teach students with LD that their learning is pathological.

BRING YOUR ATTENTION TO THE POSITIVE ATTRIBUTES

"Everyone is a genius. But if you judge a fish on its ability to climb a tree, it will live its whole life believing that it is stupid" is a saying often attributed to Albert Einstein (who was believed to be dyslexic himself). Students with LD have been constantly reminded that they possess undesirable intellectual traits within the context of academia. If higher education and writing center scholarship continue to focus their energy on only the unattractive experiences of these students, this focus will only continue to suffocate them, thereby making it more difficult for LD students to reach their full potential. Students will continue constructing barriers of shame and self-doubt in an attempt to hide their learning differences because they don't fit the mold of their typically-learning peers. Their own perception of learning differences disables their learning and creates self-fulfilling prophecies—believing they're flawed students. All entities within higher education, including writing centers, must shift their attention toward the positive attributes of learning differences. Higher education must build upon the strengths of these students by allowing them to realize their true learning potential.

In less than a decade, the Special Olympics (2009) has accomplished similar results for individuals with intellectual differences through their campaign. The R-Word: Spread the Word to End the Word campaign has influenced public policy and created a stir within pop culture with celebrities such as LeBron James, Lady Gaga, and J. Cole all issuing sincere apologies following remarks containing the word *retard*. Like individuals with intellectual differences, students with LD deserve to be understood. People with learning differences don't need to be cured. It's society's ignorance toward learning differences that needs further treatment.

This is where writing centers have the potential to truly impact higher education and students with LD. I've witnessed writing centers embracing similar roles within higher education, and now it's time to empower students with LD by advocating that they are more than capable of being exceptional students. As experts in collaboration and inclusiveness, writing centers possess the core values needed to be the voice of students with LD on college campuses.

My own story is testament to the impact writing centers can achieve when it comes to embracing learning differences. As I previously mentioned, my writing center director only knew I was interested in learning differences because of my capstone project as a writing center tutor. As a student with ADHD who has wrestled with many areas of the writing process, I questioned whether I was capable of tutoring my peers prior to my capstone project. The truth is that my capstone project was the beginning of my own transformation regarding the misconceptions about my ADHD. I finally began eradicating my disabling self-doubts and became comfortable revealing my ADHD to those around me. I wasn't ashamed about others knowing my diagnosis.

While my capstone project was a significant step in the right direction, I wasn't completely immune to the stigma surrounding my ADHD after presenting my project. In fact, I was initially apprehensive to reveal my diagnosis to complete strangers by accepting the opportunity to write this very piece. Unfortunately, insecurities still lurked in the back of my mind, trying to persuade me against it. Nevertheless, my mind's skepticism has transformed since I have begun the writing process. I have worked through my self-doubts and uncertainties surrounding my learning differences and now fully embrace my ADHD. Once again, the writing center has given me the support I needed in order to eliminate the stigma surrounding ADHD that my own mind still clung to following my capstone project.

Instead of clinging to the stigma, I'm now able to recognize that my ADHD has been remarkably valuable in shaping my life. Rather than getting frustrated when I can't pay attention, I realize my ADHD mind is simply trying to communicate useful information to me. Instead of recognizing the inattentiveness as a burden, I recognize that my ADHD mind is simply yearning for something more stimulating. Once my ADHD mind is engaged, it opens the throttle and doesn't look back. My ADHD has the ability to become enthralled with certain tasks or aspects of life, which can be extremely adaptive. It's as if my ADHD mind is off to the races engaging in something that truly matters to me as an individual. I'm no longer inattentive during these situations—I'm overattentive. The ADHD community and supporting research have identified such overattentiveness as hyperfocus.

Although the ADHD mind is known to become easily distractible, such a notion is a misnomer when hyperfocus ensues. Hyperfocus allows individuals with ADHD to block out irrelevant stimuli and intently focus on a task for hours at a time. It is important for the individual to feel passionate about the task at hand. I experience the state of hyperfocus whenever I write about something I'm truly passionate about, which is exactly the case for the subject of learning differences. Over the past six months, I've sat at the library for countless hours researching, taking notes, outlining, and editing this very piece. I can't count the number of hours, but I can count eighty-six research articles on learning differences I've read and saved on my computer. That doesn't even include the articles I have partially read and decided weren't relevant. My mind becomes completely absorbed, and hours feel like minutes. The amount of time and effort I have put into this chapter is probably comparable to the work of a master's thesis for others. I'll admit I have definitely overresearched, written several pages that veered off topic with irrelevant information, and found it difficult to cohesively organize my arguments. I wouldn't have it any other way though.

Even though my ADHD mind finds it challenging to organize ideas that pinball around in my head throughout the writing process, these ideas do render themselves useful when it comes to brainstorming. I'm able to regularly come up with a variety of possible solutions for any given situation and impulsively blurt them out as they dart across my mind. My methods may be unconventional, but they work well for my learning and writing processes. Like many individuals with ADHD, I act on my mind's natural impulses. I'm not afraid of taking risks when it comes to putting my thoughts into action.

My ADHD mind thrives on this level of hyperfocus, which spews into other areas of my life. It's virtually impossible for my ADHD mind to go through a single day living monotonously. If I commit to something that doesn't energize me, my lack of interest quickly reveals itself to those around me. Hyperfocus gives me the unceasing urge to follow my passions in life. I realize my intrinsic need to do things that stimulate my mind and allow it to engage in hyperfocus as much as possible. With a dopamine-deprived brain, individuals with ADHD are constantly seeking the stimulation our brains thrive on. My ADHD makes me live authentically. By doing things I'm truly passionate about, like tutoring, my brain is literally receiving the mental stimulation it is constantly seeking. I look at tutoring and my work with other students as mutually beneficial opportunities. While students enter the center with hopes of receiving writing guidance, I aspire to empower them by helping find their most optimal learning styles. It's collaboration in its finest form.

Students with ADHD aren't the only individuals who experience benefits because of their learning difference. All learning differences have the potential of exhibiting similar attributes. The majority of the positive research on learning differences surrounds dyslexic students. Although dyslexic students find reading and spelling challenging, they have also been shown to possess strengths with visual-spatial abilities (von Károlye et al. 2003, 430). These abilities are highly valued within a variety of fields including engineering, architecture, entrepreneurship, and visual arts. In fact, Julie Name Logan (2009) found that over one third of successful entrepreneurs are dyslexic (332).

The potential to succeed for every student with LD is there—whether it is through writing, academics, or business ventures. Through my writing strategies and experiences as a tutor and student, I have learned to change my perspective on ADHD and other learning differences. The idiosyncrasies rooted in my ADHD may create challenging situations, but I accept them as unique aspects of my mind. I refuse to ruminate on the negative misconceptions of my ADHD. Instead, I focus on the positive attributes my inattentiveness and scattered-mindedness bring to my personality. My ADHD mind plays a pivotal role in my life's success. It's imperative that other students with LD come to similar realizations.

PART VI: (DIS)ABILITY
Review

We believe it is important to note that Tim's essay stands alone in part 6 and that this positioning only highlights the need for the field to do more research on students with disabilities, as Rebecca Day Babcock (2015) suggests in her scholarship on working with students with disabilities. She writes, "There is a true need for more research on disabilities in the writing center . . . and while it is important to study tutees, there are no published studies whatsoever about tutors or directors with disabilities" (Babcock 2015, 41). Tim's chapter shows us the importance of learning from the narratives of those individuals who have learning differences in order for writing center scholars and practitioners to take on Babcock's (2015) call for future studies in writing center scholarship. His own narrative as a tutor shows readers what we need to learn from individuals with LD in order to develop more inclusive pedagogies. As we think about student engagement in our writing sessions and classrooms, shift our attention to what students find meaningful, and become passionate about in their writing assignments (Eodice et al. 2016), we can't help but think about what we can learn from individuals with ADHD and their experiences with hyperfocus. Tim's chapter and his own call for empowering students with learning differences in the center seeks to help them attain their most "optimal learning styles" as he has been able to do as a student, as a tutor, and as an individual with an LD, and his is a narrative that must be read and discussed in our centers.

As is true for the parts of this collection that focus on race, language, sexuality, gender, and class, disability is a construct we cannot examine on its own. Disability scholars Liat Ben-Moshe, Anthony J. Nocella II, and A. J. Withers (2013) write, "Disability, if understood as constructed through historical and cultural processes, should not be seen as a binary but a continuum. One is always dis/abled in relation to the context one is put in. A person has a learning disability if put in a scholarly setting" (Ben-Moshe, Nocella, and Withers 2013, 210). Tim's narrative asks readers to interrogate what they privilege in terms of how people learn and also asks us to rethink what the field considers "best practices."

DOI: 10.7330/9781607327837.p006

Multilingual scholars in the field of writing studies show the mutual learning experience that occurs through language differences (Bruce and Rafoth 2009, 2016; Cox and Matsuda 2011; Matsuda 1999; Matsuda, Ortmeier-Hooper, and You 2006; Rafoth 2015), and yet Tim's chapter begs the field to explore what we can learn from those students with LD that come to our center: as students seeking help with their writing, as tutors teaching, and as directors leading.

We see this narrative as a thought-provoking read at staff-education meetings that can serve as a starting point to future studies in writing centers. While it is important to collaborate with campus offices such as disability services and invite them to come to staff meetings, the result of these partnerships can often lead to presentations of labels and terms with quick "fixes" and tips and strategies in working with "those students" that do little to enable dialogue, interaction, and shared learning, further Otherizing these bodies. What we find important in Tim's work is that his chapter can serve as an entry point for meaningful conversations about disabilities in the writing center and about what we can learn from those who identify as disabled. We hope reading and sharing narratives like Tim's will empower others to perhaps "come out" and share similar stories they might have felt too embarrassed or ashamed to discuss—particularly in an academic setting. As this narrative indicates, we must first learn through listening and exchanging perspectives. We wonder what a shared conversation on staffing would be like after reading this chapter? How would our centers respond if we were to start a conversation on actively recruiting those who are disabled? What would that look like in terms of outreach? Is it even a possibility? How would that change our ideas and notions of tutor education? These are questions we hope the field starts to explore; Tim's stand-alone chapter, and the lack of scholarship on disabilities in the field, indicates there is a lot of work that must be done on students with LD as we continue to strive to make our centers inclusive for all.

Conclusion
IDENTITY POLITICS REDUX
A Call for Sustainable Action

Harry Denny, Robert Mundy, Liliana M. Naydan,
Richard Sévère, and Anna Sicari

This edited collection presents readers with a range of personal narratives about the realities of writing center work as it involves race, multilingualism, gender and sexuality, faith, class, and disability. It underscores
intersections among these features of identity, and by virtue of its form,
it celebrates writing as a key medium by which to exchange uncomfortable stories about everyday struggles involving identity politics that might
otherwise go unspoken. In writing and reading these narratives within
the brave space this collection comprises, we as editors have learned
things about ourselves and our colleagues we might have otherwise
never learned, and our hope is that our readers also learn from these
narratives—that they get a sense of their own identities in relation to colleagues in their field and that they get a sense of the power of exchanged
narrative as a means by which to develop writing center theory, practice,
and research. To conclude this collection, we first reflect on the thorny
nature of identity as a concept. We then reflect on the ways in which individuals, writing center communities and the field of writing center studies, broader campus communities, and the communities that surround
our campuses can benefit from reflections on identity. Ultimately, these
reflections function as a call that attempts to open the door to more
exchanges of narratives such as the ones included here, be those narratives told in informal contexts, in staff meetings, or with the aim of producing inquiry-based research in the field of writing center studies, all
of which we see as equally valid extensions of our narrative-based work.

The picture this collection paints of identity is a multifaceted one that
involves interconnected experiences that occur both inside and out of
the writing center. Our portrait of identity as a concept challenges nar-
row conceptions of the self as singular—the understanding of the self as
a socially, culturally, economically, or otherwise unified experience and

DOI: 10.7330/9781607327837.c019

performance. Instead, identity as we frame it exists as fragmented—as a nuanced and messy thing. And understanding the most noteworthy features of identity in general or of a specific identity often necessitates going beyond what is most striking about an individual, the identifier that appears as most legible on our bodies, because individuals are at once many changing pieces. By going beyond these noteworthy features and reading identity as always already complex, members of communities such as writing centers can create conditions for inclusivity through considerations of the ways in which features of our identities and our lives intersect with one another. Our hope is a response to the most common of questions: what do you know about my experience? We ask our readers to consider various experiences presented in this text and to place what they learn into the larger matrix of identity and its formation. Any other approach would provide no points of entry, no seams to allow contact and possible continuity.

As individual readers of our work engage in contemplations of their own complex identities, we urge them to develop empathy by forming alliances, and we see consciousness-raising as a means to build a greater sense of interconnectivity. Our students, staffs, and faculties exist as an amalgam of individuals who find their way to the writing center carrying far more than the assignments that on the surface bring them to our doorsteps. They bring their experiences, lived or understood through association—the narratives assigned to their bodies, beliefs, and choices. They bear the burden of the social, cultural, and/or economic symbolic markers and/or capital that determine who is afforded a greater sense of autonomy and who is not. We make no promises and offer no pre-scriptives about how to go about the process of reflecting on these complex identities. However, we do ask that those who enter and work in the writing center be self-reflective practitioners, ones who give immense consideration to how their own identities and experiences affect the outcomes of their sessions. We ask that they work to understand and come to terms with their own biases and world-views, challenging themselves to be almost naïve spectators, viewers who are prepared to suspend what may seem to be obvious in the hope of finding new avenues in conversations. We ask our readers to engage in dialogue with these individuals and their narratives, to pose questions, and to reflect. We ask them to start moving outside the neat and tidy and to embrace the messiness of disruption that will come from unearthing identities.

In our field, we collectively share narratives that unpack our identities—our anxieties, fears, angers, and hopes—because, as our title suggests, we are "out in the center." We are vulnerable and unguarded in our writing center work, and our collection's value comes in its presentation and complication of identity formation and reformation as writing center conversations allow for them. As we see it, the everyday teaching, learning, and laboring of writing centers is unique in that the personal consistently bleeds into the professional. Any exchange in a writing center consultation involves the interplay of personal details with academic and professional subjects and goals because of the fluid nature of conversation. The personal stories our contributors share challenge what is made public by way of the private. Being out in the center is a performative *act*. It's an act of making the private public; it's talking, sharing, laughing, crying, yelling, and living. Being is entirely in the moment and in large part involves action rather than consideration because to *be* is to exist on the page and in the world. It is uninhibited and it serves no past; it concerns itself not with what is to come. *Being* is to be alive—to live and breathe as art—to remind all who read along or who enter into dialogue with our contributors that this work is not solely about scholarship but rather about lived experience in all its forms.

For writing center studies to be out in the center is for our field to take up questions of identity as we do in order to create change in the composition of writing centers. For instance, one of many problems units in our field face in creating spaces for dialogue and action is one of homogeneity, and if we don't have a critical level of diversity, these conversations can't even begin to happen in meaningful ways. That means we must think about our staffing—how we hire and whom we hire. Too often, we hear from colleagues at other institutions that they don't get applicants that enable their writing centers to have a more diverse, inclusive face. Yet many of our colleagues don't get out on campus and engage with a range of places students inhabit, places where students and potential staff members might be. Some of our writing centers are fortunate to be on campuses where a critical mass for *easy* diversity is already present; we only need to do the legwork and alliance creation to find the tutors. Others work at universities that are relatively homogeneous, but we still must engage in outreach. We still must talk with faculty and administrator allies on campus. Given how many of us are already on campus building awareness of what our units do, we have natural occasions to ask peers to send a variety of students our way. Our tutors are constantly working with students, so we ought to empower them to recruit: to invite writers who demonstrate the qualities we value to apply to join our operations.

It is just as important to think about the professionals who lead our writing centers as it is to consider which students use and tutor in them. How do we recruit more people of color, multilingual writers, individuals with disabilities, or other minority or marginalized people to work as directors? We are aware that this is a deeply structural question about the pipeline of talent in higher education and the professional disciplines. If too few underrepresented individuals enter into graduate education, and if even fewer of them trickle into composition studies writ large or writing center studies, the field has all the fewer options. This reality means faculty and directors must engage in another level of mentorship by identifying talented tutors and encouraging them to work in the profession as administrators. It means faculty and directors must bring young tutors to national academic writing center conferences such as the International Writing Centers Association (IWCA) or the National Conference on Peer Tutoring in Writing (NCPTW) and support their emergent voices so they feel as if they have an intellectual presence in the field. It means faculty and directors must nurture tutors' questions into inquiry-based projects that can become robust research agendas. And we can't stop with the front end of the pipeline; we also must think about approaches to supporting underrepresented professionals wherever they are in the field, whatever sorts of institutions they appear in. This effort involves developing targeted mentoring networks, finding funding for start-up research projects, and developing active outreach and responses to their needs. Such responsiveness requires new thinking and practices that dovetail with a variety of institutional realities.

We urge the field to reflect on its own identity by considering the ways in which it perpetuates problems of stagnation its own scholarship criticizes. Certainly, we recognize our field is marginalized, perhaps due to this isolation we seem to embrace, and too much time has been spent wringing our collective hands about marginalization's perpetuation. It's long been clear that institutional and disciplinary dynamics play daunting roles in our professional status (Balester and McDonald 1999; Geller and Denny 2013; Ianetta et al. 2006). What does it mean to attend conferences where participants rarely mirror our wider populations? When we attend the conferences and we take notes, are we really listening to each other and finding ways to collaborate for institutional change? How are we engaging with scholarship to enable us to move beyond just *naming the problem* and creating a climate of change and hope? About issues of critique yet no engagement, bell hooks (2003) writes in *Teaching Community* that "when we only name the problem, when we stay compliant without a constructive focus on resolution, we take hope away. In this way critique can become merely an expression of profound cynicism, which then works to sustain dominator culture" (hooks 2003, xiv). In what ways do hooks's words speak to the dilemmas of our field? And how can we go beyond naming the problems our field faces in order to effectively respond to them?

Writing centers must be better about asking questions and providing solutions that push not only our units but also our whole institutions toward change. Countless institutional mission statements ask us to create civic-minded individuals, but creating such individuals involves more than bearing witness to the problems reported on the evening news. To create civic-minded individuals involves starting in the center and providing an opportunity for individuals to give voice to unsettling moments and realities they see and experience. The voices in this collection have a certain bold beauty in that they narrate moments such as these. Our contributors damn the torpedoes, fully aware of the risks associated with exposure, but regardless of vulnerability, they opt to remain seditious, not willing to keep with a practice that suggests a strict adherence to the binary of public and private because deconstructing this binary creates the opportunity to produce institutional change. Indeed, the voices we include function as a reminder of the pervious nature of place and the transformational nature of writing collaboration and instruction. Our contributors function as conduits that move the reader from the margin to the center and back again, fluidly reminding us to consider the lives, in all their manifestations, of those who enter the locale. And they likewise remind us we can be conduits for change within our institutions.

Critical race theory, feminist and queer theory, theory on disability, labor studies, and theories of language acquisition and multilingualism percolate in these essays, and these theories inform the ways in which we must speak more forcefully on campus about the ways in which our expertise and our experiences position us to advise and continue to learn from a wide variety of audiences. Instead of persisting in the role of "dumping ground" for institutional problems resulting from flawed or ill-considered policies (Boquet 2016, 00), writing centers must show institutions how we can inform policies and participate in or drive decision making. For example, when campuses design summer bridge programs for underrepresented students, writing centers can make valuable contributions. We value intensive individual and small-group tutoring. And we know how to make a summer bridge work, how to make it student friendly, and how to make it sustainable. We also have a good deal of knowledge about how and where students write and study and what's on their minds. We can teach policymakers quite a bit about student success and about students themselves. Writing centers have direct and indirect contact with faculty and curriculum. Our tutors and our own experience in the everyday work of writing centers can help faculty question their own practices and perhaps even reimagine them, assuming we can foster those connections without threatening the autonomy of our colleagues.

Just as we can create change through engaging the institutions we inhabit, we can influence the communities we participate in beyond our campuses. We need not morph into writing center missionaries who are out to colonize the world into our belief system, but we do need to think about how we can become advocates wherever we turn our attention. How do we listen to the needs of our communities as we create service-learning projects (Davis and Kramer 2016)? How do we see the everyday issues or concerns in our surrounding communities intersect with and inform our writing center work? And, as we know too well, sometimes the everyday gets disrupted: how do we listen and respond to public moments of crisis in our centers? Rarely does a month pass without a disaster, mass shooting, or some other horrifying event. What sort of public-service need can a writing center serve in moments such as these? We think of the work the writing center and others at the University of Oklahoma played in the healing after a tornado devastated a neighboring community, or of the community-based work the Salt Lake Community Writing Center has done so well (Rousculp 2014). Of course, we don't need an extraordinary event to spur outreach; sometimes outreach means just showing up and being an ally, like attending a callout event for a campus LGBTQ+ center, attending events at multicultural centers, or cosponsoring events with community-based organizations. The narratives of our collection show us the real need to embrace the communities in which we live and to learn from them to create sustainable change.

What we call upon readers and the wider writing center world to do is to hire with an eye for diversity and then think about how our staffs have the potential to represent a diverse critical mass that can foster a truly innovative learning environment. In writing centers, people of different abilities and from different races, ethnicities, genders, sexualities, classes, linguistic heritages, faiths, and disciplines come together to challenge and mentor one another as learners, tutors, and writers. And professionals in that mix need professional development through a curriculum that equips them with sufficient conceptual and theoretical frameworks to do the work of mentoring students well. We want writing centers to foster learning in a diverse environment with commitment to critical, transformative, and pragmatic teaching because this model can serve twenty-first-century higher education well. Certainly, not everyone who walks in the doors of a writing center wants a liberatory education, but everyone deserves support that both empowers them and mitigates their experiences in relation to societal, cultural, and political systems that render the institutional conditions of learning and teaching as always fraught.

We also call upon readers and the wider writing center world to commit themselves to the everyday and longitudinal labor of inquiry-based research, projects that should complement but never replace the kinds of narratives this collection offers. We recognize not everyone is supported, positioned, or interested in the generation of scholarly insight and the production of knowledge in the same way. But writing centers face considerable risk when they don't assume that nearly every phenomenon that arises in their spaces or across their institutions has an intellectual antecedent in the field's literature. Failing to understand the academic roots of our everyday labor, the teaching, mentoring, and learning that happens all around writing centers, relegates our ever-important work to the arena of service. The practice of producing opportunities for intellectual engagement and the academic circulation of conversations recognizes the deep expertise we carry with us into sessions. We engage learners in the lifelong process of writing and identifying as writers, and others can learn from our work. Such a commitment to inquiry also means members of our community of practice understand they must equip themselves for ongoing learning, whether that means discovering new theories of pedagogy for multilingual learners, developing innovative practices of assessment, or engaging with emergent lines of scholarship of which we might not be aware.

We draw to a close by underscoring the point with which we began: that the writing center extends into the world and that moments of crisis enable dialogue about the bodies that participate in writing center work. We must continue to learn from and listen to one another—to value our narratives and stories as important and necessary research. We must remember that there is no writing center without stories of the outside world that give shape to the center. We must remember that writing centers—like individual identities—are messy and in constant states of flux and development. And we must remember that we determine the dynamics of our spaces for collaborative learning and research by way of the writing center inhabitants that we shape ourselves as being through our actions and inactions. We determine whether our centers will be inclusive or exclusive and whether they'll exist as spaces in which we can find ways to talk about the range of uncomfortable realities and public controversies that too often remain "out there" and not in our centers—the controversies that give shape to twenty-first-century life and create potential for a future that offers more socially just possibilities.

AFTERWORD

Michele Eodice

In this book, *Out in the Center*, you find lots of complicated but clearly told tales of lived experience; this book works hard, really hard, right at the very busy intersection of intersectionality. I'm speaking of intersectionality in the sense that Kimberlé Williams Crenshaw (2018) imagines it—the reality that multiple ways of being and knowing come out, come together, and come to bear on the human experience. Many current academic publications include the term *intersectionality*, but far too few academic publications actually demonstrate how intersectionality possesses the power to explain what the fuck is really going on.

A cleaner definition is offered by Patricia Hill Collins and Sirma Bilge (2016):

> Intersectionality is a way of understanding and analyzing the complexity in the world, in people, and in human experiences. The events and conditions of social and political life and the self can seldom be understood as shaped by one factor. They are generally shaped by many factors in diverse mutually influencing ways. When it comes to social inequality, people's lives and the organization of power in a given society are better understood as shaped not by a single axis of social division, be it race or gender or class, but by many axes that work together and influence each other. Intersectionality as an analytic tool gives people better access to the complexity of the world and of themselves. (2)

One goal of this collection might be to introduce readers and their writing centers to an affordance, in this case intersectionality, that lifts and leverages their thinking about the person across from them. I want this collection to succeed in motivating readers to view their teaching and research through a lens essential for understanding the world.

Guess what? You don't get to use that lens unless you listen to the stories.

So, the collection includes dynamic, poignant, often cringe-worthy stories of how badly we treat each other, how alone and tired and scared many of us feel even in the midst of a writing center or a classroom, places made for learning and caring, or so we say. But does a collection

DOI: 10.7330/9781607327837.c020

like this make new knowledge? Are stories, narratives, and personal voices enough to move big ideas, such as equity and access? Do life stories count as credible academic contributions? Don't these writers realize their work is worth less when crafted out of the personal? There are those who might (still) be unconvinced that lived experience is reliable evidence of phenomena; unfortunately, many of them are in gatekeeper roles. To them we can say (and feel free to copy and paste this next part into your annual evaluation materials): to deny these voices the power they possess is an epistemic injustice (Fricker 2007; Godbee 2017). This collection is an authentic performance of epistemic justice—from the editors' conception of the collection all the way to the publisher's staff support—showing respect for these voices and answering the exigency to get these voices out into the world.

I'm queer, drink beer, get used to it.

The editors of this collection landed on *coming out* as metaphor and use the term to describe what identities, bodies, voices do when they proclaim—and because of the richness of the selections here, the stories embody intersectionality.

But with the mere mention of coming out, the closet immediately comes to mind. In this collection we witness not only old-school coming out ("Hi, I'm gay") but a kind of twenty-first-century coming out that sounds very different but is essentially performing the same act: "I want you to know who I am, finally. It may have taken me a long time to embrace all these identities, but I am tired of hiding some of them from you. In order for me to learn better, love better, and be healthier, I need to be who I am in all my glory, when I choose to." Perhaps the resilience of this idea—you come out of the closet, identity revealed—has held up as useful to describe other Others and their ways of hiding and revealing identities. Yet as much as we seem determined to come out, we also want to keep the closet. I am all for what Darnell Moore (2012) proposes when they ask: might it be possible to destroy the closet?

How might we construct, live into, a queer space imbued with the potential for self-empowerment, self-determination, and agency? A personal/political space that we are no longer forced to come out of but that is instead available for us to invite others *into*?

Come in, come out, overcome, and come over—to the writing center . . .

We are, I am, you are
by cowardice or courage
the one who find our way

back to this scene
carrying a knife, a camera
a book of myths
in which our names do not appear.
                    —Adrienne Rich "Diving Into the Wreck"

REFERENCES

Adler-Kassner, Linda. 2008. *The Activist WPA: Changing Stories about Writing and Writers.* Logan: Utah State University Press. https://doi.org/10.2307/j.ctt4cgqss.

Ahmed, Sara. 2004a. "Affective Economies." *Social Text* 22 (2[79]): 117–139. https://doi.org/10.1215/01642472-22-2_79-117.

Ahmed, Sara. 2004b. *The Cultural Politics of Emotion.* New York: Routledge.

Alexander, Jonathan. 2008. *Literacy, Sexuality, Pedagogy: Theory and Practice for Composition Studies.* Logan: Utah State University Press.

Alexander, Jonathan, and David Wallace. 2009. "The Queer Turn in Composition Studies: Reviewing and Assessing an Emerging Scholarship." *College Composition and Communication* 61 (1): 300–320.

Alexander, Michelle. 2012. *The New Jim Crow: Mass Incarceration in the Age of Colorblindness.* New York: New Press.

Anderson, Benedict. 1991. *Imagined Communities: Reflections on the Origin and Spread of Nationalism.* Rev. ed. New York: Verso.

Anzaldúa, Gloria. 2007. "How to Tame a Wild Tongue." In *Borderlands/La Frontera: The New Mestiza*, 3rd ed., 75–86. San Francisco, CA: Ann Lute Books.

Babcock, Rebecca Day. 2015. "Disabilities in the Writing Center." *Praxis: A Writing Center Journal* 13 (1): 38–49.

Babcock, Rebecca Day, and Terese Thonus. 2012. *Researching the Writing Center: Towards an Evidence-Based Practice.* New York: Peter Lang. https://doi.org/10.3726/978-1-4539-0869-3.

Balester, Valerie M., and James McDonald. 2001. "A View of Status and Working Conditions: Relations between Writing Program and Writing Center Directors." *WPA: Writing Program Administration* 24 (3): 59–82.

Bartholomae, David. 1986. "Inventing the University." *Journal of Basic Writing* 5 (1): 4–23.

Bawarshi, Anis, and Stephanie Pelkowski. 1999. "Postcolonialism and the Idea of a Writing Center." *Writing Center Journal* 19 (2): 41–59.

Ben-Moshe, Liat, Anthony J. Nocella II, and A. J. Withers. 2013. "Queer-Cripping Anarchism: Intersections and Reflections on Anarchism, Queer-ness, and Dis-Ability." In *Queering Anarchism: Essays on Gender, Power, and Desire*, edited by C. B. Daring, J. Rogue, Deric Shannon, and Abbey Volcano, 207–20. Oakland, CA: AK Press.

Bhabha, Homi K. 2004 (1994). *The Location of Culture.* London: Routledge.

Birnbaum, Lisa. 1995. "Toward a Gender-Balanced Staff in the Writing Center." *Writing Lab Newsletter* 19 (8): 6–8.

Black, Laurel Johnson. 1998. *Between Talk and Teaching: Reconsidering the Writing Conference.* Logan: Utah State University Press. https://doi.org/10.2307/j.ctt46nwx4.

Bloom, Lynn Z. 1996. "Freshman Composition as a Middle-Class Enterprise." *College English* 58 (6): 654–75. https://doi.org/10.2307/378392.

Bly, Robert. 2004. *Iron John: A Book About Men.* Cambridge: Da Capo.

Boquet, Elizabeth H. 2002. *Noise from the Writing Center.* Logan: Utah State University Press.

Boquet, Elizabeth H. 2004. "Gator Bait: On Teaching, Writing, and Growing Up on the Bayou." *Writing on the Edge* 15 (1): 61–76.

Boquet, Elizabeth H. 2016. *Nowhere Near the Line: Pain and Possibility in Teaching and Writing.* Logan: Utah State University Press. https://doi.org/10.7330/9781607325765.

DOI: 10.7330/9781607327837.c021

Borkowski, David. 2004. "'Not Too Late to Take the Sanitation Test': Notes of a Non-Gifted Academic from the Working Class." *College Composition and Communication* 56 (1): 94–123. https://doi.org/10.2307/4140682.

Bourdieu, Pierre. 1986. "The Forms of Capital." In *Handbook of Theory and Research for the Sociology of Education,* edited by John G. Richardson, 241–58. New York: Greenwood.

Bousquet, Marc. 2003. "The Rhetoric of 'Job Market' and the Reality of the Academic Labor System." *College English* 66 (2): 207–28. https://doi.org/10.2307/3594266.

Bousquet, Marc. 2008. *How the University Works: Education and the Low-Wage Nation.* New York: New York University Press.

Brabazon, Tara. 2015. *Enabling University Impairment, (Dis)ability, and Social Justice in Higher Education.* Cham, Switzerland: Springer International.

Brandt, Deborah, Ellen Cushman, Anne Ruggles Gere, Anne Herrington, Richard E. Miller, Victor Villanueva, Min-Zhan Lu, and Gesa Kirsch. 2001. "The Politics of the Personal: Storying Our Lives against the Grain." *College English* 64 (1): 41–62. https://doi.org/10.2307/1350109.

Brodkey, Linda. 1989. "On the Subjects of Class and Gender in 'The Literacy Letters.'" *College English* 51 (2): 125–41. https://doi.org/10.2307/377422.

Bruce, Shanti, and Ben Rafoth. 2009. *ESL Writers: A Guide for Writing Center Tutors.* 2nd ed. Portsmouth, NH: Boynton/Cook.

Bruce, Shanti, and Ben Rafoth, eds. 2016. *Tutoring Second Language Writers.* Logan: Utah State University Press. https://doi.org/10.7330/9781607324140.

Butler, Judith. 1988. "Performance Acts and Gender Constitution: An Essay in Phenomenology and Feminist Theory." *Theatre Journal* 40 (4): 519–31. https://doi.org/10.2307/3207893.

Butler, Judith. 1990a. *Gender Trouble: Feminism and the Subversion of Identity.* New York: Routledge.

Butler, Judith. 1990b. "Performative Acts and Gender Constitution: An Essay in Phenomenology and Feminist Theory." In *Performing Feminisms: Feminist Critical Theory and Theatre,* edited by Sue-Ellen Case, 270–82. Baltimore, MD: Johns Hopkins University Press.

Camangian, Patrick. 2010. "Starting with Self: Teaching Autoethnography to Foster Critically Caring Literacies." *Research in the Teaching of English* 45 (2): 179–204.

Canagarajah, A. Suresh. 2006. "The Place of World Englishes in Composition: Pluralization Continued." *College Composition and Communication* 57 (4): 586–619.

Carino, Peter. 2003. "Power and Authority in Peer Tutoring." In *The Center Will Hold: Critical Perspectives on Writing Center Scholarship,* edited by Michael A. Pemberton and Joyce Kinkead, 96–113. Logan: Utah State University Press. https://doi.org/10.2307/j.ctt46nxnq.9.

Carino, Peter. 2011. "Power and Authority in Peer Tutoring." In *The St. Martin's Sourcebook for Writing Tutors,* 4th ed., edited by Christina Murphy and Steve Sherwood, 112–27. Boston, MA: Bedford/St. Martin's.

Chase, Susan E. 2005. "Narrative Inquiry: Multiple Lenses, Approaches, and Voices." In *The Sage Handbook of Qualitative Research,* 3rd ed., edited by Norman K. Denzin and Yvonna S. Lincoln, 651–79. Thousand Oaks, CA: SAGE.

Clance, Pauline Rose, and Suzanne A. Imes. 1978. "The Imposter Phenomenon in High Achieving Women: Dynamics and Therapeutic Intervention." *Psychotherapy* 15 (3): 241–47. https://doi.org/10.1037/h0086006.

Coates, Ta-Nehisi. 2015. *Between the World and Me.* New York: Spiegel & Grau.

Collins, Patricia Hill, and Sirma Bilge. 2016. *Intersectionality (Key Concepts).* Cambridge: Polity.

Colombo, Gary, Robert Cullen, and Bonnie Lisle. 1989. *Rereading America: Cultural Contexts for Critical Thinking.* Boston, MA: Bedford/St. Martin's.

Condon, Frankie. 2012. *I Hope I Join the Band: Narrative, Affiliation, and Antiracist Rhetoric.* Logan: Utah State University Press. https://doi.org/10.2307/j.ctt4cgk2v.

Condon, Frankie. 2017. "Writing in the Margins: Language, Labor, and Class." Keynote address, annual conference of the Northeast Writing Centers Association (NEWCA), Pleasantville, NY, April 1–2.

Conference on College Composition and Communication (CCCC). 2003. "Students' Right to Their Own Language." Special issue, *College Composition and Communication*, 25 (Fall). http://www.ncte.org/library/NCTEFiles/Groups/CCCC/NewSRTOL.pdf.

Connell, R. W. 1987. *Gender and Power: Society, the Person, and Sexual Politics*. Stanford, CA: Stanford University Press.

Connell, R. W. 1995. *Masculinities*. Cambridge, UK: Polity.

Connors, Robert J. 1996. "Teaching and Learning as a Man." *College English* 58 (2): 137–57. https://doi.org/10.2307/378461.

Corder, Jim W. 1985. "Argument as Emergence, Rhetoric as Love." *Rhetoric Review* 4 (1): 16–32. https://doi.org/10.1080/07350198509359100.

Cose, Ellis. 2003. *The Envy of the World: On Being a Black Man in America*. New York: Washington Square.

Cox, Michelle, and Paul Kei Matsuda. 2011. "Reading an ESL Writer's Text." *Studies in Self-Access Learning Journal* 2 (1): 4–14.

Crenshaw, Kimberlé Williams. 2018. *On Intersectionality: Essential Writings*. New York: New Press.

Crowley, Sharon. 2006. *Toward a Civil Discourse: Rhetoric and Fundamentalism*. Pittsburgh, PA: University of Pittsburgh Press. https://doi.org/10.2307/j.ctt5hjng7.

Cunningham, David S. 1991. "Theology as Rhetoric." *Theological Studies* 52 (3): 407–30. https://doi.org/10.1177/004056399105200301.

de Beauvoir, Simone. 2011. *The Second Sex*. Translated by Constance Borde and Sheila Malovany-Chevallier. New York: Vintage Books.

Denhart, Hazel. 2008. "Deconstructing Barriers: Perceptions of Students Labeled with Learning Disabilities in Higher Education." *Journal of Learning Disabilities* 41 (6): 483–97. https://doi.org/10.1177/0022219408321151.

Denny, Harry C. 2010. *Facing the Center: Toward an Identity Politics of One-to-One Mentoring*. Logan: Utah State University Press. https://doi.org/10.2307/j.ctt4cgqnv.

Denny, Harry C. 2011 (2005). "Queering the Writing Center." *Writing Center Journal* 25 (2): 39–62. Reprint. In *The St. Martin's Sourcebook for Writing Tutors*, 4th ed., edited by Christina Murphy and Steve Sherwood, 263–84. Boston, MA: Bedford/St. Martin's.

Dewey, John. 1934. "Individual Psychology and Education." *Philosopher* 12 (1): 1–6. http://www.the-philosopher.co.uk/2016/08/individual-psychology-and-education-1934.html.

Dickinson College. n.d. "The Norman M. Eberly Multilingual Writing Center." Accessed June 19, 2007. http://www.dickinson.edu/info/20158/writing_program/2829/the_norman_m_eberly_multilingual_writing_center.

Disney, Tim, dir. 2009. *American Violet*. Chatsworth, CA: Image Entertainment. DVD.

Driscoll, Dana Lynn, and Sherry Wynn Perdue. 2012. "Theory, Lore, and More: An Analysis of RAD Research in *The Writing Center Journal*, 1980–2009." *Writing Center Journal* 32 (2): 11–39.

DuBois, W. E. B. 1986. "Of The Wings of Atalanta." In *Dubois: Writings*, edited by Nathan Huggins, 415–23. New York: Literary Classics of the United States.

DuBois, W. E. B. 1995. "The Negro College." In *W. E. B. Dubois: A Reader*, edited by David L. Lewis, 68–75. New York: Henry Holt.

Ellis, Lindsay. 2013. "An Adjunct's Death Becomes a Rallying Cry for Many in Academe." *Chronicle of Higher Education*, September 19. http://chronicle.com/article/An-Adjuncts-Death-Becomes-a/141709/.

Eodice, Michele, Anne Ellen Geller, and Neal Lerner. 2016. *The Meaningful Writing Project: Learning, Teaching, and Writing in Higher Education*. Logan: Utah State University Press.

Esters, Jason. 2011. "On the Edges: Black Maleness, Degrees of Racism, and Community on the Boundaries of the Writing Center." In *Writing Centers and the New Racism: A*

Call for Sustainable Dialogue and Change, edited by Laura Greenfield and Karen Rowan, 290–99. Logan: Utah State University Press. https://doi.org/10.2307/j.ctt4cgk6s.18.

Faludi, Susan. 2000. *Stiffed: The Betrayal of the American Man*. New York: Harper Perennial. First published 1999 by W. Morrow.

Ferris, Dana R. 2003. *Response to Student Writing: Implications for Second Language Students*. Mahwah, NJ: Lawrence Erlbaum.

Ferris, Dana R., and John S. Hedgcock. 1998. *Teaching ESL Composition: Purpose, Process, and Practice*. Mahwah, NJ: Lawrence Erlbaum.

Fish, Stanley. 2003. "Save the World on Your Own Time." *Chronicle of Higher Education*, January 23. https://www.chronicle.com/article/Save-the-World-on-Your-Own/45335.

FitzGerald, William. 2012. *Spiritual Modalities: Prayer as Rhetoric and Performance*. University Park: Pennsylvania State University Press.

Foss, Sonja K., and Cindy L. Griffin. 1995. "Beyond Persuasion: A Proposal for an Invitational Rhetoric." *Communication Monographs* 62 (1): 2–18. https://doi.org/10.1080/03637759509376345.

Foucault, Michel. 2007. *Discipline and Punish: The Birth of the Prison*. Translated by Alan Sheridan. New York: Vintage Books. https://doi.org/10.1215/9780822390169-018.

Fox, Tom. 1999. *Defending Access: A Critique of Standards in Higher Education*. Portsmouth, NH: Heinemann.

Freire, Paulo. 1993. *Pedagogy of the Oppressed*. Anniversary ed. Translated by Myra Bergman. New York. Continuum.

Fricker, Miranda. 2017. *Epistemic Injustice: Power and the Ethics of Knowing*. Oxford: Oxford University Press.

Gee, James Paul. 2001. "Literacy, Discourses and Linguistics: Introduction *and* What Is Literacy?" In *Literacy: A Critical Sourcebook*, edited by Ellen Cushman, Eugene R. Kintgen, Barry M. Kroll, and Mike Rose, 525–44. Boston, MA: Bedford/St. Martin's.

Geller, Anne Ellen, and Harry Denny. 2013. "Of Ladybugs, Low Status, and Loving the Job: Writing Center Professionals Navigating Their Careers." *Writing Center Journal* 33 (1): 96–129.

Geller, Anne Ellen, Michele Eodice, Frankie Condon, Meg Carroll, and Elizabeth H. Boquet. 2007. *The Everyday Writing Center: A Community of Practice*. Logan: Utah State University Press. https://doi.org/10.2307/j.ctt4cgmkj.

Gilyard, Keith. 1991. *Voices of the Self: A Study of Language Competence*. Detroit, MI: Wayne State University Press.

Giroux, Henry A. 1989. "Schooling as a Form of Cultural Politics: Toward a Pedagogy of and for Difference." In *Critical Pedagogy, the State and Cultural Struggle*, edited by Henry A. Giroux and Peter L. McLaren, 125–51. New York: SUNY Press.

Giroux, Henry A. 1993. "Living Dangerously: Identity Politics and the New Cultural Racism: Towards a Critical Pedagogy of Representation." *Cultural Studies* 7 (1): 1–28. https://doi.org/10.1080/09502389300490021.

Glenn, Cheryl, and Andrea A. Lunsford, eds. 2014. *Landmark Essays on Rhetoric and Feminism: 1973–2000*. London: Taylor & Francis.

Glenn, Cheryl, and Krista Ratcliffe, eds. 2011. *Silence and Listening as Rhetorical Arts*. Carbondale: Southern Illinois University Press.

Godbee, Beth. 2017. "Writing Up: How Assertions of Epistemic Rights Counter Epistemic Injustice." *College English* 79 (6): 593–618.

Goodburn, Amy. 1998. "It's a Question of Faith: Discourses of Fundamentalism and Critical Pedagogy in the Writing Classroom." *Journal of Advanced Composition* 18 (2): 333–53.

Greenfield, Laura, and Karen Rowan. 2011a. "The 'Standard English' Fairy Tale: A Rhetorical Analysis of Racist Pedagogies and Commonplace Assumptions about Language Diversity." In *Writing Centers and the New Racism: A Call for Sustainable Dialogue and Change*, edited by Laura Greenfield and Karen Rowan, 33–60. Logan: Utah State University Press. https://doi.org/10.2307/j.ctt4cgk6s.6.

Greenfield, Laura, and Karen Rowan, eds. 2011b. *Writing Centers and the New Racism: A Call for Sustainable Dialogue and Change*. Logan: Utah State University Press. https://doi .org/10.2307/j.ctt4cgk6s.

Grimm, Nancy Maloney. 1999. *Good Intentions: Writing Center Work for Postmodern Times*. Portsmouth, NH: Boynton/Cook-Heinemann.

Grimm, Nancy M. 2006. "Myth Busting: A Proposal for the Public Work of Writing Centers in Fast Capital Times." Paper presented at the National Conference on Writing Centers as Public Space, University of Illinois at Chicago, September 30, 2006.

Grimm, Nancy M. 2011. "Retheorizing Writing Center Work to Transform a System of Advantage Based on Race." In *Writing Centers and the New Racism: A Call for Sustainable Dialogue and Change*, edited by Laura Greenfield and Karen Rowan, 75–100. Logan: Utah State University Press. https://doi.org/10.2307/j.ctt4cgk6s.8.

Grutsch McKinney, Jackie. 2013. *Peripheral Visions for Writing Centers*. Logan: Utah State University Press. https://doi.org/10.2307/j.ctt4cgk97.

Grutsch McKinney, Jackie. 2016. *Strategies for Writing Center Research*. Anderson, SC: Parlor.

Harklau, Linda, Kay M. Losey, and Meryl Siegal, eds. 1999. *Generation 1.5 Meets College Composition: Issues in the Teaching of Writing to U.S.-Educated Learners of ESL*. Mahwah, NJ: Lawrence Erlbaum.

Harris, Muriel, and Tony Silva. 1993. "Tutoring ESL Students: Issues and Options." *College Composition and Communication* 44 (4): 525–37. https://doi.org/10.2307/358388.

Harrison, Faye V. 1995. "The Persistent Power of 'Race' in the Cultural and Political Economy of Racism." *Annual Review of Anthropology* 24 (1): 47–74. https://doi.org/10 .1146/annurev.an.24.100195.000403.

Hoggart, Richard. 1998. *The Uses of Literacy*. Edison, NJ: Transaction.

Hohn, Donovan. 1999. "'The Me Experience': Composing as a Man." In *Working with Student Writers: Essays on Tutoring and Teaching*, edited by Leonard A. Podis and JoAnne M. Podis, 285–99. New York: Peter Lang.

hooks, bell. 1994. *Teaching to Transgress: Education as the Practice of Freedom*. New York: Routledge.

hooks, bell. 2000. *Feminism Is for Everybody: Passionate Politics*. Cambridge, MA: South End.

hooks, bell. 2003. *Teaching Community: A Pedagogy of Hope*. New York: Routledge.

Horner, Bruce, Min-Zhan Lu, Jacqueline Jones Royster, and John Trimbur. 2011. "Language Difference in Writing: Toward a Translingual Approach." *College English* 73 (3): 303–21.

Hunzer, Kathleen M. 1997. "Misperceptions of Gender in the Writing Center: Stereotyping and the Facilitative Tutor." *Writing Lab Newsletter* 22 (2): 6–10. https://wlnjournal.org/ archives/v22/22-2.pdf.

Hutchinson, Earl Ofari. 1994. *The Assassination of the Black Male Image*. Los Angeles, CA: Middle Passage.

Ianetta, Melissa, Linda Bergmann, Laurent Fitzgerald, Carol Peterson Haviland, Lisa Lebduska, and Mary Wislocki. 2006. "Polylog: Are writing Center Directors Writing Program Administrators?" *Composition Studies* 34 (2): 11–42.

International Writing Centers Association (IWCA). 2014. "IWCA Research Grant Winners Announced." http://writingcenters.org/2014/08/iwca-research-grant-winners -announced-2/.

Isaacs, Emily, and Melinda Knight. 2014. "A Bird's Eye View of Writing Centers: Institutional Infrastructure, Scope and Programmatic Issues, Reported Practices." *WPA: Writing Program Administration* 37 (2): 36–67. http://www.wpacouncil.org/archives/37 n2/37n2isaacs-knight.pdf.

Jackson, Cassandra. 2011. *Violence, Visual Culture, and the Black Male Body*. New York: Routledge.

Jacoby, Jay. 1983. "Shall We Talk to Them in 'English': The Contributions of a Sociolinguist to Training Writing Center Personnel." *Writing Center Journal* 4 (1): 1–14.

Jarratt, Susan C. 2000. "Feminist Pedagogy." In *A Guide to Composition Pedagogies*, edited by Gary Tate, Amy Rupiper, and Kurt Schick, 113–31. New York: Oxford University Press.

Johnson, Lamar, and Nathaniel Bryan. 2017. "Using Our Voices, Losing Our Bodies: Michael Brown, Trayvon Martin, and the Spirit Murders of Black Male Professors in the Academy." *Race, Ethnicity and Education* 20 (2): 163–77. https://doi.org/10.1080/13613324.2016.1248831.

Jones, Charisse, and Kumea Shorter-Gooden. 2003. *Shifting: The Double Lives of Black Women in America*. New York: Harper Perennial.

Jones, Stephanie. 2006. "Language with an Attitude: White Girls Performing Class." *Language Arts* 84 (2): 114–24.

Justice, Laura M. 2006. "Evidence-Based Practice, Response to Intervention, and the Prevention of Reading Difficulties." *Language, Speech, and Hearing Services in Schools* 37 (4): 284–97. https://doi.org/10.1044/0161-1461(2006/033).

Kaletka, Zak. 2017. "Putting Writing at the Center of Inclusivity." University of Washington Tacoma, News & Information. https://www.tacoma.uw.edu/news/article/putting-writing-center-inclusivity.

Katsiyannis, Antonis, Dalun Zhang, Leena Landmark, and Anne Reber. 2009. "Postsecondary Education for Individuals with Disabilities: Legal and Practice Considerations." *Journal of Disability Policy Studies* 20 (1): 35–45. https://doi.org/10.1177/1044207308324896.

Kennell, Vicki R., and Beth A. Towle. 2016. "Review of *Tutoring Second Language Writers*, by Shanti Bruce and Ben Rafoth." *Writing Center Journal* 35 (3): 227–30. http://www.jstor.org/stable/43965695.

Kimmel, Michael S. 2008. *Guyland: The Perilous World Where Boys Become Men*. New York: HarperCollins.

Ladson-Billings, Gloria. 1995. "Toward a Theory of Culturally Relevant Pedagogy." *American Education Research Association* 32 (3): 465–91. https://doi.org/10.3102/00028312032003465.

Ladson-Billings, Gloria. 1999. "Preparing Teachers for Diverse Student Populations: A Critical Race Theory Perspective." *Review of Research in Education* 24 (1): 211–47. https://doi.org/10.3102/0091732X024001211.

Land, Robert E. Jr., and Catherine Whitley. 2006. "Evaluating Second-Language Essays in Regular Composition Classes: Toward a Pluralistic U.S. Rhetoric." In *Second Language Writing in the Composition Classroom: A Critical Sourcebook*, edited by Paul Kei Matsuda, Michelle Cox, Jay Jordan, and Christina Ortmeier-Hooper, 324–32. New York: Bedford/St. Martin's.

Langellier, Kristin M. 1989. "Personal Narratives: Perspectives on Theory and Research." *Text and Performance Quarterly* 9 (4): 243–76. https://doi.org/10.1080/10462938909365938.

Langellier, Kristin M. 1999. "Personal Narrative, Performance, Performativity: Two or Three Things I Know for Sure." *Text and Performance Quarterly* 19 (2): 125–44. https://doi.org/10.1080/10462939909366255.

LeCourt, Donna. 2004. *Identity Matters: Schooling the Student Body in Academic Discourse*. Albany: SUNY Press.

LeCourt, Donna. 2006. "Performing Working-Class Identity in Composition: Toward a Pedagogy of Textual Practice." *College English* 69 (1): 30–51. https://doi.org/10.2307/25472187.

LeCourt, Donna, and Anna Rita Napoleone. 2011. "Teachers with(out) Class: Transgressing Academic Social Space through Working-Class Performances." *Pedagogy* 11 (1): 81–108. https://doi.org/10.1215/15314200-2010-018.

Legg, Angela M., and Janie H. Wilson. 2013. "Instructor Touch Enhanced College Students' Evaluations." *Social Psychology of Education* 16 (2): 317–27. https://doi.org/10.1007/s11218-012-9207-1.

Leki, Ilona. 1992. *Understanding ESL Writers: A Guide for Teachers*. Portsmouth, NH: Boynton/Cook-Heinemann.

Lerner, Neal. 1997. "Counting Beans and Making Beans Count." *Writing Lab Newsletter* 22 (1): 1–4. https://www.wlnjournal.org/archives/v22/22-1.pdf.

Lerner, Neal. 2001. "Choosing Beans Wisely." *Writing Lab Newsletter* 26 (1): 1–5. https://www.wlnjournal.org/archives/v26/26.1.pdf.

Liggett, Sarah, Kerri Jordan, and Steve Price. 2011. "Mapping Knowledge-Making in Writing Center Research: A Taxonomy of Methodologies." *Writing Center Journal* 31 (2): 50–88.

Lightfoot, Jonathan. 2010. "Classroom 'Race' Talk." *Race, Gender, & Class* 17 (1/2): 148–53.

Lindholm, Jeannette M. 2000. "Listening, Learning, and the Language of Faith." In *The Academy and the Possibility of Belief: Essays on Intellectual and Spiritual Life*, edited by Mary Louise Buley-Meissner, Mary McCaslin Thompson, and Elizabeth Bachrach Tan, 55–67. Cresskill, NJ: Hampton.

Lindquist, Julie. 1999. "Class Ethos and the Politics of Inquiry: What the Barroom Can Teach Us about the Classroom." *College Composition and Communication* 51 (2): 225–47. https://doi.org/10.2307/359040.

Lindquist, Julie. 2002. *A Place to Stand: Politics and Persuasion in a Working-Class Bar.* Oxford: Oxford University Press.

Lindquist, Julie. 2004. "Class Affects, Classroom Affectations: Working through the Paradox of Strategic Empathy." *College English* 67 (2): 187–209. https://doi.org/10.2307/4140717.

Liu, Eric. 1999. *The Accidental Asian: Notes of a Native Speaker.* New York: Random House.

Lock, Robin H., and Carol A. Layton. 2001. "Succeeding in Postsecondary Ed through Self-Advocacy." *Teaching Exceptional Children* 34 (2): 66–71. https://doi.org/10.1177/004005990103400210.

Logan, Julie. 2009. "Dyslexic Entrepreneurs: The Incidence; Their Coping Strategies and Their Business Skills." *Dyslexia* 15 (4): 328–46. https://doi.org/10.1002/dys.388.

Lorde, Audre. 1997. "The Uses of Anger." *Women's Studies Quarterly* 25 (1/2): 278–85.

Lundman, Susan. n.d. "How to Make Vegetarian Chili." LEAFtv. Accessed June 20, 2017. https://www.leaf.tv/articles/how-to-make-vegetarian-chili/.

Lunsford, Andrea. 1991. "Collaboration, Control, and the Idea of a Writing Center." *Writing Center Journal* 12 (1): 3–10.

Maalouf, Amin. 2010. *In the Name of Identity: Violence and the Need to Belong.* Translated by Barbara Bray. New York: Penguin Books.

Mack, Nancy. 2006. "Ethical Representation of Working-Class Lives: Multiple Genres, Voices, and Identities." *Pedagogy* 6 (1): 53–78. https://doi.org/10.1215/15314200-6-1-53.

Malcolm X. 1940. *The Autobiography of Malcolm X.* Mattituck, NY: Aeonian Press.

Marshak, Laura, Todd Van Wieren, Dianne Ferrell, Lindsay Swiss, and Catherine Dugan. 2010. "Exploring Barriers to College Student Use of Disability Services and Accommodations." *Journal of Postsecondary Education and Disability* 22 (3): 151–65.

Martinez, Aja Y. 2016. "A Plea for Critical Race Theory Counterstory: Stock Story vs. Counterstory Dialogues Concerning Alejandra's 'Fit' in the Academy." In *Performing Antiracist Pedagogy in Rhetoric, Writing, and Communication*, edited by Frankie Condon and Vershawn Ashanti Young, 65–85. Fort Collins, CO: WAC Clearinghouse; Boulder: University Press of Colorado.

Marzluf, Phillip P. 2011. "Religion in US Writing Classes: Challenging the Conflict Narrative." *Journal of Writing Research* 2 (3): 265–97. https://doi.org/10.17239/jowr-2011.02.03.1.

Matsuda, Paul Kei. 1999. "Composition Studies and ESL Writing: A Disciplinary Division of Labor." *College Composition and Communication* 50 (4): 699–721. https://doi.org/10.2307/358488.

Matsuda, Paul Kei, Christina Ortmeier-Hooper, and Xiaoye You, eds. 2006. *The Politics of Second Language Writing: Into the Promised Land.* West Lafayette, IN: Parlor.

May, Alison L., and C. Addison Stone. 2010. "Stereotypes of Individuals with Learning Disabilities: Views of College Students with and without Learning Disabilities." *Journal of Learning Disabilities* 43 (6): 483–99. https://doi.org/10.1177/0022219409355483.

McCabe, Samantha. 2016. "UBC Writing Centre to Shut Down Tutorial Services." *The Ubyssey*, March 14. https://ubyssey.ca/news/ubc-writing-centre-to-shut-down-tutorial-services.

Miller, Susan. 1991. "The Feminization of Composition." In *The Politics of Writing Instruction: Postsecondary*, edited by Richard H. Bullock, John Trimbur, and Charles I. Schuster, 39–53. Portsmouth, NH: Boynton/Cook.

Mishler, Elliot G. 1995. "Models of Narrative Analysis: A Typology." *Journal of Narrative and Life History* 5 (2): 87–123. https://doi.org/10.1075/jnlh.5.2.01mod.

Moore, Darnell. 2012. "Coming Out or Inviting In?: Part I." thefeministwire. http://www.thefeministwire.com/2012/07/coming-out-or-inviting-in-reframing-disclosure-paradigms-part-i/.

Murphy, Christina, and Steve Sherwood, eds. 2011. *St. Martin's Sourcebook for Writing Tutors.* 4th ed. Boston, MA: Bedford/St. Martin's.

Murray, Christopher, Carol T. Wren, and Christopher Keys. 2008. "University Faculty Perceptions of Students with Learning Disabilities: Correlates and Group Differences." *Learning Disability Quarterly* 31 (3): 95–113.

National Center for Education Statistics (NCES). 2016. "Race/Ethnicity of College Faculty." Fast Facts. https://nces.ed.gov/fastfacts/display.asp?id=61.

National Council of Teachers of English. 1974. *Resolution on the Students' Right to Their Own Language.* http://www.ncte.org/library/NCTEFiles/Groups/CCCC/NewSRTOL.pdf.

Nawyn, Stephanie J., and Linda Gjokaj. 2014. "The Magnifying Effect of Privilege: Earnings Inequalities at the Intersection of Gender, Race, and Nativity." *Feminist Formations* 26 (2): 85–106. https://doi.org/10.1353/ff.2014.0015.

Naydan, Liliana M. 2016. *Rhetorics of Religion in American Fiction: Faith, Fundamentalism, and Fanaticism in the Age of Terror.* Lewisburg, PA: Bucknell University Press.

Neuleib, Janice Witherspoon, and Maurice A. Scharton. 1994. "Writing Others, Writing Ourselves: Ethnography and the Writing Center." In *Intersections: Theory-Practice in the Writing Center*, edited by Joan A. Mullin and Ray Wallace, 54–67. Urbana, IL: NCTE.

Newman, Lynn, Mary Wagner, Anne-Marie Knokey, Camille Marder, Katherine Nagle, Debra Shaver, Xin Wei, Renee Cameto, Elidia Contreras, Kate Ferguson, Sarah Green, and Meredith Schwarting. 2011. *The Post-High School Outcomes of Young Adults with Disabilities up to 8 Years After High School: A Report from the National Longitudinal Transition Study-2 (NLTS2).* Menlo Park, CA: SRI International.

Nordstrom, Georganne. 2015. "Practitioner Inquiry: Articulating a Model for RAD Research in the Writing Center." *Writing Center Journal* 35 (1): 87–116.

Okawa, Gail Y., Thomas Fox, Lucy J. Y. Chang, Shana R. Windsor, Frank Bella Chevez Jr., and Hayes LaGuan. 1991. "Multi-Cultural Voices: Peer Tutoring and Critical Reflection in the Writing Center." *Writing Center Journal* 12 (1): 11–34.

Olson, Bobbi. 2013. "Rethinking Our Work with Multilingual Writers: The Ethics and Responsibility of Language Teaching in the Writing Center." *Praxis: A Writing Center Journal* 10 (2): 1–6.

Olson, Gary, and Evelyn Ashton-Jones. 1995. "Writing Center Directors: The Search for Professional Status." In *Landmark Essays on Writing Centers*, edited by Christina Murphy and Joe Law, 47–55. Davis, CA: Hermagoras.

Pamuk, Orhan. 2007. "My First Passport." *New Yorker*, April 16. https://www.questia.com/magazine/1P3-1255473711/my-first-passport-personal-history.

Parker, Courtney Bailey. 2014. "The Spiritual Connection: Honoring Faith Traditions and Polishing 'Spiritual Literacies' in the Writing Conference at Faith-Based Institutions." *Praxis: A Writing Center Journal* 11 (2): 1–7.

Parker, David R., Stan F. Shaw, and Joan M. McGuire. 2003. "Program Evaluation for Postsecondary Disability Services." *Journal of Developmental Education* 27 (1): 2–10.

Parks, Stephen. 2000. *Class Politics: The Movement for the Students' Right to Their Own Languages*. Urbana, IL: NCTE.

Peckham, Irvin. 2010. *Going North, Thinking West: The Intersections of Social Class, Critical Thinking, and Politicized Writing Instruction*. Logan: Utah State University Press. https://doi.org/10.2307/j.ctt4cgpx8.

Peña, Edlyn Vallejo. 2014. "Marginalization of Published Scholarship on Students with Disabilities in Higher Education Journals." *Journal of College Student Development* 55 (1): 30–40. https://doi.org/10.1353/csd.2014.0006.

Perkins, Priscilla. 2001. "'A Radical Conversion of the Mind': Fundamentalism, Hermeneutics, and the Metanoic Classroom." *College English* 63 (5): 585–611. https://doi.org/10.2307/379046.

Peterson, Carla L. 2001. "Forward: Eccentric Bodies." In *Recovering the Black Female Body: Self-Representations by African American Women*, edited by Michael Bennett and Vanessa D. Dickerson, ix–xvi. New Brunswick, NJ: Rutgers University Press.

Poirier, Gregory. 1997. *Rosewood*. Directed by John Singleton. Burbank, CA: Warner Brothers. DVD.

Pratt, Mary Louise. 1991. "Arts of the Contact Zone." *Profession*:33–40.

Purdue OWL. Research. "Writing Centers Research Project: Raw Data from 2014–2015 Survey." Accessed June 21, 2017. https://owl.english.purdue.edu/research/survey.

Robyn Reaburn. 2016. "What Is the Purpose of Education." In *What Is Next in Educational Research?*, edited by Si Fan and Jill Fielding-Wells, 277–84. Rotterdam: Sense Publishers.

Rafoth, Ben. 2015. *Multilingual Writers and Writing Centers*. Logan: Utah State University Press. https://doi.org/10.7330/9780874219647.

Rich, Adrienne. 1972. "When We Dead Awaken: Writing as Re-Vision." *College English* 34 (1): 18–30. https://doi.org/10.2307/375215.

Rich, Adrienne. 1975. "The Burning of Paper Instead of Children." In *Adrienne Rich's Poetry*, edited by Barbara Charlesworth Gelpi and Albert Gelpi, 50. New York: W. W. Norton.

Rich, Adrienne. 1977. "Women and Honor: Some Notes on Lying." *Heresies: A Feminist Magazine of Arts and Politics* 1 (1): 23–26. http://heresiesfilmproject.org/wp-content/uploads/2011/09/heresies1.pdf.

Rich, Adrienne. 1994. "Diving into the Wreck." In *Diving into the Wreck: Poems, 1971–1972*, 52–55. New York: W. W. Norton.

Rich, Laura. 2003. "When Theologies Conflict: Reflections on Role Issues in a Christian Writing Center." *Writing Lab Newsletter* 28 (4): 10–11. https://www.wlnjournal.org/archives/v28/28.4.pdf.

Ridley, John, and Solomon Northup. 2013. *12 Years a Slave. Directed by Steve McQueen*. Los Angeles: Twentieth Century Fox. DVD.

Rodriguez, Richard. 1981. *Hunger of Memory: The Education of Richard Rodriguez, An Autobiography*. Boston, MA: D. R. Godine; New York: Dial.

Rose, Mike. 2005. *Lives on the Boundary: A Moving Account of the Struggles and Achievements of America's Educationally Underprepared*. New York: Penguin Books.

Rosin, Hanna. 2012. *The End of Men and the Rise of Women*. New York: Riverhead Books.

Royster, Jacqueline Jones. 1996. "When the First Voice You Hear Is Not Your Own." *College Composition and Communication* 47 (1): 29–40. https://doi.org/10.2307/358272.

Royster, Jacqueline Jones, and Gesa Kirsch. 2012. *Feminist Rhetorical Practices: New Horizons for Rhetoric, Composition, and Literacy Studies*. Carbondale: Southern Illinois University Press.

R-Word: Spread the Word to End the Word. 2009. "Resources." https://www.r-word.org/r-word-resources.aspx.

Ryan, Holly, and Danielle Kane. 2015. "Evaluating the Effectiveness of Writing Center Classroom Visits: An Evidence-Based Approach." *Writing Center Journal* 34 (2): 145–72.

Salem, Lori. 2016. "Decisions . . . Decisions: Who Chooses to Use the Writing Center?" *Writing Center Journal* 35 (2): 147–71.

Schell, Eileen E. 1997. *Gypsy Academics and Mother-Teachers: Gender, Contingent Labor, and Writing Instruction.* Portsmouth, NH: Boynton/Cook-Heinemann.

Schell, Eileen E., and K. J. Rawson, eds. 2010. *Rhetorica in Motion: Feminist Rhetorical Methods and Methodologies.* Pittsburgh, PA: University of Pittsburgh Press. https://doi.org/10.2307/j.ctt5vkff8.

Sealey-Ruiz, Yolanda, and Perry Greene. 2015. "Popular Visual Images and the (Mis)Reading of Black Male Youth: A Case for Racial Literacy in Urban Preservice Teacher Education." *Teaching Education* 26 (1): 55–76. https://doi.org/10.1080/10476210.2014.997702.

Sedgwick, Eve Kosofsky. 2008. *Epistemology of the Closet.* Berkeley: University of California Press.

Severino, Carol. 2004. "Avoiding Appropriation." In *ESL Writers: A Guide for Writing Center Tutors,* edited by Shanti Bruce and Ben Rafoth, 48–59. Portsmouth, NH: Boynton/ Cook. Previously printed in *Journal of Second Language Writing* 2 (3):181–201.

Severino, Carol. 2010. "The Sociopolitical Implications of Response to Second-Language and Second-Dialect Writing." In *Second-Language Writing in the Composition Classroom,* edited by Paul Kei Matsuda, Michelle Cox, Jay Jordan, and Christina Ortmeier-Hooper, 333–50. Boston, MA: Bedford/St. Martin's. https://doi.org/10.1016/1060-3743(93)90018-X. Previously printed as "The Sociopolitical Implications of Response to Second Language and Second Dialect Writing." *Journal of Second Language Writing* 2 (3): 181–201.

Silva, Tony, and Ilona Leki. 2004. "Family Matters: The Influence of Applied Linguistics and Composition Studies on Second Language Writing Studies—Past, Present, and Future." *Modern Language Journal* 88 (1): 1–13. https://doi.org/10.1111/j.0026-7902.2004.00215.x.

Sloan, Jay D. 2003. "Centering Difference: Student Agency and the Limits of 'Comfortable' Collaboration.'" *Dialogue: A Journal for Writing Specialists* 8 (2): 63–74. http://www.academia.edu/368354/Centering_Difference_Student_Agency_and_the_Limits_of_Comfortable_Collaboration.

Sloan, Jay D., and Andrew Rihn. 2013. "Rainbows in the Past Were Gay: LGBTQ+IA in the WC." *Praxis: A Writing Center Journal* 10 (2): 1–13.

Solórzano, Daniel G., and Tara J. Yosso. 2002. "Critical Race Methodology: Counter-Storytelling as an Analytical Framework for Education Research." *Qualitative Inquiry* 8 (1): 23–44. https://doi.org/10.1177/107780040200800103.

Sparks, Richard, and Benjamin Lovett. 2009. "College Students with Learning Disability Diagnosis: Who Are They and How Do They Perform?" *Journal of Learning Disabilities* 42 (6): 494–510. https://doi.org/10.1177/0022219409338746.

Stampler, Laura. 2014. "Lebron James Apologizes for Using Slur Again." *Time,* January 30. http://www.time.com/3116/miami-heat-lebron-james-apology-retarded/.

Stilson, Jeff, dir. *Good Hair.* 2009. Beverly Hills, CA: Chris Rock Entertainment, HBO Films.

Strassman, Mark. 2014. "Michael Brown's Mom: 'Nobody's Child Deserves to Be Treated Like That.'" CBS News, August 21. https://www.cbsnews.com/news/michael-brown-parents-reflect-on-their-loss/.

Street, Brian. 2001. "The New Literacy Studies." In *Literacy: A Critical Sourcebook,* edited by Ellen Cushman, Eugene R. Kintgen, Barry M. Kroll, and Mike Rose, 430–42. Boston, MA: Bedford/St. Martin's.

Tate, Gary, John McMillan, and Elizabeth Woodward. 1997. "Class Talk." *Journal of Basic Writing* 16 (1): 13–26.

Taylor, Tess. 2015. "Report from the Field: But Do You Have to Work?" VIDA: Women in Literary Arts. http://www.vidaweb.org/report-from-the-field-but-do-you-have-to-work/.

Tillis, Antonio D. 2011. "Notes of a Black Male Academic Border Crosser: Globalization and the Black Male Body." In *The Black Professoriat: Negotiating a Habitable Space in the Academy,* edited by Sandra Jackson and Richard Greggory Johnson III, 215–27. New York: Peter Lang.

Tipper, Margaret O. 1999. "Real Men Don't Do Writing Centers." *Writing Center Journal* 19 (2): 33–40.

Tollefson, James W. 1989. *Alien Winds: The Reeducation of America's Indochinese Refugees.* New York: Praeger.

Trachsel, Mary. 1995. "Nurturant Ethics and Academic Ideals: Convergence in the Writing Center." *Writing Center Journal* 16 (1): 24–45.

Tuan, Yi-Fu. 2008. *Space and Place: The Perspective of Experience.* Minneapolis: University of Minnesota Press.

Twain, Mark. 1884. *The Adventures of Huckleberry Finn.* London: Chatto & Windus. Reprint. 1st US ed. New York: Charles L. Webster, 1885.

United Nations General Assembly. 1948. *Universal Declaration of Human Rights.* December 10. Resolution 217A, Article 13(2).

United Nations High Commissioner for Refugees (UNHCR). 1951. *Convention Relating to the Status of Refugees (Refugee Convention).* July 28. Resolution 2198 (XXI), Article 1(c).

US Census Bureau. 2017. "Income." Last revised May 12, 2016. https://www.census.gov/topics/income-poverty/income/about/faqs.html.

US Congress. 2010. Rosa's Law. Pub. L. no. 111–256. 124 Stat. 2644.

US Department of Education, National Center for Education Statistics. 2014. *Profile of Undergraduate Students: 2011–2012.* https://nces.ed.gov/pubs2015/2015167.pdf.

US Department of Education. 2016. "Developing Hispanic-Serving Institutions Program, Title V—Definition of an HSI." https://www2.ed.gov/programs/idueshsi/definition.html.

Valentine, Kathryn, and Mónica F. Torres. 2011. "Diversity as Topography: The Benefits and Challenges of Cross Racial Interaction in the Writing Center." In *Writing Centers and the New Racism: A Call for Sustainable Dialogue and Change*, edited by Laura Greenfield and Karen Rowan, 192–210. Logan: Utah State University Press. https://doi.org/10.2307/j.ctt4cgk6s.13.

Vander Lei, Elizabeth, and Lauren Fitzgerald. 2007. "What in God's Name? Administering the Conflicts of Religious Belief in Writing Programs." *WPA: Writing Program Administration* 31 (1, 2): 185–95.

Vander Lei, Elizabeth, and Bonnie Lenore Kyburz, eds. 2005. *Negotiating Religious Faith in the Composition Classroom.* Portsmouth, NH: Boynton/Cook-Heinemann.

Villanueva, Victor, Jr. 2003. "On the Rhetoric and Precedents of Racism." In *Cross-Talk in Comp Theory: A Reader*, 2nd ed., edited by Victor Villanueva Jr. and Kristin L. Arola, 829–45. Urbana, IL: NCTE. Previously printed in *College Composition and Communication* 50 (4): 645–61.

von Károlye, Catya, Ellen Winner, Wendy Gray, and Gordon Sherman. 2003. "Dyslexia Linked to Talent: Global Visual-Spatial Ability." *Brain and Language* 85 (3): 427–31. https://doi.org/10.1016/S0093-934X(03)00052-X.

Walker, Alice. 1983. *In Search of Our Mother's Gardens: Womenist Prose.* New York: Harcourt.

Weaver, Margaret. 2004. "Censoring What Tutors' Clothing 'Says': The 'Right' Path or Violation of First Amendment Rights?" *Writing Center Journal* 24 (2): 19–36.

West, Candace, and Don H. Zimmerman. 1987. "Doing Gender." *Gender & Society* 1 (2): 125–51. https://doi.org/10.1177/0891243287001002002.

Willis, Paul. 1981. *Learning to Labor: How Working Class Kids Get Working Class Jobs.* New York: Columbia University Press.

Wilson, Nancy Effinger. 2012. "Stocking the Bodega: Towards a New Writing Center Paradigm." *Praxis: A Writing Center Journal* 10 (1): 1–9.

Woodson, Carter G. 2008. *The Mis-Education of the Negro.* La Vergne, TN: BN.

Wu, Jing, Haifan Xiao, Hongjuan Sun, Li Zou, and Ling-Qiang Zhu. 2012. "Role of Dopamine Receptors in ADHD: A Systematic Meta-Analysis." *Molecular Neurobiology* 45 (3): 605–20. https://doi.org/10.1007/s12035-012-8278-5.

Yee, Marian. 1991. "Are You the Teacher?" In *Composition and Resistance*, edited by C. Mark Hurlbert and Michael Blitz, 24–31. Portsmouth, NH: Boynton/Cook.

Yoshimasu, Kouichi, William J. Barbaresi, Robert C. Colligan, Jill M. Killian, Robert G. Voigt, Amy L. Weaver, and Slavica K. Katusic. 2011. "Written-Language Disorder among Children with and without ADHD in a Population-Based Birth Cohort." *Pediatrics* 128 (3): 605–12.

Yoshino, Kenji. 2007. *Covering: The Hidden Assault on Our Civil Rights.* Reprint ed. New York: Random House Trade Paperbacks.

Yosso, Tara J. 2005. "Whose Culture Has Capital? A Critical Race Theory Discussion of Community Cultural Wealth." *Race, Ethnicity and Education* 8 (1): 69–91. https://doi .org/10.1080/1361332052000341006.

Young, Vershawn Ashanti. 2007. *Your Average Nigga: Performing Race, Literacy, and Masculinity.* African American Life Series. Detroit, MI: Wayne State University Press.

Young, Vershawn Ashanti. 2011. "Should Writers Use They Own English?" In *Writing Centers and the New Racism: A Call for Sustainable Dialogue and Change*, edited by Lauren Greenfield and Karen Rowan, 61–72. Logan: Utah State University Press. https://doi .org/10.2307/j.ctt4cgk6s.7.

Young, Vershawn Ashanti, Aja Y. Martinez, and the National Council of Teachers of English. 2011. *Code-Meshing as World English: Pedagogy, Policy, Performance.* Urbana, IL: NCTE.

Zeiger, William. 1985. "The Exploratory Essay: Enfranchising the Spirit of Inquiry in College Composition." *College English* 47 (5): 454–66. https://doi.org/10.2307/376877.

Zhang, Phil, Jessie St. Amand, J. Quaynor, Talisha Haltiwanger, Evan Chambers, Geneva Canino, and Moira Ozias. 2013. "'Going There': Peer Writing Consultants' Perspectives on the New Racism and Peer Writing Pedagogies." *Across the Disciplines* 10 (3). https:// wac.colostate.edu/atd/race/oziasetal.cfm.

Zinsser, William. 2013. "Simplicity." In *On Writing Well: The Classic Guide to Writing Nonfiction*, 7th ed., 6–11. New York: HarperCollins.

Zweig, Michael. 2000. *The Working Class Majority: America's Best Kept Secret.* Ithaca, NY: Cornell University Press.

ABOUT THE CONTRIBUTORS

Allia Abdullah-Matta is associate professor of English and the codirector of the writing center at CUNY LaGuardia Community College. Her scholarship primarily focuses on twentieth- and twenty-first-century African/African Diaspora literature and visual culture. As an educator and writer, she strives to address the power and the politics of creative expression and voice as essential instruments of social justice practice and transformation.

Nancy Alvarez is a PhD candidate in the English department at St. John's University. Her dissertation, "Tutoring While Latina: Creating Space for *Nuestras Voces* in the Writing Center," is a qualitative study on the experiences of Latinas tutoring in writing centers housed within Hispanic-serving institutions across the United States. Her research interests include writing center studies, writing pedagogy, and language rights.

Hadi Banat is pursuing his PhD in second language studies at Purdue University. He has taught in Lebanon, the United Arab Emirates, and the United States. His research interests are in the intersections between second language writing and composition studies.

Tammy S. Conard-Salvo is associate director of the Purdue Writing Lab, and her research interests include technology, usability, and diversity in writing centers. She has publications in *Computers and Composition*, *The Writing Center Journal*, and *WLN: A Journal of Writing Center Scholarship*.

Harry Denny is associate professor of English and director of the writing lab at Purdue University, in West Lafayette, Indiana. His scholarship focuses on composition and writing center studies, cultural studies, and research methods. He has published on identity politics in writing centers, on the politics of assessment in writing programs, and on media, governmental, legal, and activist responses to HIV and civil rights.

Michele Eodice is Associate Provost for Academic Engagement and director of the OU Writing Center at the University of Oklahoma. Her research centers on collaboration, community writing, and the Meaningful Writing Project.

Talisha Haltiwanger Morrison is a PhD candidate at Purdue University, where she is a writing tutor and data usage analytics coordinator for the Purdue Writing Lab. She also teaches service-learning courses in accelerated and professional writing. Her research interests are in writing center administration, critical race theory and intersectionality, and community writing and engagement.

Rochell Isaac is assistant professor of English at LaGuardia Community College. Her research interests are interdisciplinary: literature and theory of the African diaspora, postcolonial literature, Black feminist theory, and cultural studies.

Sami Korgan recently received her MA in English from St. John's University. Currently, she is the assistant director of Student Success and coordinator of the writing center at Wells College in Aurora, New York. Her research interests are primarily focused on the values and experiences of writing center consultants.

Ella Leviyeva is a current student at Fordham Law School, where she is pursuing her JD. While an undergraduate student at St. John's University, Ella was a writing consultant at the university writing center, learning and growing alongside her peers daily.

Alexandria Lockett is assistant professor of English at Spelman College where she codirects the writing-intensive initiative and serves as the faculty mentor of the independent student-led literary magazine *Aunt Chloe*. Her essays have appeared in *Composition Studies, Enculturation,* and the *McNair Scholarly Review*.

Robert Mundy is assistant professor of English and writing program administrator at Pace University. His research focuses on composition studies, writing center theory and practice, and gender/masculinity studies. He has published on the intersection of gender and class, multicultural competence, masculinities in the media, and rhetoric of leadership communication. His most recent work has appeared in *The Peer Review: Journal for Writing Center Practitioners* and *Class in the Composition Classroom: Pedagogy and the Working Class*.

Anna Rita Napoleone is a lecturer at the University of Massachusetts Amherst. She has a PhD in rhetoric and composition. She has coauthored an article in the journal *Pedagogy* and a chapter in *Examining Education, Media, and Dialogue under Occupation: The Case of Palestine and Israel,* edited by Ilham Nasser, Lawrence N. Berlin, and Shelley Wong (Bristol, UK: Multilingual Matters, 2011).

Liliana M. Naydan is assistant professor of English and writing program coordinator at Penn State Abington. She researches writing centers and American literature, and her articles on these subjects have appeared in journals including *Praxis: A Writing Center Journal, Forum: Issues about Part-Time and Contingent Faculty,* and *Critique: Studies in Contemporary Fiction*. Her book, *Rhetorics of Religion in American Fiction: Faith, Fundamentalism, and Fanaticism in the Age of Terror* (Lewisburg, PA: Bucknell University Press, 2016), considers the interface between secularism and faith in post-9/11 literature.

Richard Sévère is associate professor of Medieval literature and professional writing at Valparaiso University. Richard earned his PhD from Purdue University. Previous to his position at Valparaiso, he founded and directed the Writing Collaboratory at Centenary College of New Jersey.

Anna Sicari is director of the writing center and an assistant professor of English at Oklahoma State University. Her research interests include writing center pedagogy and theory, qualitative research, and feminist scholarship in rhetoric and composition. She is currently working on a project that critically explores embodiment and writing program administrators.

Beth A. Towle is a PhD candidate at Purdue University, where she is the business writing coordinator for the Purdue Writing Lab. Her research interests include writing center administration, institutional critique, and first-generation and working-class issues/access. She also writes and publishes poetry and has an MFA from the University of Notre Dame.

Elizabeth Weaver currently works as an adjunct and freelance digital copywriter. She began teaching in 1997 and holds an MFA from Columbia University and a graduate certificate in composition studies from Stony Brook University. Her poems have appeared in the *Paris Review, Barrow Street,* and elsewhere.

Tim Zmudka recently received his MS in speech-language pathology from Grand Valley State University. While an undergraduate student at the University of Michigan, Tim was a peer writing consultant at the university's Sweetland Center for Writing. His passions revolve around the central purpose of assisting individuals to overcome barriers in all communication modalities, including writing.

INDEX